Nina Simonds is the author of **Classic Chinese Cuisine** and **Chinese Seasons.** Her writing has appeared in the **New York Times,** the **Washington Post**, **Gourmet, The Pleasures of Cooking,** and **Connoisseur.**

"Where was this wonderful book when I went to China? It's a must, and I'll surely take it along with me next time!"
—Jacques Pepin, author of **The Art of Cooking**

"A must for anyone who is even remotely interested in Chinese food and its culture. It will leave you fascinated by the complex and wonderfully diverse food of this vast country, and the restaurants in which it is served. Nina Simonds's expertise is matched only by her ability to convey this expertise in an informative and entertaining manner."
—Chris Schlesinger, author of **The Thrill of the Grill**

"Written by a true authority on Chinese food, this book is an indispensable and insightful guide for all lovers of Chinese food planning a trip to China."
—A. Zee, author of **Swallowing Clouds**

Also by Nina Simonds

Chinese Seasons
Classic Chinese Cuisine

CHINA'S FOOD

A Traveler's Guide to
the Best Restaurants,
Dumpling Stalls, Teahouses,
and Markets in China

Nina Simonds

PHOTOGRAPHS BY DON ROSE

Harper Perennial
A Division of HarperCollinsPublishers

The Pinyin alphabet pronunciation guide on p. 415 appeared originally in *The China Guidebook 1990*, 11th ed., by Fredric Kaplan, Julian Sobin, and Arne de Keijzer. © 1990 by Eurasia Press. Reprinted by Permission.

Photographs © 1991 by Don Rose.

FIRST EDITION

DESIGNED BY JOEL AVIROM

Library of Congress Cataloging-in-Publication Data
Simonds, Nina.
    China's food: a traveler's guide to the best restaurants, dumpling stalls, teahouses, and markets in China/Nina Simonds.—1st ed.
        p. cm.
    ISBN 0-06-273068-1
    1. Restaurants, lunch rooms, etc.—China—Guide-books. 2. China—Description and travel—1976– —Guide-books. 3. Cookery, Chinese. I. Title.
TX907.5.C6S56   1990
647.9551—dc20   90-7304

91 92 93 94 95 DT/RRD 10 9 8 7 6 5 4 3 2 1

For my father, whose passion for food was my inspiration.

❧

For Don, who has remained constant through the
best and worst of times.

❧

And for Jesse Benjamin, whose welcoming smile warmed my heart
when I returned from my travels in China.

CONTENTS

SICHUANESE COOKING
(Western)

ॐ

GUANGDONG COOKING
(Southern)

ॐ

PREFACE

I can still recall so vividly my first taste of Peking duck in Beijing. The year was 1979 (some seven years after President Nixon's historic diplomatic mission that reestablished relations between China and the United States), the month was March, and it was my first visit to China. We were eating at the Qianmen Quanjude Restaurant, one of the oldest and most famous eateries for duck, and I had waited impatiently for eleven years to experience some of China's splendors: to climb the Great Wall, to walk in Tiananmen Square, and to eat Peking duck in the country of its origin. And the moment had arrived.

The duck skin was a deep lacquer-brown and crisp without a trace of fat. The meat was tender and flavorful, and it was wrapped neatly in a thin Mandarin pancake with a generous smear of sweet bean sauce. Despite the fact that I had sampled the dish hundreds of times earlier in restaurants in the United States, France, Taiwan, and Hong Kong, never had it tasted better.

The Far East was by then a familiar place to me. In the early seventies I had spent over three years living in Taiwan, studying Mandarin and Chinese cuisine with master chefs who had emigrated from China, and I had returned countless times in later years to visit Hong Kong and Taipei. During that period my efforts to enter China had been fruitless. Then an opportunity arose to join a tour group. The tour had originated in Hawaii, and though the majority of my companions were elderly Polynesian women, there were also a number of individual travelers like myself who had begun the trip from Hong Kong.

The Hawaiians had done nothing but complain since we arrived, but our own little band of adventurous souls just relaxed and savored the experience of *finally* being in China. We overlooked the drabness of the cityscapes still remaining after the Cultural Revolution, ignored the discomforts of a country somewhat unprepared for the tasks of welcoming tourists after years of seclusion, and made it our business to experience as much as we could.

Although our itinerary included only one or two meals in restaurants, with the remainder planned in hotels, I was determined

to visit as many private eateries as possible to taste the true flavors of the areas we were visiting. And so I became the meal planner. Using my fluency in Mandarin and the advice of numerous sources, I organized parties almost every night to different restaurants in each city. In fact, we were surprised at how freely we could move around. The eateries were often dirty and run down, and at times the service was deplorable, but for the most part, the food was quite good.

We rejoiced at the excellent Peking duck and spicy lamb shashlik in Beijing. (Even the Hawaiians seemed to appreciate the fine meal and serenaded the kitchen staff with a Polynesian song and hula in thanks.) In Shanghai, we feasted on the first shad of the season, steamed until just flaky and generously doused with fragrant Zhenjiang black vinegar. In Hangzhou, after savoring the peaceful tranquillity of the gardens, we dined serenely on West Lake fish and superb vegetarian delicacies. And in Guangzhou, in an elegant pagodalike room with stained glass windows, we feasted on crisp roasted goose with plum sauce; fresh, steamed shrimp with heads intact; and delicate and delectable savory and sweet dumplings and assorted dim sum.

Still, we were subjected to a number of dismal hotel lunches that reinforced all the complaints I had heard from previous travelers to China. Many had returned insisting that the food was wretched, and that one was wiser to save all gastronomic experiences for Taiwan and Hong Kong. I, on the other hand (perhaps because I had expected so little) came home triumphant and filled with a sense of hope for the future of China's culinary masters.

Since that first trip, I have not been discouraged. After traveling to China more than a dozen times over the past eleven years, I have certainly had my moments of frustration and disenchantment in the face of a series of mediocre meals. But with each visit, I have seen progress, and I have tasted new delights. Conditions have vastly improved, and the food service industry, with the full support of the government, is intent on upgrading the overall quality of China's food.

Apart from the usual tourist travel, I have enjoyed some unique experiences in China. In 1984, at the request of the Shandong provincial government, I was invited to this remote and relatively unknown northeastern province to teach western cooking to Chinese master chefs. I spent four weeks in the area, demonstrating a number of dishes, and taking the opportunity to explore the place and sample its excellent food and wines.

Two years later, I helped to lead a gastronomic, cultural, and diplomatic tour for the New England chapter of the American Institute of Wine and Food on which we journeyed and feasted our way across the country, visiting culinary training centers, vineyards, and distilleries and establishing relations with culinary associations. And in 1988, I helped to establish a chef's exchange program at New England's foremost seafood restaurant, for which I was sent to Beijing to select the best chefs from that city to come to Boston for three months to cook authentic Chinese food using local products.

All these experiences further strengthened my appreciation of China's culinary riches and confirmed the realization that few foreigners have the opportunity to discover and enjoy them on their travels. The many who would return from a trip with ghastly tales of inedible hotel meals and sloppy service had seldom even visited restaurants. It was obvious that some type of reference work would be useful, but the enormity of putting together such a book was just too daunting.

It was then that I met Dr. Wang Qing, director of the Beijing Food Research Institute, the leading agency on food research in China and the publisher of China's leading food magazine. Dr. Wang, in her passionate and charming way, overrode my protests and insisted that such a book *had* to be written and that I was the person uniquely suited to do it. She pledged the full support of her institute in a collaboration that would establish a historic precedent.

According to Dr. Wang's plan, I would have full use of her agency's resources: the institute would provide an assistant who would accompany me on my travels across the country; they would put me in touch with a nationwide network of culinary experts; and they would help to research historical information concerning the regional styles. It seemed as if fate had determined that I should pursue the project.

Little did I realize how difficult an assignment I was embarking upon, particularly since my research in China coincided with my pregnancy and the birth of my son. I divided the country into two parts and organized my main research between two trips. On the first two-month journey, I was six and seven months pregnant, but undeterred, and with a belly the size of a basketball, I traveled throughout northern and eastern China, by train, bus, boat, plane, and car. At times, the conditions were unbearable (at one point, my work was interrupted briefly by an emergency root canal performed without anesthetic), but fueled by my determination, I worked feverishly every day, attempting to absorb as much material as possible and to become intimate with each city.

The second trip was no easier, especially since I had left my six-month-old child at home. Fortunately, I wasn't alone on either journey but was accompanied by my hardworking research assistant Cheng Zhu, from the Beijing Food Research Institute. Together, we discovered the jewels of each area, which in many cases were places, people, and food that only local residents might be familiar with.

Although *China's Food* may at first be perceived as a restaurant guide, it is meant to be much more. With each city, in addition to providing the reader with information on restaurants, markets, small food stalls, and wineries, I have tried to share some of the experiences that made my trips to China so memorable. I have also attempted to give the reader a sense of the atmosphere and history of each place, in addition to building an understanding of the rich, ageless traditions of classic Chinese cuisine.

Perhaps more important, I have written *China's Food* with the desire to share some of my passion for China and its extraordinary culinary heritage. I hope the book will become a companion for those who travel there, a guide to discovering a small eatery or market and enjoying a fine Chinese meal. And for those who choose to enjoy this book at home, I hope that *China's Food* will become an armchair adventure, allowing the reader from afar to enjoy a firsthand look at China's culture and people as well as its food.

Nina Simonds
January 1990

ACKNOWLEDGMENTS

No book of this type is ever written without the assistance of a team of people, and *China's Food* is no exception. In China, there were countless advisors all over the country (almost every Chinese considers him- or herself to be the foremost authority on food), and it would be impossible to list each person by name, but a number of people deserve special mention:

At the Beijing Food Research Institute, special thanks must be given to Wang Qing, the director; Huang Xiao Qing, her superior; and Wang Ren Xing, Huo Kai Zong, Liu Ming, Wang Xiao Tang, Wei Qing, Wang Hai Yan, Hu Yun Jiang, and Wang Xiong.

In Beijing, I am also indebted to Huang Kai, Yu Qiang, and Sui Jiang.

In Zhengzhou, Liu Yuan was especially cordial and hospitable.

In Shanghai, Shen Zhi Jun was more than generous with his time and help, as were Wang Yi Min, Cai Liang Chao, and Thomas Tsing.

In Hangzhou, my warmest thanks go to Dai Ning, Yang Ming, Zhang Gen Xing, Cai Bu Yan, Hu Zhong Ying, Lu Kui De, and Shen Guanzhong.

In Shandong, Zhan Lianming and Wan Yu Wei were invaluable in providing information and assistance.

In Nanjing, Hu Chang-ling, Yang Zhong Ming, and Li Guong Xi all shared their wealth of knowledge of the city and its cuisine.

In Xian, special thanks are due Zhang Li-Di and Yao Bin.

In Chengdu, Zhong Shen Hung, Li Chenglong, and Wang Yi Ming were all most helpful.

In Guangzhou, Yang Xiao Ping and Li Song Xiu went out of their way to aid me in my research.

And in Xiamen, special thanks to Weng Dai Hui for her time and assistance.

I could never begin to repay the debt owed to my friend Ronald Wu of China Attractions Limited in Hong Kong and his capable staff, who received my frantic Telexes and managed to perform the impossible task of procuring air tickets and hotel rooms for me and my research assistant.

In the United States, Stella and Pickering Lee, Yue Zunvair, Judy Chiu, Carl Sondheimer, Suzan Kahler, and Annemarie Victory were all indispensable in their individual contributions to the completion of this book. And I am deeply thankful to Dr. C. T. Wu for introducing me to Dr. Wang of the Beijing Research Institute and for providing information without hesitation whenever called upon.

Cheng Zhu, my industrious and conscientious research assistant, was my constant companion during my travels all over China. Zhu worked tirelessly researching, translating, sampling endless meals, and helping to make travel arrangements. I could never express my gratitude for her extraordinary commitment to this project, even under the most trying of conditions.

It has been a pleasure to work with Rick Kot, my editor at HarperCollins, and his capable assistant, Sheila Gillooly, and special thanks are also due Eric Ashworth, my agent, and Joel Avirom, for the book's lovely design.

There were many times when this book seemed to be an insurmountable task—one that I felt incapable of ever finishing, particularly after my son was born. An incredible number of friends supplied support and reassurance during this difficult period, urging me on, and I will always be grateful to them. In particular, Debby Richards, my close friend, was always available for constant advice and collaboration, as were Rosalie Quine and Marlene Sorosky.

I am deeply indebted to my family, especially my father and Ceil, who helped to take care of my son while I was away, and to my sister and brothers and aunt and uncle for their love and encouragement.

Last, I must thank Don for his support and advice, and for taking the time away from his own thriving business to trudge all over China and furnish the delightful photographs that grace the pages of *China's Food*.

INTRODUCTION

꽃

Not too long ago, it appeared that China's culinary future was bleak. In the early seventies, during the Cultural Revolution, countless fine restaurants were closed or transformed into cafeterialike mess halls, and fine cuisine was spurned as product of the decadent bourgeoisie.

The last five years, however, have seen a drastic change as the country has enjoyed a renaissance in all aspects of its culture, including its food. Restaurants are now flourishing and serving an ever-growing repertory of fine dishes to an enthusiastic audience. Older chefs have come out of retirement and are teaching their skills to a brigade of talented young cooks. Culinary academies and vocational schools now have record enrollment; free markets all over the country are filled with a wealth of fresh ingredients, and in some cases, new products. And there is a booming network of government-supported culinary associations that organize local culinary competitions and participate in national contests. In many respects, the Chinese have succeeded in restoring their cuisine to its former lofty position as a national treasure.

In China, food has always played a special cultural role not only in everyday life, for sustenance, but in religious ritual and medicine as well. Spring rolls and sticky rice cakes symbolize New Year, while mooncakes herald the arrival of the Midautumn Festival. Chicken soup with gingerroot is administered to restore strength after childbirth, and papaya is prescribed to soothe an ailing stomach. As a medical writer from the sixth century A.D. wrote: "A good doctor first makes the diagnosis and having found out the cause of the disease, he first tries to cure it by food." *

Throughout the ages, gastronomes with a refined knowledge of food and drink have been held in esteem. The haute cuisine of a given period frequently provided inspiration for poets, scholars, and artists. Exultant eulogies to food date as early as the Chou dynasty (12th century B.C.–221 B.C.), and one still can admire whimsical, still-life sketches of bamboo shoots, crabs, and fish that have survived from ancient times.

Even in China's earliest days the preparation of food was governed by meticulous guidelines. In his *Analects,* which were compiled around the fourth century B.C., Confucius himself is credited with establishing the refined standards that marked the beginnings of classic Chinese cuisine. "He did not eat what was of a bad flavor, nor anything which was ill-cooked, or not in season. He did not eat meat which was not cut properly, nor was served without its proper sauce. . . ."†

These same standards ruled up until the 1940s, when the revolution marked the beginning of the recession of China's classic cuisine. Many of the most talented chefs fled the country, seeking professional and political freedom elsewhere. Despite this loss, restaurants continued to thrive, and the government, intent on preserving its culinary heritage, published an eight-volume series of Chinese regional cookbooks titled *Famous Chinese Dishes (Zhonggho Ming Caipu).*

Yet these attempts proved to be short lived: by the mid-1960s, the Cultural Revolution began to take its repressive toll on all forms of art and literature, and unfortunately, food was not exempt. For over a decade classic cuisine suffered greatly, as scores of restaurants and culinary academies were shut down. Many of the most gifted chefs were reassigned to professions that were considered more vital to the modernization of China. The business of feeding the people still had to be attended to, but those workers

* K. C. Chang, ed., *Food in Chinese Culture* (New Haven: Yale University Press, 1977).

† *Confucius: Confucian Analects, The Great Learning, and The Doctrine of the Mean,* translated and edited by James Legge (New York: Dover, 1971).

who were assigned to be chefs in cafeterias and restaurants received little or no training. And these positions no longer commanded the respect they had held before.

Lu Yongliang, a master chef from central China who was judged one of the country's top chefs in the 1982 National Culinary Olympics, recalled in an interview published in *China Resurrects* magazine: "In 1971, I graduated from middle school and left my rural home for the city of Wuhan. I longed to become a steel-worker, but was assigned a job at the Wuchang Restaurant. I didn't feel I had a promising future. In fact, I felt ashamed to be a cook."

Master chef Zhu Fin, who in 1982 was sent to the United States to head a team of chefs from Sichuan province to cook in Washington, D.C., also remembers that period with pain and regret. Zhu began his apprenticeship during the fifties at age eighteen after graduation from art school. Following the traditional apprenticeship system, he first worked with older chefs before he was allowed to man the woks. During the Cultural Revolution, Zhu explained, the high culinary standards of former times were neither maintained nor encouraged. "The art of cooking was definitely halted during the Cultural Revolution. I had always been meticulously trained that food should taste a certain way and look a certain way, but during that time, nobody bothered.

"But starting in the early eighties, the changes have been drastic. It was like the baby bamboo shoots coming out of the ground after a spring rain. There has been evidence of the recovery everywhere. Many technical schools that closed during the Cultural Revolution reopened and are now offering training in the culinary arts."

Today, China has more than 120 vocational schools and culinary academies for training chefs, with a combined enrollment of over eighteen thousand students. There are also apprenticeship programs in major hotels and restaurants, many of which support food-service training programs for waiters and waitresses. China has again returned to a nine-level grading system for chefs. Examinations are held regularly, and chefs must fulfill strict requirements before advancing to other levels.

One of the greatest boons to the food service industry has been the introduction of joint-venture hotels and restaurants. In most major cities, businesses have opened under foreign management, luring talented chefs, bearing superior food products, from Hong Kong and abroad. Not only have resident Chinese chefs benefited from the expertise of these visiting masters, but service and hygiene have improved considerably. Furthermore, the competition has inspired state-run restaurants to upgrade their own standards.

The changed mood in most restaurant kitchens is obvious to any visitor. Chefs who once felt apathy and embarrassment are now excited, eager to perfect their technique and create new dishes. Granted, there remains room for improvement, and I still despair, from time to time, after having experienced a sloppy, mediocre meal. But on each return to China, I see growth and promise, and often, after sampling a memorable dish, I have had cause to feel that China's food is once again worthy of inspiring poetry.

How to Get a Great Meal in China— Some Pointers

A number of restaurants in China offer food that is on a par with the best being offered in Hong Kong and Taiwan, yet few tourists have the opportunity to sample it. There is a simple explanation for that fact. Most tour meals are planned in hotels rather than in private eateries, where the best food is prepared. This is generally due to logistic and financial considerations. (Restaurant meals require more time and money.) Visitors usually eat en masse with their tour groups, and travel packages normally do not have a huge budget for food. And contrary to what many may believe, fine restaurant dining in China, particularly for a multicourse banquet, is not cheap.

Food in China actually has never been better, or more consistent, but getting a great meal often requires effort and patience.

Nevertheless, visitors should not be deterred or afraid to go off on their own, either individually or in small groups.

Here are some guidelines that should reward you with a memorable eating experience—and one that can be savored for the rest of your life.

1   Encourage your tour leader in advance to plan meals in private restaurants whenever possible. It may be necessary to pay some extra money per person. If the group is unwilling, plan for yourself, with the aid of your tour guide.

2   Don't be afraid to break away from your group. Organize a small party of your own or dine out individually. Good meals are available for smaller groups, but with more people, the better the banquet and the cheaper the price. The ideal number is six to eight guests.

3   Unfortunately, eating in a fine restaurant can be on the expensive side, and foreigners, even overseas Chinese, are charged more than natives. Expect to pay for the extra effort expended. In some eateries, especially for a lighter, impromptu meal, the menu need not be planned in advance. Dishes ordered off the regular menu are often excellent and can be quite inexpensive. For a banquet meal, expect to pay more.

4   In making reservations for restaurants, enlist the aid of a tour leader, a hotel receptionist, or a Mandarin-speaking friend. Some restaurants have English-speaking employees and offer English menus, but they are in the minority.

5   Most restaurants, especially for a banquet meal, insist that the price per person be established in advance, when the reservations are made. Unless the restaurant specializes in such foods, dispense with the expensive delicacies like shark's fin soup, bird's nest, and sea cucumber. Make certain to notify the manager of your intentions. (Many banquet menus contain these dishes as a matter of course.)

6   Order regional dishes, concentrating on local specialties and seasonal ingredients, which tend to be the freshest. Consult the manager or get recommendations in advance and advise the restaurant accordingly, especially if planning a banquet meal.

7   Stress authenticity. Impress upon the manager of the restaurant, the chef, or whomever that although you are a foreigner, you want to taste the *authentic* flavor of the region. Discourage cooks from adapting the menu to their stereotypical notions of what a foreigner usually likes.

8   Occasionally, eliciting good food requires a bit of goading and flattery. Tell the manager or chef that you have tasted superb food in other parts of China, and mention specific names of restaurants and dishes that have impressed you. This may to help to establish some credibility and impress the manager and chef that you appreciate authentic Chinese fare. Dare the manager and cooks to make your meal memorable. Try to speak to them directly, even through a translator.

9   If you do have a memorable experience, take the extra time to compliment the manager and cook by shaking their hands or clapping. Show appreciation for the extra effort they have made.

A Few Other Details in Planning Meals

Transportation

If you are traveling alone or in a small group apart from a tour, the most convenient method of transportation is a taxi. If you are in a city where taxis are scarce or hard to come by, book a taxi through your hotel and make arrangements for the cab to return at the end of the meal. In many places, though, you can ask the restaurant to call for a cab or merely go out to the street and hail one on your own.

Credit Cards and General Payment

Although some of the most famous restaurants are now accepting one or two major credit cards, they are in the minority. Be prepared to pay in Foreign Exchange Certificates (FEC). Some restaurants will now accept local currency *(renminbi)* from foreigners, but they will frequently charge an extra percentage for doing so.

Appropriate Dress

Generally, dining out is a casual affair in China. Unless it is a very special party, the dress is informal. Men may wear a jacket, and women may opt to wear a skirt, but neither is necessarily required.

Serving Hours

The Chinese eat early, and restaurants, even in major cities, close correspondingly early, or if not, they may run out of the best dishes. Breakfast is served anywhere from 5:30 to 8:30 A.M. (the hours are earlier in restaurants and later in hotels); lunch runs from 11:00 A.M. to 1:30 P.M.; and dinner usually is served from 5:30 to 8:00 P.M. In Guangzhou, where there is a strong Hong Kong influence, dinner hours tend to be later. In order to get the best out of the kitchen, it is usually advisable to dine early.

Tipping

Many establishments discourage their employees from accepting tips. (The practice used to be universally illegal.) Some joint-venture restaurants will charge a 15 percent service fee. The general practice observed in most eateries is not to tip.

Beverages

The most popular drink served with meals in China is beer, and each region boasts its own or the products of several breweries. Maotai, a distilled liquor, is offered at banquets for toasts, as well as a selection of red and white Chinese grape wines. For those who prefer nonalcoholic beverages, orange crush, Coca-Cola, orange juice, and tea are the most widely available choices.

Breakfast

Most tour packages include breakfast, and inevitably, it will be a version of what the Chinese assume all westerners eat: eggs, ham, toast, and coffee. You may have the option, if the hotel is willing, to enjoy a Chinese breakfast, which usually consists of tea, congee or rice gruel, and a selection of small dishes such as peanuts, assorted pickles, salty duck eggs, and some dim sum, or dumplings. Breakfast is served very early (from 5:30 until 8:30 A.M.), and usually reservations at outside restaurants are unnecessary.

Ordering a Meal in Advance
Versus Ordering at the Restaurant

To begin with, you may not have a choice. Some restaurants—particularly when dealing with foreigners—insist on planning the meal in advance when reservations are made. And when dealing with large parties—natives and foreigners alike—most eateries are resolute about specifying the amount of money being spent per person and planning the banquet dishes ahead of time. This does have its advantages: it usually allows the kitchen to prepare dishes that require extra time and preparation, and it guarantees that a restaurant will not run out of a particular specialty of the house. Consequently, for any party larger than six people, I strongly advise ordering the meal in advance. It is also advisable to go over the menu with the manager or head chef before the meal is prepared.

With a smaller party, you usually have the option of ordering when you arrive instead of having the menu set in advance. In cosmopolitan cities like Guangzhou or Shanghai, where restaurants are used to dealing with multitudes of customers and ingredients are in ample supply, I would not hesitate to order off the menu upon my arrival at a restaurant. (I would also plan to have my dinner during the early dining hours.) This allows you the freedom of selecting any favorite dishes you might have and ordering daily specials. In smaller and less sophisticated locations, it is generally a wise practice when making reservations prior to the meal to specify the amount of money to be spent per person and to discuss menu ideas, leaving the final planning up to the individual eatery. Once again, make certain to go over the menu upon your arrival at the restaurant.

Ordering a Chinese Meal

For most Chinese, dining out at a nice restaurant is usually reserved for a special event such as a birthday, a family reunion, or a business gathering. And for such an occasion, a banquet or a more formal multicourse meal, where the price and menu are determined in advance, is traditional.

In smaller restaurants (and these days even in the larger, more expensive establishments), customers may order an informal, "home-style" meal directly from the menu once they are seated. Home-style meals are less expensive affairs, the number of dishes is limited, and the entire meal may be served at once, whereas a banquet meal will be served in courses.

Guidelines for ordering both types of meals are given below, but consult the restaurant listings in *China's Food* for advice on the best meals a specific eatery is likely to offer.

Planning a Traditional Chinese Banquet

Like most formal meals, a traditional Chinese banquet has a distinct agenda that is followed in the serving of different courses. Whereas in Europe, a soup is the classic opening dish for a meal, in China, the opposite is true: a sweet soup is often served at the end of a meal, and savory soups appear throughout to punctuate the meal's progression. Although dishes may differ in various regions, depending on the availability of certain ingredients, and the number of courses may vary from twelve to twenty-four, a basic format prevails.

The protocol for planning a formal meal in most restaurants is fairly predictable. Reservations should be made prior to the meal, and at that time a price per person is established. Customers can and should bargain, and the final cost will determine the number of courses and the quality of the ingredients used. Ideally, the customer can and should ask to approve the menu before the meal,

but usually the menu is planned by the head chef and manager. Diners are given a copy of the menu upon their arrival.

Alternatively, customers may, under the guidance of the manager, plan their own banquet menu. For those unfamiliar with a traditional Chinese banquet menu, the courses are as follows:

Cold Platter (Leng Pan)

Every Chinese banquet begins with the serving of a cold platter, which features thinly sliced cooked meats and seafood, cooked and pickled vegetables, preserved eggs, and in many instances, fried nuts. Inevitably, the ingredients will be arranged in a decorative, ornate design that may resemble a dragon, a phoenix, a peacock, or a variety of flowers. The complexity of the design and the range of ingredients will reflect the expertise of the chef and the cost of the meal. Prepared in advance and served at room temperature, cold platters allow the diner to pick informally at tidbits of food while the preliminary toasts are presented.

Wine-accompanying Dishes (Jiu Cai)

In a traditional meal, the ritual of toasting the host and guests is as important as the serving of food. Toasts are made at the beginning of the meal when dishes are presented whose flavors are considered complementary to alcoholic beverages. The wine-accompanying dishes are varied and extensive. They may include a simple stir-fried meat and seafood dish, such as beef with scallions or stir-fried baby shrimp, or deep-fried items like paper-wrapped meat and deep-fried chicken. Usually, one to four wine-accompanying dishes are served, depending on the sumptuousness of the meal.

Main Platters (Da Cai)

The heart of the meal arrives with the serving of the main platters. Roast suckling pig, a chicken stuffed with rice and assorted "treasures," Peking duck, and a whole fish steamed in its own juices are but a few examples of these types of dish. Main platters are the most impressive of the meal and represent the high point of the dining experience. One to four dishes may be served. From this point on, the meal begins its gradual denouement.

Rice-accompanying Dishes (Fan Cai)

Rice is usually served only as a polite gesture at banquet meals, but there are a number of dishes presented after the main platters that are simpler and could accompany this staple. They are served to soothe the stomach after the heavier, main-platter courses preceding them. Although rice-accompanying dishes are made with basic ingredients like vegetables, eggs, and bean curd, they usually are more refined than home-style renditions.

Entremets and the Finale

Sweet and savory pastries and soups are served between the different courses to freshen the palate and signify the ending of a segment of the meal. They are also served at the very end of the meal along with fresh fruit as a multicourse dessert finale. Depending on the sumptuousness of the banquet, four different types of pastry or more may be served, accompanied by a sweet, soothing soup. Finally, hot tea is presented as a ritual gesture. The hot liquid further soothes a full stomach and helps speed digestion.

Ordering a Traditional Home-Style Meal

Unlike a banquet, where the menu is prepared in advance, home-style meals are a more spontaneous event. The foods are meant to be eaten with a staple, which could be rice, noodles, or steamed bread.

The menu for home-style meals, even in a restaurant, involves balance and simplicity. Generally, for a party of up to six people, the meal will consist of five or six dishes: the choice of a meat and or a chicken entrée, plus a seafood, a vegetable, and a bean curd entrée, with the addition of a soup is appropriate. Adjust the number of dishes to the size of the group, adding more if necessary.

When ordering from the menu, follow these guidelines:

- Choose specialties of the chef and regional dishes. If necessary, consult the waiter and look around at what others are ordering.
- Consider seasonal items and order any that are appealing and available.
- Select dishes with contrasting cooking methods. Dishes should complement one another in taste, texture, and technique.

A Note on the Chef-ranking System in China

As in Europe, cooks in China traditionally were trained in apprenticeship programs sponsored in restaurant and hotel kitchens. Today, in addition to this method of schooling, there are more than 120 vocational and culinary academies where students can learn from scratch or seasoned chefs may refine their skills.

Chinese cooks, like the Europeans, are classified into two main categories: *Hong An*, or sauciers (those cooks who specialize in savory dishes and sauces) and *Bai An* or patissiers (chefs who are masters at sweet and savory pastries or dim sum). Within these two categories, there are seven levels, depending on the cook's tenure, training, and expertise. The highest title awarded to a chef is a "special first" level rating and in order to achieve this rank, a cook must have been working for fifteen to twenty years; he must excel at the required techniques; he must be able to train other cooks; and he must have an extensive knowledge of other subjects relating to food.

Alternatively, a third-level cook, the lowest rank, must have the ability to cook a required number of local specialties; he must be expert at cutting, pickling, and general food preparation; he must be able to plan a menu depending on the ingredients on hand; and he must be able to train an apprentice. Third-level chefs must have seven years of practical experience before achieving their rating.

First- and special-level chefs are tested every two years, and the panel of judges generally includes local culinary experts, visiting food authorities from the provincial and national culinary associations, and high-ranking municipal officials.

Most agree that during the Cultural Revolution, culinary standards were appallingly bad. Over the past ten years, the Chinese government—particularly through its national and regional culinary associations—has made a concerted effort to reinstate and strengthen the chefs' grading system. Examinations are held regularly in cities all over the country, and today any kitchen of note, in either a hotel or a restaurant, employs a staff of special-level cooks. The management also generally encourages its cooks to upgrade their training and rank on a regular basis.

Chinese Teas

For most foreigners, tea is as intrinsic a part of a Chinese meal as chopsticks. But while tea is considered ubiquitous in Chinese restaurants in the western world, in China, except for a dim sum parlor where snacks are served, tea is rarely served with the meal. Instead, it is presented as a preliminary, welcoming ritual for a household visit or an elaborate banquet and as a concluding gesture to honor a departing guest.

Throughout China's history the serving of tea has been synonymous with tradition. There is much dispute as to when tea first made its auspicious appearance in China. It is believed to have grown wild in East Asia as early as A.D. 350. Some credit the Emperor Shen Nong, the founder of Chinese agriculture, who lived 2737–2697 B.C., as the inventor of the drink. It is said that the emperor was fond of experimenting with all types of wild grass, and one day, while he was boiling some water, a few tea leaves innocently fell into the pot, producing the first brew.

It is certain that tea-drinking was very much in evidence as early as the Three Kingdoms period (A.D. 220–265), when it was frequently enjoyed by members of the imperial court. From then on the drink rapidly gained popularity in the south and east and slowly moved north. During this period, it was served as a tonic to stimulate the body and as an antidote to combat the effects of overindulgence in food and drink.

But the tea of earlier times was a far cry from the refined versions of the drink brewed today. It was during the Tang dynasty (618–907) that a poet named Lu Yu, who later came to be revered as Tea God, established himself as the master on the subject by writing its definitive text, which came to be known as the *Classics of Tea*. Lu Yu was responsible for raising tea-making to a fine art, impressing upon the Chinese the importance of several aspects of the brewing process in order to produce a superior product. According to Lu Yu, the proper vessels were crucial, as was the type of water. (Water culled from pure mountain springs was the best.) Tea leaves continued to be boiled, as in earlier times, until the Song dynasty (960–1279), when the method was revised to allow steeping. During the Song, tea-making was elevated still further to a fine science with several new varieties making their appearance, many of which tea lovers still relish to this day.

There are three main types of Chinese tea, which are classified according to the way the leaves are treated after picking.

Green Teas

Some tea connoisseurs maintain that green teas picked directly from the tree are the finest tasting, and especially prize those picked in early spring. Green teas are merely dried leaves that have not been cured. The flavor is slightly astringent, and many find it refreshing, particularly after a filling meal. This category also includes semigreen teas or flavored brands, the most prominent example of which is jasmine. According to tea purists, green and semigreen teas are more delicate than other varieties and should be steeped only in water several degrees below the boiling point. The most famous brand of green tea, which is considered the finest, is the Dragon Well (Longjing) variety picked at the Dragon Well Monastery in Hangzhou. Other noted varieties are White Cloud (Bei Yun), Longevity Eyebrow (Shou Mei), and Lion's Peak (Shi Feng), which is a variety of Dragon Well tea. The majority of green teas are grown in eastern and southern China.

Black Teas

Once tea leaves have been picked, they may be cured or toasted, and in this form they are known as black or red teas. These teas tend to have a hearty, robust flavor that is considerably more substantial than the flavor of the green varieties. Black teas should always be made with boiling water to bring out their fullest taste. Black teas are as popular abroad as they are in China, and the best-known variety, Keemum (Qimen), from Anhui province, became the most sought after tea for export during the Qing dynasty. Keemum is also believed to have inspired the brand known as English Breakfast. Some tea drinkers maintain that, with its deep, red color and appealing fragrance, Keemum is the ideal black tea. Another noted variety is Lapsang Souchong from Fujian province, which has a strong, smoky taste. (Some classify Lapsang Souchong as a blend rather than a distinct variety.) Yunnan province produces a famous black tea known as Puer. Besides having a fine flavor, it is treasured as a digestive aid. Although Puer has come to be synonymous with a red or black tea, more than one hundred different varieties of teas may be categorized under the Puer name, including green and oolong strains.

Oolong Teas

Once picked, some tea leaves are partially fermented, producing a broad range of teas known as the oolong, or semifermented variety. While flavors differ according to the particular brand, oolongs tend to be more subtle and less sharp than their fully fermented cousins. Some contend that oolong teas are the most desirable of all, combining the appealing characteristics of both black and green varieties: they have a refined, yet distinctive flavor with a deep, attractive hue. As with fermented teas, oolongs should be brewed with boiling water to properly develop their taste. The most famous form of oolong tea is the British brand known as Gunpowder oolong, but most purists would agree that this tea pales in comparison to the finest Chinese varieties. Tie Guanyin, or Iron Goddess of Mercy, and Oolong, or Black Dragon, are rated the most highly among oolong experts. Both varieties are grown in Fujian province in eastern China and in Taiwan. Cantonese are partial to Shui Xian or Water Nymph, which is cultivated in Fujian, Taiwan, and Guangdong province in southern China.

Flower Teas

While most purists would restrict the classification of teas into the three preceding categories, *hua cha*, or flower teas, which are made by infusing different treas with dried flower petals, have become increasingly popular in China and abroad. Flower teas are believed to have originated during the Song dynasty when dried flowers were blended with tea leaves to improve the flavor of inferior brands. As time passed the range of flowers used as flavorings grew to include petals of the rose, cassia, lotus, plum, and orchid. Jasmine is sometimes labeled a flower tea rather than a semifermented brand, since the process involves smoking or curing tea leaves with jasmine petals. The most refined and desirable of all flower teas is made by brewing water with dried chrysanthemum petals. The color is pale, the flavor is sweet, and the fragrance is intoxicating.

Chinese Wines, Spirits, and Beers

Three cups are the gateway to bliss;
A jar and the world is all yours.
The rapture of drinking, and wine's dizzy joy,
No man who is sober deserves.

—LI BAI (701–762)

Throughout the ages, the Chinese have shown exuberant passion for wine and spirits. Poets and scholars have extolled the delights of imbibing alcoholic drinks, and wine has played a prominent role in Chinese ritual and decorum. Ceremonial bronze drinking vessels have been exhumed from tombs dating back to the Shang era (eighteenth–twelfth centuries B.C.), and some even believe that excessive indulgence in drink was responsible for the dissolution of that dynasty.

There is little concrete information about when fermented brews first appeared in China or how wine was invented. One story credits a forgetful cook with having left some rice and water standing in a covered earthenware pot some thirty-five-hundred years ago. He sampled the contents and then promptly served the brew to the members of the imperial court, who all became completely inebriated. The drink was christened *jiu* and the emperor felt compelled to impose specific rules concerning its intake: he insisted that it be served in small cups; that food always be eaten with the drink; and that some form of mental or physical activity must be performed while drinking to prevent overindulgence. Perhaps it was as a result of these commands that food and drink became intimate partners, for from then on, proper social behavior demanded that any type of alcoholic beverage be accompanied by some food, most often in the form of wine-accompanying dishes or snacks.

Apart from rice, the Chinese made wine from wheat, millet, sorghum, and corn, depending on the region. Seasonings such as cassia, pomegranate blossoms, and Sichuan peppercorns were added to enhance their flavors. And since wine was often administered as a tonic, various herbs were used to improve its curative powers.

Jiu, wine, became the ubiquitous term used to refer to all fermented brews, even distilled spirits and grape wines, which arrived later. The Chinese generally divide their traditional wines and spirits into three main groups: yellow, white, and flavored, a category that also includes medicinal drinks.

Yellow wines *(lao jiu)* are the most prominent variety of Chinese alcoholic beverage, and their most popular form is rice wine. All rice wines are made by fermenting glutinous rice, water, and yeast, with a starter added. Young wines are clear, and their alcoholic content may be about 8 percent. They generally are used for cooking. The superior rice wines, which age longer, turn a deep yellow, thicken slightly, and are more suitable for drinking; they might be served at a Chinese banquet. Their alcoholic content is about 15 percent or higher.

Although there are hundreds of rice wines, Shaoxing wine, a famous brew from Zhejiang province in eastern China with a 2,300-year history, is considered the best. The key ingredient that sets it apart from all other rice wines is believed to be the pure spring water from Jian Lake. It is also more potent, with an alcoholic content of 18 percent. The wine made for general consumption is aged from three to five years, although there are rumored to be a few gallons that have been fermenting for sixty years.

For those buying Shaoxing wine, it is available in different grades:

Nuer hong, which is packaged in a shapely turquoise porcelain container, is considered the top grade. In ancient China, it was customary to bury a batch of wine a month after a daughter was born, allowing it to ferment until she was married. In keeping with this tradition, *nuer hong* rice wine is aged the longest period of all the Shaoxing varieties—at least five years. It has a deep, brown color and a rich flavor. It is traditionally served on very special occasions but may be ordered at any type of banquet as a toasting wine.

Hua diao, a secondary grade, is also available in a porcelain container, but the flavor and color are slightly lighter than *nuer hong*. It is considered to be the all-purpose banquet wine, and foreigners might find it more suited to their palate, since it is slightly less pungent.

Jia fan (or *chia fan*) is another type of Shaoxing brew, but one in which more rice is added in the fermentation process—hence the Chinese name, which means "added rice." *Jia fan* is thicker and sweeter than other grades. It is sold in a brown earthenware crock and is, among Chinese customers, the most popular variety of Shaoxing wine. Although it is primarily considered a wine for drinking, some chefs like to use it in their cooking.

Yuan hong, the lowest grade of Shaoxing wine, is sold in clear bottles with a red label. In China, this is the most readily available brand of Shaoxing and is popularly used for cooking. Since this type is aged the least amount of time, the color and flavor are lighter than all other grades. It is also the least expensive.

Any grade of Shaoxing is traditionally served heated slightly in cooler weather and at room temperature during the rest of the year.

Distillation is believed to have been invented in Sichuan province as early as A.D. 800, but it was not widely used until the Song era (960–1279), when the Chinese applied the process to several types of grain. Millet and sorghum were the most popular grains, but rice, corn, and wheat were used as well. Distilled spirits are grouped under the category of white or "white dry" *(bai gen)*. Most of these drinks are extraordinarily potent, with an alcoholic content of 100 proof and higher. There are thousands of types of "white" liquors made in different regions of China, but the following are preferred by connoisseurs.

- Maotai—anyone who has attended a Chinese banquet will never forget the experience of sampling Maotai. (Some liken the flavor to that of jet fuel.) This clear, seemingly benign drink, which is made from millet and wheat, has an alcoholic content of 106 proof. It is made in Guizhou province in southwestern China, and sources attest that the drink originated as early as A.D. 1105.
- Fen Jiu—this distilled drink, a type of sorghum-based *(gaoliang)* liquor, is primarily distilled from sorghum. It is mainly produced in Shaanxi province in central China and has a flavor some consider to be even harsher than that of Maotai. In fact,

some liken the experience of drinking this wine to imbibing barbed wire. Fen Jiu has an alcoholic content of 130 proof.

- Xifeng Daqu—although not widely available abroad, this sorghum-based spirit is quite celebrated in China. With a history of over two thousand years, it is made in Xifeng in Shaanxi province in central China. *Daqu* liquor is made with sorghum in a distillation process similar to that used for *gaoliang,* and while the flavor differs slightly, the fiery qualities are equally potent.
- Wu Liang Ye—another sorghum-based spirit, this fiery drink also includes wheat, rice, corn, and millet. It is a famous product from Sichuan province, and although rated one of the top five liquors in China, it is not widely available outside the country.

"Flavored" wines and spirits, which make up the third category of Chinese *jiu,* are usually fermented or distilled in the traditional manner with a base of rice or sorghum and the addition of a Chinese seasoning, medicine, or herb. The most famous is Rose Petal Liquor (Meigui Liu Jiu), which has a sorghum base to which fresh rose petals are added. Tianjin is the home of the most noted brand, but it is especially popular among the Cantonese, who also use it to spice their marinade for pork and duck. The name "Rose Petal" may evoke mellowness, but the drink is sweet and fiery with a 130 proof alcoholic content.

Bamboo liquor (Gu Ye Qing) is another popular flavored liquor whose most famous brand is produced in Shaanxi province. With a *gaoliang,* or distilled sorghum base, bamboo liquor boasts the addition of a dozen Chinese herbs, including bamboo leaves. It is believed to aid blood reproduction and is drunk as a digestive aid.

Wujiapi jiu, or Five Skin Wine, is another medicinal sorghum-based liquor with a 110 proof alcoholic content. It is made with the Chinese herb *Acanthopanax* and is especially popular in cooler weather, since it is believed to improve circulation and helps to battle rheumatism.

Other varieties in the extensive category of "flavored" and medicinal wines include osmanthus brandy and ginseng-flavored brandy, as well as spirits flavored with such exotic items as snake venom and deer antler. In addition, fruit liqueurs are numerous, with the most popular being those made with orange blossoms, apricot, kiwi fruit, black plums, and litchis.

Although grapes are believed to have been cultivated in Shanxi province in northern China as early as the Tang dynasty (618–907), when wines are also believed to have first been imported from the west, wine-making was not widely practiced among the Chinese until the beginning of the nineteenth century when the Germans began manufacturing in earnest in Shandong province in northeastern China. The Chinese, however, continued to prefer wines made from other types of fruits, most notably plums and flower petals.

Most Chinese grape wines are overly sweet, and their quality is not on a par with those found in other parts of the world, but the situation is slowly improving. Today, with the introduction of joint-venture wineries from France, Chinese companies are seeing a renaissance in the production of quality grape wines, brandy, and cognac, particularly in the Tianjin area. Several quality wines are being bottled there, with the two most widely available brands being Dynasty, which makes a decent medium-dry white wine, and the Heavenly Palace Winery, which exports Spring Moon, a pleasant white table wine. Tianma Winery, in Tianjin, is also beginning to produce and export a good-quality brandy.

The Germans first introduced beer to China during the early 1900s, opening breweries in northern China. Up until the last ten years, it was a drink enjoyed more enthusiastically by foreigners. Today, beer is the most popular alcoholic drink in China, and every major city boasts at least one local brewery. The bestselling brand in China and abroad is Tsingtao from Qingdao city in Shandong province, but other breweries have begun exporting their products: both Great Wall and Five-Star Beer from Beijing are now also available in a limited number of countries outside China. Although foreigners tend to like their beer ice-cold, be forewarned: in most restaurants in China, it is available only at room temperature or warm.

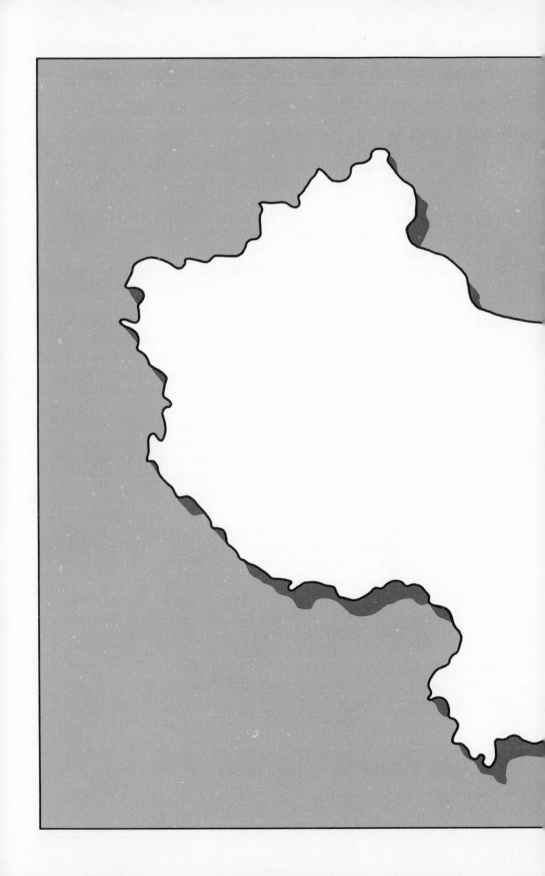

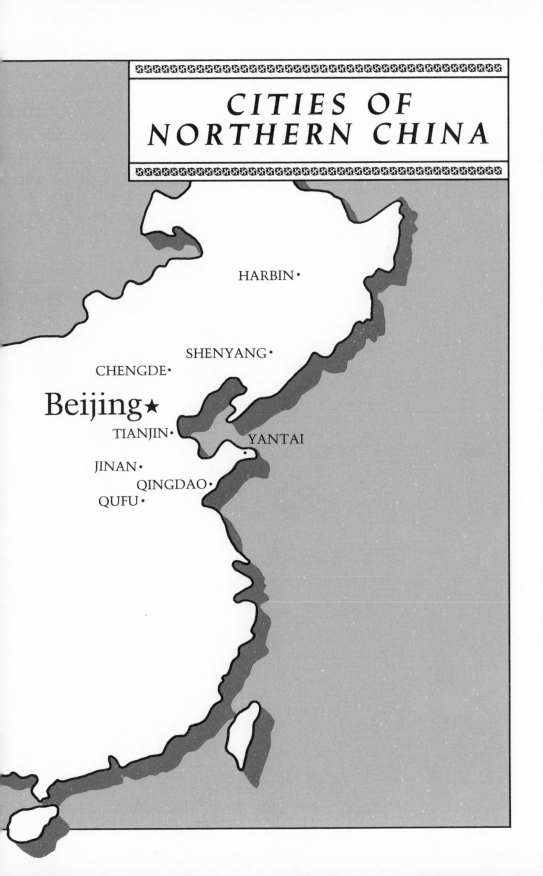

CITIES OF NORTHERN CHINA

HARBIN·

SHENYANG·

CHENGDE·

Beijing★

TIANJIN·

YANTAI

JINAN·

QINGDAO·

QUFU·

NORTHERN COOKING

F or most foreigners northern cuisine immediately conjures up visions of roast duck. To be sure, duck is a noted dish in the city's classic repertoire: numerous restaurants offer the traditional Peking duck banquet complete with lacquer-coated duck skin wrapped in delicate Mandarin pancakes, often accompanied by an infinite series of courses making use of the individual duck parts, which may be stir-fried, grilled, deep-fried, or braised.

But northern cuisine is far richer and more varied than most visitors realize, and few discover the exquisite, and somewhat opulent delicacies of the imperial court, the refined and fresh flavors of Shandong province, the meaty but succulent offerings of Mongolian and Muslim cooking, and the robust and homey street foods to be found in stalls throughout the city.

Situated on the great plain dividing Inner Mongolia and the famed Yellow River, Beijing is the meeting point of the provinces of Shandong, Hebei, Shanxi, Shaanxi, and Henan, as well as the area formerly known as Manchuria. Each region contributes a host of products and divergent influences. In addition, because it has been the capital of China for close to a millennium, Beijing has drawn visitors from all parts of the country, and through the years, cooks have incorporated regional dishes from every area into the local culinary style. Even today, eateries all over the city offer the authentic flavors of Sichuan, Canton, and Shanghai, as well as those of the north.

Geographically, Beijing lies on a central plateau in the northern hemisphere. Accordingly, one would assume the climate to be temperate, but owing to the flatness of the surrounding terrain, Beijing is unprotected from the violent weather of the northwestern steppelands. Summers tend to be hot and humid, while winters are frigidly cold. The growing season is short, and the region does not enjoy the bounty of fruits and vegetables available year round, as in the south. While apples, peaches, pears, and grapes are transported from Shandong to the city in warmer times, root vegetables like cabbage, bok choy, leeks, and onions predominate most of the year.

One of the distinguishing features of northern regional cooking, due to the cooler climate, is the presence of wheat-based staples: steamed breads, noodles, dumplings, and pancakes replace rice in everyday fare. Meat also plays a significant role in the northern diet. The substantial presence in the city of Muslims, who shun pork for religious reasons, accounts for the popularity of lamb and beef. Like their forebears in Inner Mongolia and surrounding regions, Muslim chefs customarily boil or grill meat over an open fire, serving it plainly. In Beijing, the refined influence of the Han cooks has gradually prevailed, resulting in a more delicate version of many Muslim dishes. Mongolian firepot and Mongolian barbecue are two examples. The meat is cut into paper-thin slices, often marinated, and cooked in boiling broth or on a charcoal grill. It is then served with a spicy dipping sauce. Another import is lamb shashlik, where cubes of lamb are marinated in assorted spices, threaded on skewers, and cooked over a charcoal brazier.

In striking contrast to robust Muslim fare is imperial palace cuisine, which is extremely sophisticated. Most imperial dishes require lengthy, detailed cooking procedures, as well as costly delicacies such as shark's fin, bird's nest, fish lips, and bear's paw. Imperial dishes are diverse, reflecting the varied tastes and palates of the individual rulers for whom they were created. And a number of imperial recipes are representative of the food of Shandong, a province to the east. In ancient times Shandong chefs were highly respected for their culinary skills and were brought in to run the imperial stoves. Shandong cuisine takes full advantage of the province's bounty of vegetables, fruits, and seafood. The seasonings are mild and the sauces are light, so that the natural, fresh flavors of the foods are accentuated.

Like those of any other city in China, Beijing's food stalls contribute their share of regional specialties, featuring a sublime assembly of snack foods: fluffy steamed buns stuffed with various fillings, hand-thrown noodles served in spicy broths, crusty dumplings, and skewers of miniature crab apples coated in a neat layer of crackling caramel.

Northern cuisine, with its diverse and contrasting elements, is easily among the most wide-ranging schools of classic Chinese cooking.

BEIJING

Beijing was not a city that I warmed to immediately. Certainly, I was amazed and moved by the Forbidden City, and awed and enthralled by the grandeur of the Summer Palace and the Temple of Heaven. But its outskirts were very off-putting, with their endless rows of characterless, identical high-rise buildings, and there was something cold and a little forbidding about the city and the mood of its people.

As it happened, I had made that first trip in 1979, at the height of the activity surrounding the Freedom Wall, an event that heralded the end of the persecution of the Cultural Revolution, and proved to be an exciting but uneasy time in China. On subsequent visits, however, I became familiar with the city and accustomed to its vastness, and finally I found myself captivated by its unique charm. Like any capital, it is an intriguing place, seething with the politics and history of the entire country. As evidenced recently, in May and June of 1989, and throughout the Cultural Revolution, Beijing—and particularly Tiananmen Square—is China's primary staging ground for political rallies and protests.

Throughout its three-thousand-year history, Beijing has seen its share of tumult. First settled in the twelfth century B.C. under the name of Ji, the city was later destroyed during the Qin dynasty (221–206 B.C.) and rebuilt during the Han (206 B.C.–A.D. 220). It first came to be known as Beiping or "northern peace" in 1368, during the Ming dynasty. In 1403 it became the capital of China and was renamed Beijing or "northern capital," and remained as such until the early 1920s, when for the next twenty years of turbulence the capital was moved to Nanjing. In 1949, after the founding of the People's Republic of China, Beijing again was christened the capital by Mao Zedong.

Beijing is a city markedly influenced by the changing of its seasons. Since the land is flat, it is subject to the whims of the elements. During the short spring, cool nights give way to sunny, dusty days; in summer, the city assumes a humid stillness. In the winter months, the temperature may be frigid, but the sun usually prevails, producing a dry, bracing cold. Autumn is when Beijing's weather is ideal, with clear, sunny days crowned by vivid sunsets and followed by crisp, cold evenings.

Beijing's population is a blending of Han, Mongolian, and Muslim, with some minorities from Tibet and the remote western province of Xinjiang. Like its people, the city's food is a study in contrasts. At small snack houses customers revel in the humble delights of northern regional snacks—crusty, pan-fried dumplings, bowls brimming with hearty soups, and skewers of fragrant cumin-flavored barbecued lamb shashlik. Nearby, magnificent restaurants, their exterior and decor preserved from the Qing dynasty, (1644–1911), prepare the sophisticated delicacies of the imperial palace kitchens, which they offer on precious porcelain. Then there are the vast impersonal eateries featuring Peking duck and rinsed lamb pot, built after China reopened its doors to the west in the late seventies. And most recently, western-style bakeries and fast-food chains have begun to litter the urban landscape, offering crusty French loaves, whipped-cream pastries, and fried chicken and biscuits with brown gravy.

Needless to say, it is a city that offers something for everyone, and whether you dine in majestic splendor in pagodas that overlook Beihai Park or stroll through the soaring main pavilion of the Summer Palace, Beijing is a city that will captivate and enchant both your mind and your stomach.

BEIJING FANDIAN (BEIJING HOTEL) CHINESE DINING ROOM
First Floor

—

33 Dong Changan Jie
Tel.: 5137766
Hours: 11:30 A.M.–10:00 P.M.

While the Beijing Hotel has acquired an impressive reputation for its banquet dinners, I must take issue with such claims. In my experience, the food has been mediocre and the prices have been ridiculously inflated. (If you can even book reservations, the base cost is usually over U.S. $100 per person.)

Although it's hardly banquet fare, I do recommend one dish prepared at the Beijing Hotel: the dumplings *(jiaozi)*, which can be ordered on the first-floor Chinese dining hall, are positively first rate. Years ago, I was tipped off to them by a Chinese acquaintance, and after countless dumpling orgies, I must admit that they are some of the best I have ever tasted. Stuffed with meat and cabbage, and generously seasoned with garlic chives, they make a filling and inexpensive meal. If you are a fan of dumplings, this is the place to feast. There are two choices—northern-style or spicy Sichuanese. I prefer the plain ones, but sample both, and choose your own favorite. I like to round out the meal with several orders of the hotel's pickled cabbage *(pao cai)*.

The dining room is somewhat cavernous, the tablecloths are not always clean, and the service is often inexcusably slow, but all my irritations disappear after the first mouthful of those steaming dumplings. Usually the pickled cabbage is served immediately and can be eaten to quell hunger pangs.

The menu is Chinese and English. There are many other dishes on the dining-hall menu, but I have found many to be unsatisfactory in flavor and sloppy in execution. Reservations are unnecessary.

BEIJING JIAZHOUKAOROU (BEIJING MONOGOLIAN BARBECUE RESTAURANT)

▬

16 Deng Dajie
Tel.: 5112142
Hours:
11:30 A.M.–2:30 P.M. (lunch),
5:30–8:30 P.M. (dinner)

Just up the street from Qianmen, the south gate in Beijing, is a new strip of restaurants that was built in 1987. The most promising eatery in the lot has a bright neon sign announcing "Bar-B-Q." And for anyone who has had the pleasure of enjoying a Mongolian barbecue in Taiwan or elsewhere, these words are enough to send you scurrying up the stairs to the second- (for local currency) or third-floor (for Foreign Exchange Certificates) dining room.

Although Mongolian barbecue is available at other restaurants in the city, the Taiwanese version offered here is a wonderful do-it-yourself, all-you-can-eat affair. Diners begin by piling thin slices of raw meats and shreds of assorted vegetables into an empty bowl, sprinkling the lot with their own mixture of seasonings. The bowl is then handed to a chef, who cooks the contents in seconds on a huge, charcoal-fueled brazier. The diner may then eat the stir-fried meat and vegetables as is or stuff them into hot, flaky sesame buns, which magically appear at the table when the cooked food arrives.

The sesame buns are slightly doughy, and the selection of meats and vegetables might not be so extensive as in some restaurants, but the cooked barbecue is very good, and for 22 yuan or a little more, customers can eat their fill, returning as many times as they please. Included in the cost is a bowl of somewhat bland but nonetheless soothing corn soup.

The Mongolian Barbecue Restaurant is the joint venture of an overseas Chinese investor from Taiwan and a Chinese company. On the day we dined there tables of Caucasians and Chinese were calmly enjoying the food at the third-floor dining room, while the lower floors were packed with local residents reveling in the newness of the experience. (Westerners may be familiar with the all-you-can-eat smorgasbord concept, but few Chinese have ever encountered such a remarkable thing.)

(continued)

Reservations should be made the day before for large parties. If the group is small, seats should be available. The restaurant does accept a host of credit cards, including Visa, American Express, and Diner's Club.

BEIJING KAOYA DIAN (WALL STREET DUCK)

—

Hepingmen, north of
Liulichang Jie
Tel.: 334422, 338031–2
Hours:
10:30 A.M.–1:00 P.M. (lunch),
4:30–8:00 P.M. (dinner)

Beijing is famous for its roast duck, and perhaps the largest and glitziest of the restaurants serving the dish is the Hepingmen branch of the Beijing Roast Duck Restaurant. Its sister restaurant, located off of Tiananmen Square, is far more humble and older (see page 75), but reservations there must be made quite a bit in advance. Since the Wall Street Duck is a far bigger establishment, with forty-one private dining rooms and seating for 2,500 people, tables are easier to come by.

Although there have been reports of customers being rushed and the restaurant's requiring a hefty minimum per person before assuring a reservation, we did not encounter either of these problems. Our meal there was above reproach, and perhaps our treatment was better than that given most diners, for we were dining with one of the most famous culinary historians in China.

We were seated in one of the private dining rooms, which had a pleasant if thoroughly bland decor. The service was somewhat slow, but our waitress was accommodating. Since we were there for the duck dinner, we sampled a number of duck specialties, for which this restaurant has gained just renown. Before the arrival of the duck, we were presented with an exquisite rendition of duck web, meat, and liver bathed in a fermented wine rice sauce. The sauce was slightly sweet and heady with the flavor of rice wine lees. Also served were delicious deep-fried duck livers lightly coated in bread crumbs, and duck wings that had been boned and stuffed with slivers of black mushrooms and stir-fried with hearts of green vegetable.

The highlight of the meal, as expected, was the roast duck, with crisp skin and tender meat.

In Beijing, restaurants serve as accompaniments both pancakes, which are delicately thin, or flaky sesame cakes *(shao bing)*. The sweet bean sauce that accompanies the duck and is spread on the pancake or sesame cake is especially flavorful here. The duck soup, however, which traditionally follows the main course, was flavorless.

Prices at this eatery are steep. For about 100 yuan per person, with a party of six to twelve, one can enjoy a cold platter, four to five entrées, including the roast duck, plus soup and fruit for dessert. Beverages are extra, but shouldn't be too expensive. Since this is the most popular duck restaurant for foreigners, reservations must be made at least forty-eight hours in advance.

BEIJING SANXIA JIULOU (BEIJING SANXIA RESTAURANT)
▬

76 Xirongxian
Tele.: 651678
Hours:
10:30 A.M.–1:30 P.M. (lunch),
6:30–9:30 P.M. (dinner)

From the street, the Beijing Sanxia Restaurant might not look all that impressive, particularly in the face of the splendor of the Sichuan Restaurant across the way. But the first clue to the quality of this eatery is the handwritten (and in slightly mangled English) message to customers that is posted on the front window, ensuring them of the dedication of the restaurant toward preparing good food and inviting all to come in, try, and offer advice. The only advice we could give was to keep up the good work.

Opened in 1987, the Sanxia is a joint venture between a Sichuan provincial catering company and the Beijing government. Twenty chefs from Sichuan province reign in the kitchen, overseen by master chef Chang Ke Qin, who won a gold medal in the National Culinary Competition held in Beijing in 1988.

The first floor holds simple tables where customers can enjoy elaborate dishes or the simpler pleasures of Sichuanese fare, such as dumplings in hot oil or *dan dan* noodles. On the second floor, nine stately private rooms with doorways draped in red velvet curtains hold tables for banquet parties.

Some of the restaurant's noted specialties are camphor-smoked duck *(zhang cha ya)*, spicy fish-

(continued)

flavored crispy fish *(yu xiang cui pi yu)*, stuffed bean curd *(koudai doufu)*, braised fish *(tai bai yuan yu)*, and steamed spareribs in fragrant rice powder *(feng zheng yuan leng tu tiao)*—not to mention the old classic Ma Po bean curd *(Ma Po doufu)*.

For banquets, customers should make bookings two days in advance, but for smaller groups who prefer to order directly from the menu and don't mind the plain setting on the first floor, tables are usually available. (During peak meal hours, there may be a brief wait.) Depending on the number of courses, banquets may cost about 80 to 100 yuan per person, whereas if you order à la carte from the menu, the price should average about 30 to 40 yuan per person.

BEIJING WANGFUJING QUANJUDE ("SICK DUCK" ROAST DUCK)

—

13 Shuaifu Yuan, Wangfujing Dajie
Tel.: 553310, 551642, 554669
Hours:
11:30 A.M.–1:00 P.M. (lunch), 5:30–8:00 P.M. (dinner)

For years this restaurant has been known as the "Sick Duck," since it is just down the street from the Capital Hospital. But I suspect that its unusual name also distinguishes this eatery from its two cousins, the Qianmen Roast Duck and the Hepingmen Roast Duck restaurants. All are owned by the same company, and some regulars claim there is little difference in the food they serve.

The Wangfujing Quanjude, however, does hold a special place in my own heart, for it was here, on my first trip to Bejing in 1979, that I sampled my first Peking duck in Beijing, and the meal was superb. I can report, also, that recent visits have, despite one or two dishes that were disappointments confirmed my initial impressions. The only problem remains obtaining reservations. Since the restaurant is quite small, seats are not easy to come by. (To be safe, bookings should be made at least forty-eight hours in advance.)

The restaurant serves excellent Peking duck, with a delectable version of sweet bean sauce. (Each chef adds his own seasonings to this condiment, making its flavor at each restaurant distinctive.) The "Sick Duck" also claims responsibility for having created the classic specialty steamed duck custard, an eggy custard fortified with duck fat. Today, if you attend an authentic Peking duck dinner in Hong Kong or Taiwan (as well as many restaurants in China), this dish is a standard part of the feast.

The "Sick Duck" is older and slightly funkier than the Wall Street Duck, and to me, its atmosphere is slightly more appealing. There are five or six private rooms, and unless you have a large party and are spending a great deal of money, you will most likely be seated in one of the small dining rooms with other Chinese parties. The dining rooms are plain with the ubiquitous burgundy carpeting and Chinese calligraphy, but pleasant. The linen is meticulous, and the service is quite good, albeit a trifle curt. Among the other highly regarded dishes are the stir-fried duck meat with green peppers, deep-fried duck livers, and stir-fried shrimp with water chestnuts.

Unfortunately, the "Sick Duck" tends to be somewhat rigid with its bookings: it seldom allows foreigners to order spontaneously from the menu. The usual procedure is to specify a price, and it will plan the menu after the reservation is made. When booking the table, you should specify any dishes you aren't interested in eating. The minimum per person is at least 70 yuan, but to get a full meal with Peking duck and four or five entrées, expect to pay about 100 yuan or more per person.

CHENG JI SI KAN JIUJIA (GENGHIS KHAN RESTAURANT)

—

Liangmaqiao Lu, Chaoyangqu
Tel.: 471614
Hours:
8:00 A.M.–3:30 P.M. (lunch),
5:00 P.M.–12:00 A.M. (dinner)

Few restaurants in China are as entertaining as the Genghis Khan. It is worth a visit if only for the theatrical experience of dining in its simulated Inner Mongolian tents. It is a thirty-five-minute drive from Beijing center, but in a city where getting to almost every destination requires some time, the distance is only a slight inconvenience.

Although the Genghis Khan has a large main dining room, try to eat in one of the small tents, where gay red, white, and blue half-moon banners line the walls and various Mongolian artifacts such as brass kettles, firepots, and boots are casually arranged. By day natural light from a central skylight shines upon an oasis of potted greenery in lush profusion. Waitresses, all said to be imported from the steppelands, are dressed in native Mongolian garb and supply a traditional Mongolian song and dance once the meal has been served.

The restaurant is the creation of E. Rdunbigle, its manager. An Inner Mongolian originally from Beijing, Rdunbigle spent a great deal of time in Inner Mongolia during the Cultural Revolution. According to the restaurant's assistant manager, it was during this period of exile that he conceived the idea for the Genghis Khan, but it was only in 1986 that he was finally able to realize his dream. Since then, his eatery has been drawing many curious locals and foreigners.

For about 80 to 90 yuan, you can dine here quite sumptuously on one of several set menu packages. The full-price meal begins with red-cooked beef slices and a vegetarian platter composed of shredded cucumbers, bean curd, and softened rice sheets tossed in a spicy dressing. Next, a selection of hot dishes, including braised oxtail and assorted stir-fried dishes, is served. Accompanying them are crisp fried cakes (slightly tough) with a minced lamb, garlic, and chive filling. Barbecued lamb strips, redolent with coriander and sesame seeds, are threaded on skewers and served piping hot from the grill.

The reigning pièce de résistance is a leg of lamb barbecued until tender in the roasting pit and served whole by the waitress, who then rather ineptly attempts to carve it. The best advice is to grab a knife and carve the meat yourself. The lamb comes with three dipping sauces —a soy sauce–garlic mixture, a garlic chive oil, and a fiery chili oil. The meal ends with the serving of a traditional Mongolian firepot (see page 336).

Beverages are extra, and lunch reservations are unnecessary. For dinner, bookings—particularly during the colder weather, when Mongolian dishes are especially in demand—should be made twenty-four hours in advance.

DONG DAN CAI SHICHANG (DONG DAN MARKET)

▬

Jianguomennei Dajie
Hours: 8:00–11:00 P.M.

If you are in the mood for an entertaining after-dinner walk, or feel especially adventurous about sampling some Chinese street stall food, the Dong Dan Night Market in front of the Dong Dan Market proper will satisfy either desire.

By day the sidewalk is lined with stalls selling all types of clothing from stone-washed denim jeans to gay-colored panty hose. At night, the makeshift shops disappear, and the area is transformed into a veritable food carnival. Cooks clad in white outfits hawk their products, calling out to strollers to encourage them to taste their dishes, and holding up deep-fried quail and freshly grilled lamb shashlik as bait.

The snacks are varied and reflect the change in the seasons. Year-round offerings include crisp scallion pancakes, caldrons of fried noodles with assorted meats and vegetables, steamed buns and breads, fried bean curd with a spicy chili dip, and pan-fried egg rolls with myriad fillings. In the warmer weather, ice cream, grilled corn, and slices of fresh fruit are popular. As winter approaches, the tropical fruits disappear to be replaced by hot sweet soups and baked sweet potatoes.

Sanitation is not a top priority, as cooks stack used bowls and chopsticks pyramid-style in huge tubs of clear water for rinsing. But the odors are enticing, and even if you choose not to eat, there is much pleasure to be had in watching others relish the tantalizing food.

DONGLAISHUN FANZHUANG (DONGLAISHUN RESTAURANT)

—

16 Jinyu Hutong,
Dongchengqu
Tel.: 550069, 556465
Hours:
11:00 A.M.–1:30 P.M. (lunch),
5:00–8:30 P.M. (dinner)

Donglaishun has long been considered one of the most popular and traditional restaurants serving Muslim food in the city. One of the five restaurants housed in and managed by the East Market complex, it is located in the center of the bustling market area of Beijing, just ten minutes from the Beijing Hotel.

Reservations are especially in demand in the winter months when customers pack the eatery to gorge themselves. A year-round favorite is rinsed lamb pot (shuan yang rou), a Chinese-style fondue. For this dish, a huge brass pot fueled by charcoal is filled with bubbling broth and placed in the center of the table. Diners then dip paper-thin slices of lamb, cabbage, cellophane noodles, bean curd, and other ingredients in the soup to cook. The cooked food is then dipped into a serving sauce, which can be adjusted by each customer to taste. Flaky sesame buns and pickled garlic cloves also are served. Many diners like to stuff the cooked meat in the delectable buns, which are also handy for eating many of the entrée dishes sandwich-style.

Donglaishun also offers some delicious appetizers and entrees. Some of the best appetizers are the spiced beef (jiang jianzi), cabbage with chili (la baicai), fried walnuts, (zha taoren), and cold braised chicken (leng shao ji). For entrées, stay with the lamb dishes, however much you may be overwhelmed by their profusion and tempted instead by the chicken and duck entrées. The best of the lot are the baked shashlik of mutton (kao yangrou chuan), which is grilled tender lamb shish kebab beautifully seasoned with a hint of five-spice powder; dry stir-fried mutton (gan bao yangrou), a superb dish with thin shavings of lamb seasoned with scallions; soft-fried fillet (ruan zha liji), seasoned with bamboo shoot shreds and coriander; and braised mutton in red sauce (pa yangrou tiao).

Within the last two years, the restaurant has added a new wing, which has numerous private rooms. The decor is somewhat bland, but it is

(continued)

clean and innocuously pleasant. But the food is what draws people to this eatery, and generally it is excellent. Prices, depending on the dishes ordered, can be on the expensive side, and for a filling meal with a rinsed lamb pot and several entrées, expect to pay at least 80 yuan per person. Since this is one of the most popular restaurants in the city, reservations should be made at least twenty-four hours in advance.

DU YI CHU SHAO MAI GUAN (DU YI CHU SHAO MAI RESTAURANT)

—

36 Qianmen Dajie
Tel.: 5112093
Hours: 6:15 A.M.–9:30 P.M.

The Du Yi Chu is famous throughout Beijing for its steamed open-face dumplings *(shao mai)*. That is the exclusive offering at this tiny eatery where hordes come, sit at the round tables, and devour mountains of freshly steamed dumplings generously doused with vinegar.

This is a very simple place for the adventurous eater who wants to experience a bit of local color. The dumplings are good, stuffed with a pork and shrimp filling, but slightly doughy. Prices are cheap; the dumplings are weighed and sell for about 75 cents per ounce.

A CULINARY HISTORIAN IN CHINA

—

*W*ang *Ren Xing is eating. But his method and manner are not those of the casual diner. His concentration is total as he drinks in the fragrance, texture, and color of each dish.*

His face is intent, eyebrows knitted together and forehead beaded with sweat while he tastes his food. He relishes each mouthful—the deep-fried duck liver, lightly coated with breading and crispy on the outside, the duck web, meat, and liver bathed in the fermented wine rice sauce, the red-cooked duck wings with tender stir-fried hearts of green vegetable, and finally, the Peking duck—tender meat and crisp skin brushed with a bold stroke of sweet bean sauce and stuffed into a crispy sesame-seed bun. At last, temporarily satiated until the next dishes arrive, he begins to talk about the food before him.

"Today, most restaurants only use one version of cooking Peking duck—where the duck is hung in a vertical oven and roasted," Mr. Wang explains, "but traditionally, there were other methods. The first is a technique known as men, *where the duck is literally smothered with the heat. First the duck is roasted in a hot oven, then the oven is completely sealed off, the heat is lowered, and the duck continues cooking for about forty minutes. The other method is* cha shao *or barbecued, where the duck is roasted on an open spit. Most duck restaurants in this city use the first method of cooking in a vertical oven."*

Mr. Wang is no ordinary gastronome. He is considered one of the most knowledgeable culinary historians in China, particularly in the area of northern Chinese cooking. His expertise is acknowledged in Beijing by restaurateur and master chef alike, as well as by members of culinary associations in the most distant provinces of China.

Mr. Wang's age and appearance belie his knowledge. He looks to be in his mid-thirties, but he is actually forty-three years old. He has already published eight books. And despite a voracious appetite for all types of food, he is painfully thin. Perhaps the calories are burned away by the intensity with which he approaches each endeavor in his frenetic schedule.

In addition to writing books. Mr. Wang is an associate editor of China's Food, *the foremost monthly food magazine; he is the* resident culinary historian of the Beijing Food Research Institute, the leading agency for food research in China; and he is a frequent consultant to restaurants and hotels in Beijing, which, from time to time, stage re-creations of historical banquets or notable individual dishes. In 1988 he helped to research and plan the menus for the first Imperial Food Festival, featuring Qing dynasty dishes, organized by the Beijing Huizhong Hotel.

He is singularly dedicated to his study of Chinese culinary history, a pursuit that only recently has been taken seriously in China. Last year, Mr. Wang took a sabbatical without pay to devote himself to the study of Japanese. He now reads and speaks it fluently, which is essential in his research, since so many Japanese texts contain historical information regarding Chinese culinary matters, and much of the corresponding material in China was destroyed during the Cultural Revolution.

Oddly enough, his present occupation was determined by a death in his family when he was a boy, but his curiosity earmarked him early on for some type of research. "I always asked questions about everything," Mr. Wang explained. "I was a very curious child. Everything fascinated me.

"My father was a cook here in Beijing who made shao bing (flaky sesame buns). After I graduated from middle school, I went to the university, but my mother died and I had to go to work to help support the family. There were three children and I was the oldest. There was no question about my leaving school, but I was upset and disappointed. That was in 1964. The government sent me to a small restaurant to be a chef, and I did that for eight years, but even while I was working there, I pursued studies of my own. Every afternoon from two to four o'clock when there weren't any customers I would go to the Beijing library to study. The other employees would watch the restaurant, play chess, or talk, but I went to the library to study."

Mr. Wang's early research was practical, investigating problems of cooking. His first book, which was written in 1978, explored the history of hotels in China with minor information on Chinese culinary history. From there he went on to write about Chinese holidays and food ritual, traditional foods and cooking methods, eating in the imperial manner, and ancient culinary culture.

His books could hardly be considered bestsellers in China, for the bulk of his audience is limited to the culinary schools and restaurant kitchens. Mr. Wang acknowledges that being a culinary historian presents a challenge. "It is a difficult topic to research because you must read a lot of ancient texts. In China, only professors have access to these books and can understand them, but they don't really comprehend the relevance of culinary history."

Despite the hardships, Mr. Wang is undeterred, confident of the importance of his work. "Confucius said that Chinese food is a source of Chinese culture," he said. "You can see it clearly if you visit the Museum of History here. There are many ancient Chinese vessels and 70 percent of them are cooking vessels. Through these implements we can understand much about past life-styles and civilization.

"Similarly, in a later period, Su Dongpo, a poet from the Sung dynasty, incorporated cooking ideas in his poetry. He used a sha guo clay pot, one of the oldest forms of a Chinese cooking vessel, to create a classic dish. Then he wrote a poem outlining the recipe.

"Huangzhou produces good pork," Mr. Wang slowly recites, "which is cheap as dirt. The rich spurn and won't eat it. The poor know not how to cook it. Keep the fire low; use very little water. I take a bowl of pork first thing in the morning. I like it this way—mind your own business."

FAMILY LI'S RESTAURANT

—

11 Yangfang Hutong, De Nei
Dajie
Tel.: 6011915
Hours: lunch and dinner daily
by appointment only

Because there is no sign indicating the location of Family Li's Restaurant, one of the most exclusive eateries in Beijing, most customers get lost and spend hours attempting to locate the place. Even with the correct number, finding the entrance is a trying business.

And then there's the matter of getting a reservation: for lunch, arrangements must be made two to three weeks in advance, and for dinner, the wait is one month. Still, customers like Armand Hammer, Lawrence Tisch, David Rockefeller, Donald Sutherland, Bette Bao Lord, and the American, British, Canadian, Italian, and Swiss ambassadors to China keep coming.

What is it that draws these luminaries and hundreds of other avid fans back to the restaurant? Is it the imperial palace cuisine, which the twenty-nine-year-old daughter Li Li has managed to duplicate with her father's help, or the fresh ingredients that the family meticulously uses for their dishes? Perhaps it is the singular experience of dining alone in the heart of a Chinese household, with the entire family helping to cook and serve the food.

The restaurant opened in 1985 after Li Li, who had recently graduated from the Chinese Social University with a degree in nutrition, won first prize in a nationally sponsored family dinner contest. The shy, willowy contestant received extraordinary publicity, and she decided to put it to use by opening a tiny restaurant in her family's home. Converting her bedroom into the dining room with one table, the family of six distributed the duties and volunteered to help.

Although the family has never had a restaurant proper, Li Li is continuing a heritage that began with her great-grandfather, who was a steward in charge of "life affairs" for the imperial court of the Qing dynasty (1644–1911). In that position, he oversaw the running of the imperial household and collected recipes from the imperial chefs.

Li Li's father, Li Shanglin, also has always had a fascination with food. As a child, he would watch the chefs creating imperial dishes and would study the recipes his father had gathered. Mr. Li went on to become a professor of applied mathematics, but he never lost his love of food. During the Cultural Revolution, he was barred from working and took up the task of cooking for his family. After the Red Guard destroyed the three hundred recipes that Li Shanglin had preserved from his father's work, he would spend part of every day trying to recall and record them.

Just as her father would stand, as a child, and watch the cooks in the imperial household, so too would Li Li take her place by his side as he cooked for the family, memorizing his technique and the recipes. When at fifteen she failed the college entrance examinations, she took over the role of cook for the family, experimenting daily

(continued)

with new dishes and attempting to recreate some of the fine cuisine of the imperial court. While her father remained her chief mentor, her mother, who was a pediatrician, gave her lessons in nutrition, and her artistic brother helped her to invent unique cold-platter designs.

From the opening day, the restaurant has been a great success. The first customers were invited guests from the Ministry of Health. So impressed were they with the meal that they told other officials and friends. Pujie, younger brother of Puyi, China's last emperor, also heard of the eatery and visited, intent on sampling dishes created from the imperial palace recipes. Soon articles appeared in the Chinese newspapers, and there hasn't been a quiet evening in the Li household since.

At first, the restaurant was only open on weekends, while Li Li attended classes at the Social University, but since she graduated, hours have been extended to include daily lunch and dinner—a daunting schedule, considering it takes about twelve hours to prepare every meal.

On a recent visit, while Li Li quietly worked in the kitchen readying a meal, Li Shanglin talked about the lengthy preparations involved in its organization. "First, Li Li and I plan the menu, trying to think about what's available. Then every day my wife, who is also retired, and I go to the market, Friendship store, Friendship supermarket, and free market looking for the ingredients. We try to get the freshest ingredients for each dish." To illustrate the family's fanatic concern for freshness, he shows us a fish tank where a live fish is swimming, unaware that it will soon become the sweet-and-sour fish course for our luncheon.

"Then we must clean the ingredients, cut and chop everything, and make it ready before the guests arrive," Li Shanglin continues. "People usually leave after ten o'clock, and then we have to clean everything, so we usually don't get to bed until after midnight. The next day we start all over again with the shopping."

Li Shanglin says the family does not make a great deal of money (about 200 yuan per month) from the restaurant, since ingredients are so expensive. They also pay a monthly stipend to neighbors, because the families are so closely clustered around the tiny courtyard. And indeed, there is no evidence of conspicuous consumption apart from the two refrigerators, which are obviously necessary for the business.

There is some talk that Li Li may leave the restaurant. Her father and mother have already anticipated some possible changes and have made plans. "Li Li may want to get married or go abroad to study, so my first daughter, my wife, and I will continue the restaurant. That's why it's called Family Li's restaurant," he says. "All our relatives and friends help."

A meal at the Lis may be fairly simple in execution, but its meticulous preparation is obvious. Our lunch began with four cold dishes, including chicken shreds in a gingery Sichuan peppercorn sauce, pickled cucumber slices, and tossed celery strips with mustard sauce. We then proceeded to soft-fried scallops, pork tenderloin in a wine rice sauce, deep-fried prawns, stir-fried bean sprouts, a whole Mandarin fish in sweet-and-sour sauce, excellent Peking duck with Mandarin pancakes, and a delicate chicken soup with tender chunks of winter melon.

Every meal served at the restaurant is different, and prices tend to run about 500 yuan for a table of eight to twelve people. Again, reservations must be made weeks in advance.

FANG SHAN FANDIAN (FANG SHAN RESTAURANT)
—

Island of the Hortensias
Beihai Gongyuan, Qiang Dao
Tel.: 442573, 443481
Hours:
11:30 A.M.–1:30 P.M. (lunch),
5:30–8:00 P.M. (dinner)

To my mind, there is no restaurant in China more spectacular than the Fang Shan. Laid out in the ancient manner, the restaurant consists of a series of magnificent interconnecting dining rooms (some more attractive than others), all decorated in the imperial Qing manner and overlooking scenic North Lake in Beihai Park.

By far the most splendid of the eleven dining rooms is located in one of the taller buildings. There the thronelike chairs surrounding the table are all upholstered in brilliant imperial yellow. One wall is lined with wooden doors that open onto a tiny balcony that looks out on the lake. If you can possibly book this room, do so, though as it is usually reserved for only the most expensive banquets.

The Fang Shan is known throughout China as one of the country's foremost restaurants, but some visitors have found the help surly and ill mannered and the food occasionally mediocre. After sampling a number of meals here, I have had both experiences, but the positive times outweigh the negative ones. And when the chefs are "on," the food here is nothing short of superb.

For a restaurant that has achieved such prominence, it is interesting that its history is not as venerable as others in Beijing. Its story began in 1911 when the Qing dynasty came to an end, and the imperial chefs were dismissed from their duties. In 1925, when Beihai Park was opened, a former official to the imperial kitchens invited three of its former master chefs, Sun Sahoran, Wang Yushan, and Zhao Chengshou, to open a teahouse that served tea and dishes based on imperial recipes. The restaurant flourished and in 1956, Fang Shan moved to the buildings it now inhabits. Although it appears small, it can serve up to three hundred people daily.

Many of the dishes on the menu originated as the favorites of the Empress Dowager Ci Xi, and as she was known to have a fondness for snacks, some of Fang Shan's most notable specialties are pastries, sweet and savory. Among them are the small steamed cornbreads (xiao wotou). These were created by imperial chefs in memory of a cornbread given to the Empress Dowager by a villager when she was fleeing Beijing in 1900 to escape the Allied forces.

Another specialty *(rou mo shao bing)*, a flaky sesame cake stuffed with ground meat and eaten sandwich-style, was inspired by a dream of the Empress Dowager. The next morning she awoke and found, to her wonder and delight, that the food of her dreams was on her breakfast menu. So extreme was her happiness that she rewarded the chef handsomely. This dish is still one of the most popular items on the menu. Other pastries include yellow mung bean cakes *(wandou huang)*, and red bean rolls *(yundou juan)*.

Although the restaurant is celebrated for some extraordinarily elaborate dishes, many of them in the shape of dragons and phoenixes, the kitchen also offers some less complex but no less refined dishes. Foremost among them are The Three Treasures *(guan men San Xian)*, a clear steamed soup with chicken, black mushrooms, and sea cucumbers, the stuffed Mandarin fish *(huaitai guiyu)*, fried duck stuffed with shrimp and walnuts *(hao ren ya feng)*, sweet-and-sour fillets of pork *(zhua chao liji)*, and mushrooms and rape stalks *(xianggu cai xin)*.

The prices vary according to the dishes ordered, but for a truly memorable meal, one can easily pay 160 yuan per person and up for a party of eight to twelve. If one has the time, money, and desire, a special Han and Manchu banquet, served traditionally at royal weddings and deaths of emperors or imperial concubines, is available *(Man han quan xi)*. In 1980, eight Japanese ordered this extraordinary meal. The banquet extended over six evenings and featured 234 entrees, 48 hors d'oeuvres, and countless pastries and fruits. The total cost of the meal was roughly 12,000 yuan (about U.S. $3,000).

Reservations for any meal should be made at least twenty-four hours in advance, and during the busy tourist season, three to four days is recommended.

KAOROU JI
(KAOROU JI RESTAURANT)
—

14 Qianhai Dong Yan
Tel.: 445921
Hours:
11:00 A.M.–1:00 P.M. (lunch),
5:00–7:30 P.M. (dinner)

Overlooking a lake with lily pads serenely floating on its surface, the setting of the Kaorou Ji could not be more picturesque. It is for this reason—along with its excellent barbecued meats—that the Kaorou Ji has achieved such popularity with both native Chinese and foreign residents. It is relatively undiscovered by tourist groups, however, perhaps owing to its distance—a good twenty-five-minute ride from the center of the city.

The Kaorou Ji began business in 1848 as a single tent set up Mongolian style around two large charcoal braziers. Traditionally, it was a particularly favored retreat during the lotus season (from mid-July through mid-September), when members of the emperor's court would flee from the heat of the city to the cool tranquillity of the lakeside.

The restaurant, which now occupies a somewhat stately two-story building that was constructed in 1951, stands a short distance from the emperor's courtyard, which was used during the Yuan, Ming, and Qing dynasties. Unfortunately, there is only one private room upstairs, with huge windows that look directly out on the Shichahai Lake, but during the hot summer months customers can dine outdoors on a veranda.

The menu offers a number of fine dishes capably executed under the command of master chef Guo Wenju, who has held this position for forty years. The main attraction of the restaurant is its barbecued meat, for which paper-thin slices of lamb are grilled with a generous portion of coriander and slivered green peppers. During the winter skewered lamb is also served. The preparation of both dishes involves marinating the meat in a mixture of soy sauce, sugar, rice wine, and coriander. The meat is cut with a special huge cleaver, and despite the pressure that has been put on the manager to convert to an electric meat slicer, to his credit he insists on continuing the old tradition of cutting the meat by hand.

Chef Guo also takes pride in the fact that the restaurant uses yellow oak for its grilling and maintains meticulous control of the fire so that the barbecued meats are guaranteed to be perfectly cooked. (Our meat was deliciously juicy, a testament to his care.) You can see the old grill, which is claimed to have been in use for the past hundred years, as you walk up the stairs into the private room.

Sesame buns *(shao bing)*, considered by many to be the best in the city, are served with the roasted meat. The buns are flaky and crisp on the outside and soft within. Split open the buns and stuff them with the meat mixture, and then eat them with your fingers or pick them up with chopsticks. For other dishes, you should consult the waiter, guiding him away from suggestions of shark's fin and other costly delicacies.

Since there is only a single private room, make reservations several days in advance; otherwise, for a small party, alternative seating arrangements can be made if twenty-four-hour notice is given. Prices are moderately expensive: for a full meal complete with barbecued meats and other entrees, expect to pay approximately 90 to 100 yuan per person.

"KENDEJI JIAXIANGJI" (KENTUCKY FRIED CHICKEN)

Qianmen Dajie
Tel.: 3016860
Hours: 9:00 A.M.–9:30 P.M.

There are few sights as comical or as disconcerting as the three-story Kentucky Fried Chicken in Beijing, standing majestically opposite the Mao Memorial. Its location seems almost a slight to the memory of the Chinese leader, who publicly shunned and outlawed all remnants of western bourgeois culture. But the restaurant has prevailed in spite of him, the largest and highest-grossing outlet in the world of the Kentucky Fried Chicken chain.

At first, its owners feared that curious Chinese customers would flock to this fast-food mecca for a taste, never to return. But time has shown that despite the high prices and long lines, local residents keep coming back for more of the crispy fried chicken and flaky biscuits.

Upon entering, you may be mentally transported back to the United States (or perhaps Japan, where Kentucky Fried Chicken outlets are found in every major city). The gleaming, stainless steel fryers and bright neon signs proclaiming Pepsi and Sprite look just like the originals, as do the trays with their portions of fried chicken and scoops of mashed potatoes swimming in a pool of brown gravy. But the illusion fades pleasantly when you notice sweet young Chinese women wearing the neat brown and yellow uniforms.

If you like Kentucky Fried Chicken at home, then you won't be disappointed: the food is a reasonable duplicate of the stuff made in the States. Prices, however, are higher: a fifteen-piece chicken bucket runs about 55 yuan, while a fried chicken dinner can be had for 10.

QIANMEN DAJIE
(QIANMEN STREET BAZAAR)

—

The area surrounding Qianmen Gate is worth discovering, particularly if you have exhausted your thirst for exploring the Forbidden City or roaming through the stores in Wangfujing Street. Make certain to hold securely to your purse (pickpockets are rampant) and prepare yourself for the Chinese crowds enjoying some of Beijing's best street food.

On the sidewalk directly across from front gate are rows and rows of Chinese fast-food stands. Cooks deftly toss ingredients on their portable stoves, surrounded in a tight circle by people on stools. Chopsticks clenched, the customers impatiently await the serving of the stir-fried meat with peppers, tomatoes, and cucumbers, hot off the fire. At a neighboring stall the cooked food is artfully arranged in portable Styrofoam boxes, offering the convenience of fast-food Chinese takeout. And over all, the air is thick with the smell of roasted meat wafting from the charcoal grills loaded with skewers of lamb shish kebab.

On the right is the stand Da Wan Cha, known for its ample portion of freshly brewed tea with the reasonable price tag of two cents. For over eight years the price has remained the same, since the owner has vowed not to raise it. So successful has been his strategy that there are now Da Wan Cha outlets in other cities of China.

Several doors down is the famous Yue Sheng Zhai, a shop that specializes in red-cooked beef. As you pass, your nostrils will be assailed by the rich aroma of star anise, soy sauce, and braising spices. This shop has been selling its signature dish for at least sixty or seventy years.

Around the corner and across the street on Qianmen Dajie is the legendary Qianmen Quanjude (see page 75), which has long been considered one of the finest eateries for Peking duck in the city. Several doors down is the Du Yi Chu Shao Mai Guan, a tiny hole-in-the-wall shop that specializes in steamed open-face dumplings (see page 58).

One of the most unusual shops to visit in the bazaar is around the corner from Qianmen Dajie on Liang Shi Dian Jie, a small alley to the right of Qianmen Street. The Liu Bi Ju is noted for its pickles and fermented condiments, and one step into this shop will give any visitor a bird's-eye view of the immense diversity of Chinese pickles. The pungent odor of fermenting vegetables here is intoxicating. Behind the counter, women dressed in white aprons stand ready with tongs to help customers. Before and behind them are numerous clay pots filled with over sixty varieties of preserved foods, ranging from salted, pickled, and fermented turnip to pickled cucumbers, spicy apricot kernels, and many varieties of preserved chili peppers.

A large wooden plaque hanging on one wall charts the history of the store, which first opened in 1503. It was not long before Liu Bi Ju attracted a popular following, and the condiments were so highly regarded that officials of the imperial palace frequently were dispatched to buy pickles for the ruling monarchs. Today, according to local sources, standards remain as high.

The Qianmen Bazaar is open at all hours of the day and night, but the prime time for walking and viewing the sights is from late morning to early evening.

LAO SHE CHAGUAN (LAO SHE TEAHOUSE)

■

3 Qianmen Dajie
Hours: 9:00 A.M.–9:00 P.M.

One would hardly expect to find a traditional Chinese teahouse adjacent to Kentucky Fried Chicken, but that is where Yin Shengxi, general manager of Beijing's Big Bowl Tea Trade Company, chose to open the Lao She Teahouse, a replica of the classic teahouses of ancient China. Yin established the teahouse as a gathering place for artists. "Artists and I have a common goal," he explained in an article printed in the *China Daily* in April 1989, "to vitalize traditional Chinese culture."

Yin Shengxi is famous in Beijing as a self-made millionaire. Ten years ago, he sold large bowls of tea for two fen in the market on Quianmen Street; today his tea business has expanded to Shenzhen, Zhuhai, and Hainan provinces. He has also instituted the China Tea Culture Society, a group Yin hopes will promote tea culture and tea trade.

In designing the Lao She Teahouse, Yin has made every attempt to capture the flavor of the traditional teahouse of days past. Waitresses wear long *qipao*, the traditional tight-fitting Chinese dress with a high collar. The walls are lined with striking bold-brush calligraphy hangings, and tables and their accompanying stools are made of dark wood. At night, customers can listen to traditional Chinese music or Peking opera performed from a stage in the front of the room.

Customers buy meal tickets in the gallery located across the hall from the entrance of the teahouse. One is presented with a choice of a 10-, 15-, or 20-yuan meal, depending on the variety of snacks desired. A wide selection of teas is offered, including the special Yuqian, Longjing, Maojian, and Zhulan varieties.

For our visit, we settled on a simple, fragrant jasmine. The tea was served in lovely brass pots, accompanied by little dishes of candied fruits, melon seeds, and assorted cakes. At other tables, groups of students were clustered, quietly sipping tea and munching on melon seeds. It was a soothing respite from the chaos of Kentucky Fried Chicken next door.

Yin has been quoted as saying that he would like to open traditional teahouses in the United States, as well as in other parts of China. "Now that Kentucky Fried Chicken has laid eggs in China," he asks, "why can't we sell Chinese tea in their home?"

QIANMEN QUANJUDE (QIANMEN ROAST DUCK)

■

32 Qianmen Dajie
Tel.: 750505
Hours:
10:30 A.M.–1:00 P.M. (lunch),
4:30–7:00 P.M. (dinner)

As appearances go, the entrance of the Qianmen Roast Duck is hardly impressive. The burgundy carpet is slightly dingy, and the stairway leading to the main dining room is poorly lit. But pay no attention to these minor details. If you are lucky enough to obtain a reservation, this is truly where the best Peking duck in the city is served. And as you may well believe from the condition of the carpet, the Qianmen Roast Duck has been serving excellent food for over 120 years.

The restaurant had the most humble of beginnings. Yang Chen Ren, the original owner, began his career by selling cooked chicken and duck on the street. As business prospered, he bought a small restaurant, but when success eluded him he renamed the eatery Quan Ju De, which roughly translates to mean "Everything Is Included." In fact, the menu was quite simple: The standard meal was "four-way" duck, which featured cold, stuffed duck neck, roasted duck, stir-fried vegetables in duck oil, and duck soup made with bones. Today the menu offers over two hundred dishes using every conceivable part of the anatomy of the duck.

As of this writing of this book, the original two-story building is in the process of being renovated, and an extensive addition is to be added at some point. Until then, the number of tables is limited, and during the busy season from March to November, reservations may be required several days to a week in advance.

But the food is definitely worth the wait and bother. At a recent meal, the roast duck was delicious. The skin was crisp, and meat slices were butter-tender. The duck came with a choice of

(continued)

steamed Mandarin pancakes or sesame rolls, and the sweet bean paste had a rich, mellow flavor. Deep-fried duck rolls made with ground duck meat in a lightly breaded coating were superb, as were grilled duck hearts redolent with fresh coriander and scallions.

As is the case in several other famous restaurants in Beijing, the management will not discuss the menu with foreigners, preferring instead to plan the meal according to the amount spent per person. For most parties of four to twelve, expect to pay about 80 to 100 yuan per person and assume the staff will do its best to please.

The restaurant takes most major credit cards, including American Express, Visa, and Master-Card.

ROSENBEC'S BAKERY

Qianmen Dong Dajie
Tel.: 557731
Hours: 7:00 A.M.–9:00 P.M.

If while in Beijing you find yourself craving a croissant or some type of pastry, Rosenbec's offers both. The bakery is a bustling place where a slightly adapted version of western-style pastries are scooped up by Chinese locals as fast as they come out of the ovens. The croissants aren't as flaky as the original French version, but Rosenbec's does turn out a good, fragrant product. The bakery also features raisin rolls, cream- and custard-filled pastries, red bean paste rolls, and a specialty known as soy milk pound cake. These baked goods are perfect for an excursion or a picnic, since they keep quite well, even after one day.

Rosenbec's also serves ice cream cones, but if you are looking for more substantial fare, go next door to one of its two restaurants, which offer some unusual but decent western dishes in a fast-food atmosphere. Service is cafeteria style, and daily specials include a selection of sandwiches with cabbage soup, potato salad, and curry-fried rice. In the inner dining room, the menu is more ambitious, with such dishes as chicken Kiev, Neapolitan spaghetti, and fried prawns.

The main draw here is people-watching, and the restaurants are also a favorite Chinese student hangout. (There were a number of western foreign students enjoying the fare as well.) Prices are fairly inexpensive, and the favored drink is—you guessed it—Coca-Cola.

SICHUAN FANDIAN (SICHUAN RESTAURANT)

—

51 Xirongxian Hutong, Xuan
Nei Dajie
Tel.: 656348
Hours:
11:00 A.M.–1:00 P.M. (lunch),
5:00–7:30 P.M. (dinner)

Along with the Fang Shan, the Sichuan Restaurant is certainly one of the loveliest eateries in Beijing. Serene courtyards connect the many dining rooms, culminating at the rear of the restaurant in the Imperial Banquet Hall, magnificently appointed with stately columns, an exquisite tiled ceiling, imperial yellow tablecloths, and ornately carved wall murals.

According to the "Brief Description" posted on the bulletin board in the center of the courtyards, the Sichuan Restaurant first opened in 1959, thanks largely to the efforts of Zhou Enlai, who had a passion for Sichuanese food. Originally, the building was a mansion of a prince called Chan Ke, who was the twenty-fourth son of a ruler of the Qing dynasty.

Since its opening, the Sichuan has been considered one of Beijing's best restaurants. I first ate an excellent meal there in 1979, and on a recent visit, it more than lived up to its fine reputation. Since we had a very small party, we preferred to order directly from the menu rather than in advance and were consequently seated in a small, drab, but clean side room. If you have a large party (more than six), and it is a busy evening, the restaurant will probably insist on establishing a budget per person and setting up the menu in advance. The price for such a banquet ranges from 50 to 300 yuan per person, depending on the dishes ordered. My suggestion, as always, is to discourage the sea cucumbers and bird's nest, which are the most costly items, and order any of the following dishes, many of which are among the restaurant's specialties: crisp prawn rolls *(dan pi xia juan)*, dry-cooked beef *(gan shao niurou si)*, sweet-and-sour fish *(tang cu yu)*, smoked duck *(zhang cha ya)*, Sichuan dumplings *(Sichuan huntun)*, and Sichuan cold noodles *(ma la liang mian)*. Outstanding home-style items include fish-flavored pork shreds *(yu xiang rou si)*, spicy and fragrant in their fiery sauce, and the Ma Po bean curd, which was superb and tender, as were the vegetable hearts with straw mushrooms *(xianmo caixin)*. Two delicious appetizers are the cold dry crisp beef *(dong ying niurou)* and the "strange-flavored" chicken *(guai wei ji)*.

The menu is in Chinese and English. Reservations are necessary whether you are ordering from the menu or reserving places for a banquet, and since this is one of the most highly regarded places in the city, you should book at least twenty-four hours in advance. During high tourist season, with a big party, it would be wise to allow at least forty-eight hours.

SONGHELOU (PINE AND CRANE RESTAURANT)

10 Taijichang Dajie
Tel.: 545223
Hours:
11:30 A.M.–1:30 P.M. (lunch),
5:30–7:30 P.M. (dinner)

Although not generally frequented by tourist groups, the Beijing Songhelou has gained just renown among native and foreign residents since its opening some fifteen years ago. This eatery is a branch of the famous Songhelou in Suzhou, which has a national reputation for its superb eastern Chinese specialties. After visits to each establishment, I have found that the food at the Beijing branch easily surpasses that of the Suzhou eatery. And for a departure from the heavy lamb and duck dishes of northern-style Chinese cooking, it is well worth a visit.

Located just five minutes from the Beijing Hotel, the Songhelou is quite a modest little place. The downstairs holds two dining rooms for locals, and four private banquet rooms can be found upstairs. Over the years I have had the opportunity to dine on both floors, and while on the main floor food ordered directly from the menu is excellent, foreigners might find the tidiness of the private rooms more to their liking.

Another advantage of booking a banquet (although it is more costly) is that the chefs are given the opportunity to prepare some superb dishes, which in my experience have been impressive both in taste and appearance. In general, the eastern cooking style seeks to accentuate the natural flavor of the ingredients, using understated sauces and a light hand with seasonings. While there are some heavier red-cooked specialties, redolent with their soy sauce–based braising mixture, for the most part the cooking is a radical departure from the heavy, hearty qualities of Beijing cooking. Some dishes that are worth considering are the Squirrel Fish *(Songshu Guiyu)*, red-cooked chicken *(huang men ji)*, stir-fried eels *(xiang you shanhu)*, and black mushrooms with cabbage *(xianggu youcai)*.

Since there are only a few banquet rooms, reservations should be made at least forty-eight hours in advance. Prices assuredly will not be cheap. For a full banquet here, expect to pay 100 yuan or more per person for a table of ten to twelve.

VEGETARIAN RESTAURANT BEIJING INTERNATIONAL HOTEL

—

9 Jian Nei Dajie
Tel.: 5126688
Hours:
11:30 A.M.–2:00 P.M. (lunch),
5:30–9:00 P.M. (dinner)

Since the Beijing International Hotel opened several years ago, its restaurants have hardly come to be noted for superb dining, but that may change with the addition of the vegetarian eatery on the second floor. The chief cook, Sui Jiang, despite his relatively young age of thirty-six, is a master who has studied his craft in Huangzhou, Xiamen, and Fujian, as well as Beijing.

The restaurant itself is quite modest, but airy and comfortable. Mint-green carpet, chairs, and linen offset the bamboo chandeliers. A huge wooden Santa Claus with reindeer greets customers at the entrance. We were told it had been installed for the holidays, but it looked as if it might be there permanently.

The food here will not disappoint either the ardent vegetarian or the uninitiated diner. Few culinary experiences can equal that of an outstanding Chinese vegetarian meal. Artistic mock-meat creations are coupled with the pungent flavorings of gingerroot, scallions, and sesame oil, which are used abundantly to compensate for the absence of meat.

Most meals being with an assortment of cold dishes, and the vegetarian ones, such as cauliflower in mustard sauce, are especially good. Small dishes of spicy condiments such as pickled chili peppers, sweet-and-sour garlic cloves, and preserved bean curd are also available and may be sampled prior to or during the meal.

Chef Sui is well-versed in vegetarian versions of such classics as sautéed shredded eel, made with deep-fried strips of Chinese black mushroom, and mock Peking duck, in which crisp pieces of bean curd skin are smeared with sweet bean sauce and wrapped in Mandarin pancakes. Sui also has created some new dishes that are well worth trying, such as his mock prawns with a carrot, water chestnut, and black mushroom filling bathed in a rich sweet-and-sour sauce *(Lohan da xia)*, mock stir-fried crab *(chao xie fan)*, and mock braised goose *(gua lu su er)*.

Each course is served in carved wooden vessels imitating those from the Han period some two

(continued)

thousand years ago. The overall effect is charming and unique.

Reservations should be made the day before, especially for a banquet. An English menu was being prepared and should be available shortly. For a simple meal from the menu the price should be about 50 to 60 yuan per person. For a full-scale banquet, expect to spend about 100 yuan per person.

XILAISHUN FANDIAN (XILAISHUN RESTAURANT)

194 Fuchengmen Nei Lu
Tel.: 549309, 549028
Hours:
11:30 A.M.–1:30 P.M. (lunch),
5:00–8:00 P.M. (dinner)

Few foreigners are familiar with this restaurant, which opened some forty years ago but has only lately gained an impressive reputation with the addition of master chef Qiao Chunsheng to the kitchen roster. Chef Qiao, who has a movie-star handsome face, won silver and copper medals at the Fifth International Culinary Competition held in Prague several years ago, as well as two gold medals at the Chinese National Culinary Competition held in 1982.

The restaurant is small and quite modest, with only one banquet room upstairs, though additional rooms are planned for the future. You must book early—particularly since the real dining experience is tasting Chef Qiao's specialties.

Xilaishun, like its *shun* cousins, specializes in Muslim cooking, featuring rinsed lamb pot *(shui yangrou),* fried mutton with sesame seeds *(zhima yangrou),* and lamb shashlik. Also try to sample the chef's Peking duck, which many Chinese officials contend is the best in the city. Another excellent dish is the Lantern Chicken *(denglong ji),* in which chicken meat and bamboo shoots are seasoned in a spicy sauce, wrapped in a piece of heatproof cellophane, and deep-fried. The cellophane balloons out, making a spectacular presentation and sealing in the flavors of the ingredients. We also sampled a delicious chrysanthemum firepot, a more refined seafood version of the lamb classic.

Prices are moderate; a multicourse banquet will cost about 90–100 yuan. Reservations should be made forty-eight hours in advance.

YILI KUAI CANTING
(YILI FAST FOOD)

▬

145 Xirongxian Hutong
Tel.: 651131, 553518
Hours: 10:00 A.M.–9:30 P.M.

For an entertaining diversion, you might consider visiting the first Chinese fast-food restaurant in Beijing. Yili, a prominent confectionary company which manufactures breads, cakes, and candy, opened this small eatery some six years ago to cater to the demand for fast-food convenience. Some of the favorite dishes are glorified in colorful pictures displayed around the dining room, including a cherry-red hotdog in a bun with an accompanying cup of steaming Maxwell House coffee, a hearty roast beef sandwich positioned next to a large jar of Maxwell House, and a tempting juicy hamburger—likewise accompanied by a steaming cup of you-know-what coffee. (Despite repeated questions to the nattily dressed manager, we could not get an explanation for this partiality to Maxwell House.) Otherwise, the general atmosphere is dim and rather dingy.

The menu is quite eclectic, with a selection of western sandwiches and some Chinese items like curried fried rice (the favored choice of half the customers seated in the restaurant), noodles, and bean curd soup. The food is unexceptional, but not bad as most fast-food places go.

The most compelling reason to visit Yili Fast Food is for the people-watching. You can sit contentedly (with your own steaming cup of coffee) and gaze at the crowd, a blending of Beijing's young sophisticates and students, most of whom are fashionably dressed in hip, upscale outfits. The background music during our visit was Stevie Wonder and Michael Jackson. All this and more for around 20 yuan.

YOUYISHUN FANZHUANG (YOUYISHUN RESTAURANT)

—

11 Xuanwumen Nei Dajie,
Xidan
Tel.: 662110
Hours:
11:00 A.M.–1:30 P.M. (lunch),
4:30–8:00 P.M. (dinner)

Like its cousin, Donglaishun, Youyishun specializes in Muslim cuisine, with particular attention to lamb. The management here claims that its lamb, which is raised on special farms outside the city, has its own unique smell and taste. It also states that its kitchen hosts the most talented master cutter of lamb in the city, a man who can turn out mountains of paper-thin slices of meat in minutes.

Youyishun first opened in 1948 as a private enterprise, but, like other restaurants in China, it was taken under government ownership in the fifties. It is highly regarded as one of Beijing's finest Muslim eateries, and judging from our experiences, its reputation is well deserved.

The prices are not cheap, but the expertise of the chefs and service are clearly first rate. Master chef Feng Yong Fu, who is a special-level cook, has overseen the kitchen for the past forty years, and the service has been supervised by a veteran who also has been there since the beginning.

We had an exquisite meal, in which all the dishes were selected by the manager; even if the menu is planned in advance, however, it is wise to go over the selections before you dine.

For our banquet, the linen napkins were neatly folded into the shape of swans, an extra touch often performed at superior establishments. The cold platters of red-cooked beef and salted beef (a preserving process resulting in something similar to corned beef) were delicious, as were the sweet-and-sour cucumbers. The minutely shredded stir-fried chicken and fish (chao long feng si) with a generous seasoning of fresh coriander, were extraordinary. Braised chicken thighs (jiang chao ji tui) were red-cooked to a buttery tenderness, as was the braised beef (wei niurou). The deep-fried lamb (shao yangrou) was tender, hearty, and not in the least gamey tasting. One of the most unusual dishes, a house specialty, is dates and yams in a crisp roll *(tang liu juan guo)*. For this dish, the fruit and yam filling is wrapped in a thin bean-milk skin filling, deep-fried until crisp on the outside, and lightly tossed in a slightly cloying syrup.

For the meal finale, the kitchen is well versed in a number of pastries, sweet and savory, but I recommend the simple almond bean curd *(xingren doufu)*, which is refreshing and light, especially after the heavy meat dishes.

For a full-scale banquet expect to pay at least 100 to 120 yuan per person. There are limited banquet facilities, and because the main dining room tends to be slightly squalid, it is wise to book at least twenty-four hours in advance, establishing a price in the same call.

ZHEN SU ZHAI FANZHUANG or BEIJING SUCAI CANTING (BEIJING VEGETARIAN RESTAURANT)

▬

74 Xuanwumen Nei Dajie
Tel.: 653181, 654296
Hours: 10:00 A.M.–9:00 P.M.

Since it first opened in the 1930s the Beijing Vegetarian Restaurant has been a haven for both vegetarians and those interested in sampling the refined art of Chinese meatless cooking. Over the years, I have enjoyed many vegetarian meals in Hong Kong and Taiwan, and the dishes that we ordered directly from the menu in this restaurant compared favorably with the best I had previously eaten.

The Beijing Vegetarian Restaurant is quite modest in appearance. Upstairs in the main dining room, the tablecloths and seat covers are a pleasant sky-blue color, and lacy curtains with a bamboo motif hang from the windows. The burgundy carpet could use cleaning, but the waitresses are friendly, helpful, and efficient.

Those who have never enjoyed the subtle artistry of Chinese vegetarian cooking are in for a surprise. Unlike many western vegetarian recipes, which tend to be bland, Chinese dishes are generously flavored with pungent ingredients such as like sesame oil, gingerroot, and smoky black mushrooms. And many of the dishes are styled in appearance as mock replicas of their meat, poultry, or fish counterparts.

Among the most widely acclaimed "mock" entries on the menu are the fried and braised yellow croaker (gan shao huang yu), sweet and sour spareribs (tang cu pai gu), and Eight Treasure whole duck (Ba bao zheng ya). Except for the spareribs, these dishes must be ordered in advance, but you can walk into the restaurant and order directly from the menu deep-fried eels (shanyu), sesame duck (zhima ya), mock stir-fried chicken with green peppers and peanuts (gong bao ji ding), vegetarian steamed buns (sucai baozi), and the vegetarian cold platter, which has a selection of delicious cold snacks.

For a large party, reservations should be made at least twenty-four hours in advance, and if you have the time, definitely order some of the specialties prior to the meal. For a modest meal ordered from the menu, the cost should be about 40–50 yuan per person. For a banquet, expect to pay about 80–90 yuan per person with a party of eight to ten people. American Express cards are accepted here.

TIANJIN

A visitor's first impression of Tianjin is likely to be that it is a huge, rather characterless, industrial city, set on a crowded harbor. And since it is one of China's five largest cities and its largest commercial seaport, such a reaction is hardly surprising.

But if you have some time to explore, you will discover that Tianjin grows on you with each passing day, and that it and its surroundings do hold many charms. There are the rather quaint but picturesque sections where aging Victorian mansions built by the British, French, and Germans in the late 1800s still sit in stately but crumbling glory. There's the garish but impressive three-story complex known as Food Street, which teems with activity and houses shops, bakeries, and restaurants. Just outside the city proper are some of the foremost grape wineries in the country, many of them in joint-venture agreements with French winemakers, where you can plan an informal visit and stop in for a simple tour, tasting local wines.

Since its humble beginnings in the Song dynasty (960–1279), Tianjin has played a prominent role in trade. Its original name is Zhi Gu, or buying and selling, and it was not until 1404, during the Ming dynasty, that it was renamed Tianjinwei by the Duke of Yen. In 1412 the Grand Canal, linking the city to the sea, was opened, and for the next few centuries Tianjin prospered—but not without incident. The city was invaded by the British in 1858, and two years later, a treaty was signed giving the Europeans free rein over the city and establishing it as a primary trade center and port. Soon fierce antagonism developed between the foreigners and the local Chinese, resulting in the Tianjin Massacre of 1870, when a number of European missionaries were killed. In 1900, during the Boxer Rebellion, the city was attacked, but foreign residents retained their stronghold. When Tianjin was overtaken by the Communists in 1949, the Chinese finally reclaimed their dominance in the city and set about rebuilding its economy. The city suffered a setback in 1976, when it was ravaged by a severe earthquake, but today, to all appearances, Tianjin is thriving and contributing impressively to the nation's economy.

Because of its close proximity to Beijing, the culinary offerings of Tianjin are strikingly similar to those of the capital, particularly roast duck. The city's restaurants also cater to the palates of a cosmopolitan clientele, offering excellent Cantonese, Sichuanese, Shandong, Japanese, and western dishes.

DENG YING LOU FANDIAN (DENG YING LOU RESTAURANT)

—

94 Binjiang, Heping Qu
Tel.: 702071 (third floor banquet rooms)
702069 (first floor restaurant)
Hours:
11:00 A.M.–2:00 P.M. (lunch),
5:00–8 P.M. (dinner)

Don't be put off by the somewhat shabby entrance and dirty, spotted carpet of this eatery. Instead, proceed up the stairs to the third floor (assuming you have booked a private room in advance), where another world awaits. There you will find four private rooms, each with its own theme, but all of which feature wall carvings in the imperial motif, and fixtures in beautiful dark wood. If you haven't had the foresight or the time to reserve one of the private rooms, you can still enjoy a slightly bawdy time in one of the main dining rooms, where the air may be a trifle smoky and your meal served against the roar of lively conversation and enthusiastic toasts.

The Deng Ying Lou, according to the very capable second-floor manager, Guo Jia Feng, handles about fifteen hundred customers per day, making it one of the most popular restaurants in the city. And in its eighty-year history, the restaurant has earned a just reputation for its flavorful Shandong-style cooking.

We received a report from a foreign resident who had a disappointing meal there, but it was a banquet arranged by Chinese locals on a slim budget. Our experiences, when we ordered directly from the menu, were above reproach, after we insistently rejected the suggestions of costly delicacies and confined ourselves to the more modest Shandong dishes.

The most highly recommended dishes are the crispy-skin chicken *(xiang su ji)*, which was one of the best versions I had tasted anywhere in China, delicious in its five-spice-powder coating, clear-steamed fish *(qing zheng yu)*; Three Flavors *(San Xian)*, a clear-steamed soup with pork, shrimp, and black mushrooms; Shandong-style chicken with mushrooms *(Shandong mogu ji)*; and delicious *bao zi*, or stuffed buns, filled with sweet and savory filling. Our particular favorite was the vegetarian version *(sucai bao)*, filled with bean threads, egg, and fresh coriander.

When you order from the menu, prices are moderate, averaging about 50 to 60 yuan per person. For a full-scale banquet and entry into one of the private rooms, expect to pay about 100 yuan per person for a table of ten to twelve. Order some of the Shandong specialties, and the price may not be quite as high.

Reservations for the private rooms should be made about forty-eight hours in advance, and for a table in the main dining room, bookings can be made a day or several hours before, unless special dishes are requested.

GU JING JIUJIA (GU JING RESTAURANT)

1 Nanshi, Shipin Jie
Tel.: 252737
Hours:
11:30 A.M.–2:00 P.M. (lunch),
5:30–8:00 P.M. (dinner)

On the opposite corner of Food Street from the Hong Kong Restaurant is the Gu Jing Jiujia. This pleasant restaurant is the exact opposite of the slick, sophisticated ambience of the Hong Kong eatery. But the food, in its own right, can be equally as good.

Don't be put off by the rather desolate storefront on the street entrance, which looks like a liquor store but sells a host of local Tianjian products. Leave the dusty bottles and canned goods behind and proceed up the stairs to the main dining room, which is modest in size, holding about ten tables. There are several private rooms, but the restaurant itself is small enough so that it doesn't become overly noisy or smoky. And it is tastefully furnished with billowy pink curtains and framed Chinese three-dimensional scenes.

The cooking style here is Sichuanese, and many of the dishes we tried were excellent. Dry-cooked beef shreds (gan shao niurou si) were dry and crisp, with tender shreds of carrots and celery, and just the right sprinkling of Sichuan peppercorn powder in the spicy sauce. The Ma Po bean curd (Ma Po doufu) was nicely seasoned with a fiery sauce that contrasted beautifully with the creamy curd. Silver-thread rolls (yin si juan) also were delicious, puffy, and light with a delicately yeasty flavor. The hot-and-sour soup (suan la tang) and braised chicken (tie ban dou shi ji) are also recommended.

The Gu Jing first opened under a different name and in another location in 1985, and two years later, moved to its present address on Food

(continued)

Street. Although young, it has already established a reputation as serving some of the best Sichuanese food in the city. Every Friday the most renowned Sichuanese master chef in Tianjin comes in to cook and keep the kitchen in line.

Prices are extremely moderate, and if ordered directly from the menu, dinner shouldn't cost more than 50 to 60 yuan per person. Banquet prices, of course, will run higher. Diner's Club is accepted, and while reservations for lunch are unnecessary, they should be made for dinner about twenty-four hours in advance.

JI SI LING (KIESSLING RESTAURANT)
▬

33 Zhejiang Lu
Tel.: 32020, 32561
Hours: 9:00 A.M.–10:30 P.M.

For a bit of Tianjin local color there is no better place to go than the Ji Si Ling, located in the heart of the city. Originally opened some years ago as a German bakery, this eatery quickly established a reputation as serving some of the best European food in the city.

These days, the menu is still European, but Chinese chefs have taken over, and the food bears hardly any resemblance to its former authentic self. Even the pastries, once among the Kiessling's reigning glories, look greasy and unappetizing. The decor is worth a visit in itself—heavy red velvet drapes, colored neon lights, pink linen-sheathed chairs, and an astonishingly surreal wall-length mural in the far lower dining room.

But the real fun is to just stop in in the middle of the day and relax with a cup of coffee, a Coca-Cola, or an ice cream, and just take in the Chinese audience, families and friends enjoying the western treats.

KAHAN JAPANESE RESTAURANT
—

Tianjin Hyatt Hotel
198 Jiefang Bei Lu
Tel.: 318888
Hours:
11:30 A.M.–1:30 P.M. (lunch),
6:00–10:00 P.M. (dinner)

It is not my usual practice to eat at western restaurants in China, but the Hyatt Hotel is centrally located and perfect for a refreshing drink, cup of tea, or pit stop in a whirlwind day of sightseeing. And it was for all the above reasons that we first wandered into the hotel and stumbled upon the restaurants here. We had heard some good reports from locals, and after trying things for ourselves, were pleased with the meals there.

The Kahan Japanese Restaurant, although pricey, is attractive and airy with high and low wooden tables, sliding rice-paper doors, and an impressive wall of windows that allows the customer a scenic view of the Hai River. While there are several private rooms, decorated in the spare but appealing Japanese manner, a seat at one of the tables in the main dining room will allow you to watch the master chef prepare certain dishes at the front of the restaurant.

The food is quite good, albeit slightly bland. The customer can choose from a varied selection of à la carte items, such as various forms of sushi, sashimi, and classic Japanese entrées, or opt for the set meal, which includes a sampling of different combinations of Japanese dishes. The traditional set dinner, priced at approximately 135 yuan, offers appetizers, fish consommé, sashimi, a grilled dish, prawns and vegetables, a hot pot, some tempura items, miso soup, pickles, and fruit. Reservations are unnecessary for lunch but should be made at least several hours in advance for dinner.

LINGNAN CHAOXIAN CANTING (KOREAN RESTAURANT)

—

158 Jiefang Bei Lu
Tel.: 312693
Hours:
11:30 A.M.–1:30 P.M. (lunch),
5:30–8:30 P.M. (dinner)

A fairly recent arrival in Tianjin, the Lingnan Chaoxian Canting offers a refreshing alternative to dining at a noisy local eatery or in the artificial serenity found at a restaurant located in a western hotel. Since it's a public restaurant, there's a bit of local color, but being a joint venture, it is well managed and clean.

The long wooden tables with their tabletop stoves and stately chairs also provide a change from the usual look of most Chinese restaurants, which asserts itself only in the ornate, lacquered murals.

The menu offers some classic Korean specialties such as marinated sliced meat and seafood that is cooked by the customer and dipped into a spicy sauce. The meat here tended to be slightly tough but once grilled, it was lent a fine flavor by the marinade. The ever-present kimchee, or pickled cabbage, was quite good. (We reordered several helpings.) There's also a varied selection of hot and cold noodle dishes. We found the soups to be a trifle bland (hence the extra orders of kimchee).

Although the Lingnan Chaoxian Canting's Korean food is not outstanding, the dishes generally were good, and foreigners might find this a welcome change after a sea of Chinese banquets. Prices are higher than in most Chinese eateries, but cheaper than the western hotel restaurants. Dinner, depending on the selection of dishes, should average about 40 to 60 yuan per person, including beer and soft drinks.

FOOD STREET, OR NANSHI SHIPIN JIE

One of the most prominent gastronomic attractions in Tianjin, for locals and foreigners alike, is a visit to Food Street. Located in the southern part of the city, Food Street is a three-story mall complex housing restaurants, coffeehouses, bakeries, and food shops. Among the upscale eateries here are the Hong Kong restaurant and an outlet of the famous Goubuli shop, which specializes in stuffed steamed buns. (See the note in the Local Tianjin Specialties Section.)

On the first floor is a charming restaurant that looks more like a French bistro than a small eatery in China. Xian Heng Fen Juang does, however, feature the traditional Chinese lacy curtains and small rooms with handsome wood molding and elegant calligraphy hangings. The featured food here is Confucian, a more refined version of the Shandong style.

As you proceed upstairs you'll pass a small Chinese bakery (Jing Wei Zhai) which is worth looking in on. The specialty here seems to be turning out Chinese renditions of western sweets. As we walked by, colorful cakes were being packed into Styrofoam cases. Adjoining the bakery was a small tearoom.

On the second floor there are several shops worth visiting. The first, Guo Ren Zhang Shi, might aptly be described as a peanut boutique. Much as the United States has seen the appearance of a slew of popcorn stores that sell every conceivable flavor of popcorn, so too does this store offer an astonishing variety of peanuts.

Just down the way is a similar shop, but this time the product is beans. Here you can find sugar-coated soybeans, candy-coated lima beans, plus pumpkin seeds, sunflower seeds, dried apricots, fried peanuts with garlic, and baked peanuts with a black, aniselike outer coating (one of my favorite types).

Another unusual place to stop on the second level is San Mao (Three Hairs) Restaurant, named for a popular Chinese cartoon character who has three hairs on his head. Local Chinese plan birthday parties for their children at the San Mao, and it is not unusual to see several in progress simultaneously. Like McDonald's or other fast-food chains, it serves treats such as hamburgers, fried chicken, noodles, various types of ice cream desserts, and soft drinks.

SHENHU ZHI HAI JIUBAJIAN (SEA OF KOBE BAR)

Tianjin Grand Hotel
Youyi Lu, Hexi Qu
Tel.: 319000 Ext. 21413
Hours: 7:00 P.M.–12 A.M.

This small bar/restaurant is one of the charming finds of Tianjin. Situated in an unlikely location off the lobby of the Tianjin Grand Hotel, it is an ideal stop for a few authentic Japanese dishes, as well as for an entertaining look at *karaoke*, the popular Japanese pastime where anyone from the audience can get up and sing a familiar song, with the aid of a video disc and a microphone. The entertainment doesn't usually begin until after nine or ten, but one can enjoy the food from the moment the doors open.

There are only nine tables in this cozy eatery, each one a booth plushly upholstered in red velvet. The bar, which has ten seats, is fully stocked, with a particularly fine selection of all the top brands of cognac, the favored Japanese businessman's drink.

Zhuang Guixiang, the capable and friendly Chinese manager, speaks fluent Japanese and passable English and has been keeping standards high since the bar's opening in 1984. The restaurant offers sashimi once a week when the supply of fresh fish comes in, and regularly serves other Japanese classics, such as yakitori, an excellent miso soup, and a selection of noodle dishes and soup pots. There also are daily specials.

The full menu is translated into English. Plan on spending about 60 to 80 yuan for a filling meal, with an additional charge for drinks.

TIANJIN'S BLOSSOMING WINE INDUSTRY

According to historical documents, grape wine was introduced to China as early as the Han dynasty (206 B.C.–A.D. 220). Soon afterward, grapes were transplanted to provinces in northern China, where they thrived. Today, although grapes are grown in several areas, the primary wine-making region remains in the northeastern triangle of three provinces: Henan, Hebei, and Shandong. The most promising area of growth, as far as the wine-making industry and Sino-French joint ventures are concerned, is in Tianjin, a location thought to be prime because of its climate and its close proximity to Beijing.

Modern wine-making (as we know it) was initially implemented in China by Germans near the end of the nineteenth century. The Chang Yu Winery in Yantai on the Shandong peninsula is considered to be one of the oldest vineyards in China. In 1892 wine-making pioneer Zhang Bishi, after living abroad, established a vineyard there by importing varietal grapes and machinery from France and Germany. (See page 146.)

Western methods arrived in Tianjin only much later. According to James Suckling, a senior editor for The Wine Spectator, the person responsible for the introduction of western winemakers as business partners is Benny Cheung, a former teacher turned entrepreneur. In 1980 Cheung helped to establish the first joint venture winery, which produces Dynasty table wine and brandy. (Dynasty's French counterpart is none other than Remy Martin.) Today, Dynasty produces a number of varieties, including medium-dry and extra-dry white wine, made primarily with Muscat grapes, a dry red wine, made with Cabernet Sauvignon grapes; a Beaujolais; a rosé; and a brandy. Dynasty also is connected to the Celestial or Heavenly Palace winery, which shares the same facilities but is an exclusively Chinese venture. It produces a Riesling, a dry red wine, a dry and semidry white wine, a Beaujolais, and a rosé. Although the Dynasty wines, which are exported widely to Europe and the United States, are generally of a much higher quality than Celestial wines, the Heavenly Palace Winery's Spring Moon, which is also being exported abroad, is a decidedly pleasant white table wine. (The name of the wine, we were told, was inspired by Bette Bao Lord, wife of the former U.S. ambassador to China and author of the novel

Spring Moon.) *Nearly all Dynasty and Heavenly Palace wines are available in hotels and most restaurants in China.*

The Dynasty facility is open to visitors, although there's not much to see apart from gleaming stainless steel vats and on certain days functioning mechanized bottling machines. The grapes are grown in other areas and transported to the winery during the season. The French winemakers guarantee control of their product with computer programs to guide the fermentation. The French, we were told by the Chinese assistant manager, usually visit the vineyards about four times per year.

It was an adventure, however, to visit the newly established Tianma Associated Wine and Spirits Company in another suburb of Tianjin. The Tianma company, which was begun in 1985, is another Sino-French joint venture, and unites several regional Tianjin government companies and Martell Far East Trading Company, a division of Martell, the renowned makers of French cognac.

We were personally greeted on our arrival by the twenty-seven-year old viticulturalist and winemaker, Regis Loevenbruck, who hails from Cognac, France. Loevenbruck, has his hands full with the enterprise. He oversees and manages the twenty-person operation, spending April through June and September through November in China, with the remaining period in France. It was only after a three-year struggle untangling the bureaucratic red tape that he was able to produce brandy and white wine for local markets and export.

According to Loevenbruck, Martell has a fifteen-year agreement with the Chinese, and has already invested approximately $1.5 million in the venture, including the cost of the equipment, which was imported directly from France. At first, a consulting team was brought in from Hong Kong to direct the flavor of the grapes and the wine, and although Loevenbruck periodically consults with them, for the most part he is now on his own, dealing with the seemingly impossible task of creating quality wine and brandy in this tiny building about fifteen miles from Tianjin. Since Loevenbruck doesn't drive, he takes a taxi every day from his room at the Hyatt Tianjin in town. (He has been so busy every day since his arrival that he has not had time to look for an apartment.) On many evenings, especially during the harvest, after working a sixteen-hour day he is simply too tired to make the journey back to Tianjin. He then pulls out a simple cot in his office and sleeps there.

Through his efforts Tianma's brandy and wine have nearly reached his quality standards. We sampled both and were quite impressed: the white wine, which is being marketed under the name Summer Palace, was dry but fruity—some of the best we had ever tasted in China—and the Dragon Royal brandy was smooth and pleasantly heady. Although Loevenbruck wants to improve the products even further, almost any change in policy—even the smallest—is a struggle.

Loevenbruck is dealing with a staff that knows virtually nothing about the art of wine-making, and although he has introduced incentive programs, it is still hard to mobilize the workers. Despite the hardship, he has managed to maintain a fierce sense of optimism and enthusiasm for his work in China. He intends, in whatever spare time he can find, to learn how to speak fluent Mandarin to facilitate communication between himself and his employees. And he will, he adamantly maintains, soon produce the best-tasting white wine and brandy in the country. After seeing what Loevenbruck has managed to accomplish in merely two years, one feels certain that he will succeed at just about anything he wishes.

TIANJIN KAOYA DIAN (TIANJIN ROAST DUCK HOUSE)

—

146 Liaoning Lu
Tel.: 702660, 703335
Hours:
11:00 A.M.–1:30 P.M. (lunch),
5:30–7:30 P.M. (dinner)

We had heard about the excellent Peking duck available at the Tianjin Roast Duck House from a number of local sources, but they hardly prepared us for the massive crowds and near chaos at this eatery. And for those meticulous about sanitary codes, this is hardly the place to visit.

It is, in fact, a noisy, boisterous, and *very* popular local establishment that happens to serve excellent roast duck. In fact, it was probably some of the best roast duck we sampled in China, crispy-skinned with firm, juicy meat. The accompanying pancakes were on the thick side, but the sweet bean sauce was delicious. Before the duck, we were served a cold appetizer platter with cucumbers, shrimp, and bean threads, which was quite good. And prawns were appealing in a tomato sauce.

One of the most extraordinary aspects of dining at the Tianjin Roast Duck is to witness the vast numbers of ducks cooked nightly to accommodate the masses of customers. And they're all freshly prepared and served straight from the oven, a practice that, according to a food authority in Beijing, is becoming obsolete, as more restaurants cook the ducks in advance and reheat them for customers before serving.

Prices are moderate, about 60 to 80 yuan per person for roast duck with some side dishes. The price for a banquet is approximately 100 yuan per person. Reservations should be made about twenty-four hours in advance.

LOCAL TIANJIN SPECIALTIES
—

Like most cities, Tianjin has its noted dishes, and after hearing that you have visited Tianjin everyone in China will immediately ask if you have sampled any of the following foods. Many Chinese who visit the city like to take samples of them back home.

- *One of the most famous foods native to this city is the Goubuli steamed bun. Unfortunately, the main branch of the Goubuli was closed the day we planned to eat there, so we were unable to taste this famous snack, but it is celebrated not only throughout China but also in Japan and Hong Kong. These buns derive their name from the nickname of the original owner, Gao Guiyou, who opened the shop over a hundred years ago. Their filling is said to be made of the finest pork and shrimp, and the skin is usually thin. A branch has been opened in Beijing, but the buns made there are said to pale in comparison to the flavor of the originals.*
- *Shibajie, or deep-fried dough twists, are so named because the original shop that created this pastry some seventy years ago is located on Shibajie Street. Made with flour and water, the dough is rolled into thin coils that are twisted into wreathlike shapes, sprinkled with sesame seeds, and deep-fried. You will see vendors selling piles of the crisp and slightly sweet Shibajie all over the city, as well as Chinese visitors carrying away boxes to take back to relatives and friends.*
- *Another local specialty is known as Erduoyan, a deep-fried cake whose name literally means "eardrum." Although erduoyan cakes are a national favorite, we found them to be quite greasy and somewhat tasteless. They do make a nice gift for any Chinese friends in other cities, as an inexpensive souvenir from Tianjin.*

XIANG GANG JIULOU (HONG KONG RESTAURANT)

29 Shipin Jie
Tel.: 250866, 250492
Hours:
11:30 A.M.–2:00 P.M. (lunch),
5:30–8:30 P.M. (dinner)

Upon entering the Xiang Gang Jiulou one is instantly transported to Hong Kong, to all the glitz and suave service of a bona-fide Hong Kong establishment.

The decor is the most obvious element borrowed from the South. Mirrors bordered in burnished wood line the walls, and wooden beams are intermittently draped with lifelike plastic grapevines. Wooden booths along one wall of the restaurant are upholstered in plush burgundy, creating a cozy and charming atmosphere. The rest of the restaurant is crowded with tables covered with starched white linen and high-backed chairs. Chinese piano music plays liltingly in the background, and the bar is stocked generously with top-grade western and Chinese whiskeys, liquors, and beers.

Established as a joint venture between a local company and a Hong Kong firm, this restaurant offers the best of both worlds as far as food is concerned. Fresh local vegetables and meats are used, as well as seafood and other choice delicacies imported from Hong Kong and Guangzhou. The meticulous service and management are reminiscent of those in most high-calibre Hong Kong eateries. (During our meal, the manager seemed to be everywhere at once, constantly monitoring the kitchen, stirring and inspecting the hot, freshly cooked rice, and scrutinizing the service in the front of the restaurant.) One of the few drawbacks of the Hong Kong restaurant is that the kitchen is located in the basement (a common situation in restaurants in China), so that transporting food causes some delays in service.

The menu, which is eight pages long and translated from Chinese to English, offers an extensive selection of Cantonese dishes, including shark's fin, abalone, conch, pigeon, and a generous sampling of "double-boiled" soups (a Cantonese specialty in which the soup is "open-steamed" in a container to achieve a clear, concentrated broth).

The seafood dishes that we tasted were all superb. The clear-steamed flounder was cooked to perfection and doused with just the proper amount of soy sauce and hot oil over its garnish of fine shreds of gingerroot and scallions. Crab, which had been flown in from Guangzhou, was outstanding, if a trifle expensive. It was simply cut into pieces in its shell (the classic Cantonese style) and stir-fried quickly with gingerroot and scallions. We happily sucked out and prodded at the sweet meat. Stir-fried rape stalk also was excellent, seared to the proper degree of crisp tenderness. Pan-fried noodles with yellow garlic chives and bean sprouts rounded out the meal beautifully.

Other specialties of the restaurant include roast suckling pig, clear-steamed chicken, prawns on a "roasted iron" plate, and roasted young dove.

Prices are quite high; you can probably expect to pay a little less than 100 yuan per person for a fine lunch or dinner, such as the one described above. But if you order more delicacies, expect to pay accordingly. For lunch, reservations are unnecessary, although during peak hours, there might be a short wait. For dinner, especially when special dishes are desired, reservations should be made at least twenty-four hours in advance.

CHENGDE

It is said that when Emperor Kangxi of the Qing dynasty first saw the misty mountains and peaceful rivers of Chengde on a tour of northern China in 1703, he became enchanted. He also wisely recognized that it would serve as a useful meeting ground for establishing contact with the Mongolian nobles and Tibetan clergy inhabiting the area. For his own pleasure and that of his coterie of imperial officials and concubines, he built a magnificent summer palace at Chengde around 1713. And to win the favor of the Mongols and Tibetans, he embarked on an ambitious project that resulted in the building of eleven lama temples, many of which were duplicates of the originals in their homeland.

Today a peaceful five-hour train ride on a course that winds through the scenic countryside outside of Beijing will take you to Chengde, now a small town where the summer imperial retreat (also known as the Mountain Resort) and nine of the remaining temples are open to the public. Chengde is a sleepy little place, a marked and even welcome contrast to Beijing. The Mountain Resort, which is conveniently located in the center of town, contains a large, peaceful park endowed with lakes and greenery. The Lama temples, which can be reached by car, are dotted among the majestic hills surrounding the town, and many offer a tranquillity and solitude hard to come by in Beijing.

Chengde also boasts one or two surprises: every morning, the center of the town becomes alive with stalls and tables set up free-form in the square where white-jacketed cooks throw masses of dough, transforming them magically into fine noodles. They also deftly stuff dumplings with meat and vegetables and stack them into bamboo layers for steaming. You can walk among the small stalls breathing in the pungent aroma of scallion pancakes merrily sizzling in a flat iron skillet, or sample a handful of steamed buns stuffed with meat or vegetables, enjoying the flavor as you view this spontaneous carnival of Chinese fast food.

QI WANG LOU, OR CHENGDE BINGUAN (CHENGDE GUESTHOUSE)

Although Chengde does not have an especially wide selection of great restaurants, potential visitors need not hesitate, since most sightseeing in the area can be done in two days or so. By far the best place to stay is the Chengde Guesthouse. Set atop a mountain slope overlooking the city and park, the guesthouse is built in the imperial style with wings facing a courtyard adorned with a peaceful rock garden. The restaurant here is quite good. Unfortunately, during peak season it is generally reserved for guests, but with the proper arrangements for a banquet or a special meal (space allowing), outside foreign customers can usually eat here.

While it is not distinguishable from most others in small hotels, the dining room is fairly clean and the waitresses are patient and quite friendly. If you are a guest staying at the hotel and you haven't made other arrangements, you will automatically be served the standard four- to five-course meal. Though it is simple food—stir-fried vegetables and scrambled eggs with tomatoes (in season) are typical dishes—it can be surprisingly flavorful and fresh. The dining room also serves some excellent open-face steamed dumplings *(shao mai)*, and nicely crisp silver-thread rolls *(jin si juan)*. On certain nights the hotel will honor the guests with game dishes, a specialty of the region. The deep-fried deer rolls, made of ground meat rolled in bread crumbs, are superb. For 500 to 600 yuan for a table of twelve, you can order a banquet of assorted game specialties—or a host of other banquet dishes. The chef in charge of the kitchen is considered one of the most talented in the city, having earned a silver medal in the culinary competition of 1988. He is also quite adept at preparing classic northern Chinese and Sichuan dishes. For special arrangements, contact the front desk and consult with the manager of the dining room.

ZHONGGUO SHOUDU DA JIUDIAN (CAPITOL HOTEL RESTAURANT, OR BEIJING XIYUAN ROAST DUCK RESTAURANT)

127 Xiaonanmen
Tel: 223501, 223506 Ext.
"Restaurant"
Hours: 11:30 A.M.–8:30 P.M.

The Capitol Hotel Restaurant—otherwise known as the Roast Duck Restaurant (Kaoya Fandian)—is a simple place that holds only ten to fifteen tables, but it is very clean, and in peak hours, there's always a wait. This eatery is a joint venture with the the famous Xiyuan Hotel in Beijing and as such is very well-run. In fact, the manager is often seen roaming about during mealtime, making certain that tables are cleaned punctually after customers have left and that service is flowing smoothly.

The serving procedure here is unusual. After a waitress takes their orders, customers must take the initiative to go to the counter in the front of the restaurant. There, arranged in a glass case, is an assortment of simple cold dishes that are meant to be served as palate-pleasers before the hot food arrives. Customers may select any that happen to please their eyes or simply forgo them, ordering soft drinks (the ubiquitous orange crush) or beer. All items from this counter—both cold platters and beverages—are paid for separately. Foreign customers should not be shy about making their presence known and should not allow the Chinese to elbow their way in front of them.

Some of the best dishes here are the unpretentious, spicy Sichuanese ones, such as the stir-fried cabbage, or the slivers of pork with garlic chives (probably available only on a seasonal basis). Definitely order whatever versions of the stir-fried vegetables are in season as well as the hot-and-sour soup, fish-flavored pork shreds, Geng Bao chicken with peanuts, and deep-fried Squirrel Fish. The Peking duckling, which is one of the restaurant's noted specialties, looked rather fatty.

Although the customers are mainly Chinese, westerners definitely will feel welcome here. The prices are extremely reasonable, averaging about 50 to 60 yuan for a filling lunch or dinner.

HOU SHEN MIAO JIE
(FOOD STALLS IN FRONT OF
WESTERN GATE OF PARK)
—

*I*f you're an adventurous eater (actually, the conditions looked fairly sanitary), pay a visit to the block of noodle stands and stalls offering dumplings and other local specialties located almost directly across from the Western Gate of the Mountain Resort Park. The stalls appear in the wee hours of the morning and stay open until early afternoon. Even if you're wary of sampling the food, it's worth taking a stroll through the festive area. You can watch mesmerized as young cooks pick up ropes of dough, whirling them repeatedly into the air like an edible lasso until they form thousands of strands of delicate noodles. They are then thrown into a pot, boiled for a few minutes, and strained into a huge bowl where a fragrant meat and vegetable sauce is poured on top. Some of the thicker noodles are deep-fried and eaten straight from the fryer as a crunchy treat. Piles of steamers are stacked with open-face dumplings, buns, and egg pancakes stuffed with meat and assorted vegetables.

ER XIAN JU NONG MAO SHICHANG
(CHENGDE'S FREE MARKET)
—

*F*urther up the street from the Western Gate food stalls is Chengde's colorful free market. There you can inspect freshly killed pork and a variety of newly picked vegetables. To the left of the tables and wagons heaped with food is a miniature flea market with all kinds of clothing, knickknacks, and sundry items. While there is a lot of worthless stuff about as in any flea market, you may find amid the junk some treasured souvenirs of your stay in this quaint city.

SHENYANG

Shenyang is not yet included on the standard tourist itinerary, but it does receive its share of foreigners. Since it is the largest industrial city in northern China and the capital of Liaoning province, western and Japanese businessmen are frequent visitors.

Shenyang was first settled some two thousand years ago but it was not until the eleventh century that the city came into its own as one of the foremost trading centers of the northern steppelands. In 1625 the Manchu leader Nurhachi named Shenyang as the northern capital, which it remained until 1644. During the Japanese Occupation, Shenyang was used as an industrial base for all of northern China.

I was especially looking forward to seeing this northern city, since it was my first visit to what was known as Manchuria, but apart from the imperial palace, built in 1625, there is little here to remind you that you are in the heart of Manchuria. Still, it is an interesting place, a little too industrial for my tastes but free of the usual hordes of tourists, and one that offers some excellent food. The cuisine of Shenyang does not differ noticeably from that of Beijing. Mongolian firepot is believed to have originated in this area, but most restaurants here feature the classic specialties of northern regional cooking.

It was in Shenyang that we were first introduced to the undiscovered secret of state guesthouses which open their dining rooms to foreigners. In one such establishment we were attended solicitously by a large staff and dined on superb pan-fried dumplings, perfectly fried to a crusty brownness. The hot-and-sour soup was so refined and perfectly seasoned that we ordered bowl after bowl, exclaiming over each spoonful.

"FEIFEI XICAN FANGUAN" (FEIFEI WESTERN-STYLE-FOOD RESTAURANT)

6 Li, Minzu Jie, Heping Qu
Tel.: 432006
Hours:
11:00 A.M.–2:00 P.M. (lunch),
5:00–9:00 P.M. (dinner)

With its four banquettes and seven tables covered with bright green lace tablecloths and its blaring music, the Feifei Restaurant is a curious little place and just a bit garish. But maybe such touches are a sign of the coming of a new age to China.

Mr. Zhao, the bespectacled owner, is a charming and somewhat earnest man with perfumed hair, a silk shirt, and suspenders, and is president of the Western-Style Food Society in Shenyang. Zhao originally trained in Chinese cuisine, studying for some twenty years, but in 1985 he switched to western-style, learning Russian cooking in Harbin. He also spent some time at the famous German-owned Kiessling Restaurant in Tianjin. Reflecting its owner's diverse background, the Feifei's menu offers a selection of German, French, Russian, and Japanese specialties. It seems that Mr. Zhao is determined to leave no stone unturned.

The Feifei first opened in February 1988, four years after Mr. Zhao opened another western restaurant to great success. Its prices are not cheap (about 20 yuan for a dish of several deep-fried prawns and 8 yuan for chicken Kiev), but the food is not bad, and it's fun to go and watch the Chinese customers enjoy the potato salad, pickles, and western dishes, as they struggle a little with knife and fork and dump large quantities of salt and pepper on their food, savoring the novelty of the entire experience.

Ideally, reservations should be made in advance, but you can take your chances and wait, if necessary.

LAO BIAN JIAOZI GUAN (LAO BIAN DUMPLING HOUSE)
—

6 Zhbongyang Lu, San Duan, Shenhequ
Tel.: 447941
Hours: 11:30 A.M.–6:30 P.M.

Lao Bian Jiaozi Guan, which originally opened in 1829, is a venerable institution in Shenyang, one whose reputation has spread outside China. (In 1984, two branches appeared in Kyoto and Sapporo in Japan.) As we discovered in Shenyang, its fame is well-deserved; the dumplings we sampled were simply delicious.

Don't expect a formal restaurant with an elegant interior: the Lao Bian is an unpretentious dumpling joint, located near one of the most colorful free markets in the older section of the city, which you may want to walk around before or after your meal. Upon entering the restaurant, you will notice to your right, behind the glassed-in area, white-coated young women preparing cold dishes such as boiled peanuts, shredded cucumbers, and shredded chicken salad. There are also plates stacked with finely minced garlic and chili paste, among the locals a popular dipping sauce for the dumplings.

The first floor is a clamor with milling waitresses skillfully passing out platters heaped with mountains of boiled dumplings. At every table customers deftly use their chopsticks to shuttle the dumplings continuously from the platter, to the spicy dip, and finally to their mouths. Foreigners and private parties will find the atmosphere is much more sedate in the banquet rooms upstairs.

For about 50 yuan per person, any foreign customer can come in off the street and fill his or her belly with the excellent dumplings. The usual variety is stuffed with ground pork and garlic chives, but for a little more money and a request in advance the restaurant will prepare a banquet feast (ideally, for at least six people) of six different dumpling fillings and a selection of hot entrees. Typically, the dumplings may be filled with minced scallops, squid, wood ears, bamboo shoots, cucumbers, or green beans. The vegetable fillings will change with the season. In spring, the stuffing may be made with a mixture or shrimp and garlic chives; in the summer, pumpkin or luffa squash and celery prevail; the autumn offers dumplings made with cabbage, fresh kidney beans, and peppers; and in the winter, the filling again becomes hearty with cabbage and lots of ground meat. The main cooking method is boiling and open-steaming, but in a multicourse banquet, the dumplings will also be fried and baked.

For a banquet, reservations should be made at least twenty-four hours in advance; otherwise, you can just walk in and order the plain boiled dumplings. Either way, it is certain that your dumpling cravings will be sated—at least temporarily. MasterCard and Visa are accepted here.

LIAONING BINGUAN (GUESTHOUSE DINING ROOM)

—

27 Zhongshan Lu, Er Duan,
Heping Qu
Tel.: 433644, 433645
Hours:
11:30 A.M.–1:30 P.M. (lunch),
5:30–8:00 P.M. (dinner)

The stateliness of this magnificent building will capture your eye as soon as you make your grand tour of Shenyang. Set back on a circular driveway, the Liaoning is a grand hotel in the thirties style. The somewhat somber marble lobby is a bit dreary but still intriguing, with an outlet of the finest antique store in the city to the left as you walk in. And because of its location in the heart of the city, the dining room is a famous meeting place for both foreign and local businessmen. Although the food has a reputation of being quite good, we found the seasoning to be bland and the food overall to be only passable. We did not, however, plan a banquet in advance, but walked in and ordered from the menu. The restaurant specializes in Beijing, Sichuan, and Shandong dishes and offers the standard items—chicken with peanuts, hot-and-sour soup, stir-fried noodles with meat and vegetables, and steamed breads.

There is one place in this hotel that is *not* to be missed, and that is the combination bar and billiard room. Actually, to do it justice, it should be described as a tavern or pub. Its three slate billiard tables are reputed to be among the finest in China. Its bar is fashioned completely of marble and surrounded by gleaming wood with mirrors and ornate leaded glass doors. It is a magnificent room and an unexpected pleasure in the heart of northeastern China. The bar itself is fully stocked with top-grade western liquor and whiskey and is open until midnight.

LIAONING YOUYI BINGUAN (LIAONING FRIENDSHIP HOTEL)

—

1 Huanghe Dajie, Chi Duan
Tel.: 66581–2–3 (Speak to
Manager Ma Zhuren)
Hours:
12:00–1:00 P.M. (lunch),
5:30–8:00 P.M. (dinner)

The Liaoning Youyi is unquestionably one of the hidden culinary treasures of Shenyang. Situated on the grounds of the state guesthouse, it might appear to be an exclusive club for VIP's and heads of state, but it is very much open to the public. The grounds alone are worth a visit, so if the weather permits, plan a little extra time for a stroll. The hotel features ten stately guesthouses (some of which are rented by corporations doing regular business here, and are beautifully restored), a health club, and the main building, where the central dining room is situated.

The public dining room is airy and large, with a slightly formal atmosphere, but the help couldn't be friendlier or more accommodating. The cuisine is predominantly Sichuanese, but the food is so meticulously prepared and refined that one might consider it more northern-imperial-Sichuanese. Although the menu contains a page of western dishes, ignore them and stick to the Chinese items. We found that almost every selection was worthwhile.

The stir-fried chicken with peanuts *(geng bao ji ding)* was somewhat spicy but beautifully seasoned with dried hot red chili peppers. Red-cooked eggplant *(hong shao qiezi)* was fragrant with ginger and garlic, a perfect complement to the hot, fluffy rice. The pan-fried dumplings *(guo-tie)* were *superb* (some of the best I have *ever* tasted), crusty, thin-skinned, and stuffed with ground meat and garlic chives. In addition to their pan-fried form, dumplings are available boiled or steamed. Hot-and-sour soup *(suan la tang)* also was exceptional, with superfine shreds of pork, bamboo shoot, sea cucumbers, and eggs. An exquisitely fresh rendition of hearts of cabbage lightly seasoned with sesame oil rounded out the meal. The generous selection of appetizers includes curried cauliflower, sweet-and-sour cucumbers, and barbecue or roast pork. Stuffed meat pies are also available, but they should be ordered in advance.

The menu is in English and Chinese. You can call and order the entire meal in advance, estab-

(continued)

lishing a price and allowing the dining room manager to select the dishes, or you may order when you arrive. A simple but superb meal can cost as little as 25 yuan per person, depending on the size of the group. For a multicourse banquet with expensive delicacies the tariff can run as much as 80 yuan per person with a table of eight to ten.

At times it might take some persistence to get into the Liaoning Youyi, but do make the effort. If you are traveling with a China International Travel Service (CITS) guide, they should be able to make arrangements for you. Otherwise, ask the clerk at your hotel to call and make a reservation, asking for Manager Ma.

LU MING CHUN FANDIAN (LU MING CHUN RESTAURANT)
—

Shi Hao Qi Duan Da Xi Lu
Heping District
Tel.: 24487, 25128
Hours: 11:30 A.M.–8:00 P.M.

First opened in 1939, the Lu Ming Chun has become one of Shenyang's most popular and highly respected eateries. The head chef and assistant manager, Liu Jing Xian, is famous throughout Liaoning province. He is a radio and television personality; he has written a book about the regional Liaoning style; and he has won a gold medal at the First National Culinary Competition held after the Cultural Revolution in 1983. Chef Liu's expertise has led to the restaurant's becoming a regional center for training chefs.

On one of the days we visited, three of Lu Ming Chun's chefs were being tested for promotion from the second level to the first. They had been selected in a previous competition from two hundred others who had come from all over the province. (In order to even qualify, contestants must have trained for ten years.) Chef Liu, along with three mayors from cities in the province and other chefs and dignitaries, was judging the dishes. Each chef had to create and prepare sixteen original dishes for the exam, and each one seemed to surpass the other in design and flavor.

The normal menu at Lu Ming Chun combines cuisines of three different styles: imperial palace (very refined and including shark's fin, bird's nest, and other costly delicacies), Muslim cooking (heartier, with the use of lamb, Monglian firepot, and shashlik), and northeastern specialties (including game dishes, such as grouse and a bear's paw, plus monkey mushroom, a wild fungus).

Foreign customers will be shown to the dining room on the second floor, where the decor—walls lined with bamboo wallpaper, and floors covered by Oriental carpets—is somewhat nondescript but a shade above that of many establishments. The waitresses, who are attired in filmy red dresses, are very helpful and attentive.

Some of the best dishes of the restaurants are the oven-baked shrimp *(shen kao da xia)*, crispy-skin duck *(xiang su ya)*, scallion-oil fish *(cong you yu)*, imperial pot turtle soup *(jiu guo yuan yu)*, monkey head mushrooms *(houtou leng xu)*, and a seasonal dish made with cabbage and bamboo shoots *(pa shan bai)*.

Reservations should be made a day or two in advance, and for a party of four to six, with about six dishes, the price will be about 100 yuan per person. If you are interested in ordering bear's paw, the order should be made about one week in advance, and the price will be about 200 yuan per person.

HARBIN

The flatness of the terrain is what first strikes you on landing at the airport in Harbin. On the road into the city the only view as far as the eye can see is acres and acres of freshly planted crops. It's no wonder, since Harbin is situated squarely in the center of northeastern China's Manchurian plain.

On my first visit to Harbin, I arrived on a hot, sunny day in early summer. A dry wind blew across the road, and golden wheat bent gently back and forth with the breeze. A farmer led his horse slowly across a field, and I would not have been surprised to see a tribe of wandering nomads making its way across the landscape.

Harbin itself was a pleasant surprise. With its broad, tree-lined avenues, grand stucco buildings, and majestic monuments, it has a decidedly Russian flavor, and indeed, Russians have played a major role in the building and shaping of this city. They first settled in the area in the 1800s, after the Chinese and Russians established an agreement extending the Transsiberian Railroad, making Harbin a major junction and opening a channel between the two countries. Following the Russian revolution in 1917, still more Russians settled in the city, until they outnumbered the Chinese. In 1932, the Japanese invaded Harbin and occupied it until 1945, when they were defeated by the Russian army. They withdrew a year later, along with many of the Russian residents.

Today some remnants of Russian influence remain even in the food. The diet of the Harbinese is rich in potatoes and crusty brown bread. Each morning, the Modern Bakery, a local favorite, teems with residents standing in line for cocoa, toasted egg bread, and bowls of sweetened yogurt. Next door, in its restaurant, customers feast on stuffed cabbage rolls and chicken Kiev, all served with healthy side orders of potato salad and pickled cucumbers and tomatoes. And in the summer, the city's sidewalks are alive with small stands serving dishes of soft ice cream, a food introduced by the Russians that has come to be relished year-round by all Harbinese.

Chinese cooks have made their mark here as well. Among the noted specialties of the area are delicacies like bear's paw, grouse, and nose of the camel deer. But simpler northern dishes are equally popular. At the the Lao Du Yi Chu Fandian, one of the city's oldest and most popular eateries, you can feast your way through fifteen courses of different stuffed dumplings. While the Chinese are unusually adventurous eaters, they inevitably wind up longing for their dumplings.

Harbin is lively throughout most of the year, but it is especially chaotic in January, when the city assumes the appearance of one of its Siberian neighbors and hosts the Ice Festival, a celebration for which the central park is transformed by luminous ice sculptures meticulously carved into lanterns, palaces, pagodas, and intricate mazes. Be aware that what seems like all the rest of China will arrive for the festival, and that hotel and restaurant reservations will be extremely difficult to come by.

FU TAI LOU FANDIAN (FU TAI LOU RESTAURANT)

—

19 Dadi Xi Shisan Daojie
Tel.: 47598, 44721
Hours: 11:30 A.M.–7:30 P.M.

The Fu Tai Lou's modest appearance does little to impress the foreigner with its status in Harbin, and its interior is hardly better. But after we sampled some of the specialties of the house, this eatery more than lived up to its reputation as one of the best restaurants in the city.

The manager who oversees the fourteen private rooms on the second floor, where most of the foreigners are seated, bragged modestly about the many customers from all over the world who had visited. And, she boasted, the restaurant is even listed in the international phone book (probably for foreigners who want to make reservations for guaranteed seats during the Ice Festival).

The private rooms are actually more like cubicles, with barely enough room for a table. Most are unadorned, but clean, and most afford a view of all the dishes being carried to other rooms. If you need some inspiration for ordering, this can be quite helpful, but, if service is as slow as it was when we visited, it might prove to be a test of endurance.

The Fu Tai Lou originally opened as a tiny eatery near the Russian border, where it found favor with the locals. About 1930 the owner moved it to its present location in Harbin and it does a thriving business: the second floor alone serves two to three hundred people daily.

The Fu Tai Lou specializes in Shandong-style cooking and Peking duck, but since it is in the heart of wild game country, bear's paw, deer, and pheasant are also among the menu's noted items. The price for these dishes can be steep, and all must be ordered at least two days in advance.

Some of the most outstanding dishes sampled here were the deep-fried birds made of chicken and shrimp *(bai niu hui chiu)*, and the French eggs *(faguo dan)*, which were deep-fried fresh eggs simmered in a tomato sauce studded with bits of tomatoes, carrots, and assorted vegetables. A simple braised mustard cabbage with dried shrimp was also good, and a dish of sweet and sour barbecued pork *(cha shao rou)* was superb. The highlight of the meal was the *shao bing,* flaky, spiraled pancakes made of dough and shortening combined in a manner similar to that used in making puff pastry. The *shao bing* are usually served as a staple (instead of steamed bread) along with the entrees.

Depending on the menu, prices for a banquet will average about 100 yuan per person. For a humbler meal, with fewer game specialties, the price will be much more modest. Reservations should be made about forty-eight hours in advance. During the Ice Festival, as with all eateries, plan a month in advance.

HUA YUAN CUN BINGUAN (FRIENDSHIP PALACE HOTEL)

Haiguan Jie
Tel.: 30911
Hours:
7:00–8:30 A.M., (breakfast),
10:30 A.M.–1:30 P.M., (lunch),
5:00–7:30 P.M. (dinner)

The restaurant of the Friendship Palace is by no means one of the foremost places to eat in Harbin, but it's clean, a bit glitzy in an endearing Chinese kind of way, and if you stick to the set menu, the food can be quite decent. It is also consistent, and the menu is printed in Chinese and English. Most of the customers are guests at the hotel, but with the proper advance reservations, other foreigners may eat here. Actually, if you find yourself staying at one of the other hotels in the city, you may be forced out of necessity to try a simple meal here, since the food at the competitors can be deplorable.

Don't be tempted by the western dishes and Chinese delicacies. Stick to the simple stir-fried meat and vegetable dishes—the chicken with vegetables, pork with cucumbers, and the stir-fried cabbage or green beans (depending, of course, on what's seasonally available). You also have a choice of accompaniment of steamed rice or steamed buns, a good and refreshing alternative.

This restaurant does have an unusual practice of allowing its help to eat with the customers before the dining room has closed, so don't be surprised if your waitress takes her lunch hour at a neighboring table while you are still partaking of your meal.

LAO DU YI CHU FANDIAN (LAO DU YI CHU RESTAURANT)

58 Dao Li Shisan Daojie
Tel.: 42808, 45017
Hours: 10:00 A.M.–7:00 P.M.

One of Harbin's finest and most unusual eateries is the Lao Du Yi Chu Fandian. Its specialty is dumplings, and one can sample a fifteen-course meal with myriad dumpling fillings. Although I would vote the dumpling banquet in Xi'an to be a shade superior, any opportunity to enjoy this meal should be taken.

It is hard to imagine a lovelier restaurant setting in China. Even from the outside, the Lao Du Yi Chu invites attention. Set off on a side street from the main boulevard, the exterior is rather quaint with ornate Chinese bric-a-brac and long wooden columns. Foreigners will be led to the third floor, where there are six private rooms. The walls of this floor are lined with bold hangings of calligraphy from well-known artists and calligraphers singing praises of the dumplings. Three of the larger private rooms are quite magnificent. Black wooden wall panels, which also serve as dividers to split up the rooms for smaller parties, portray vivid scenes of ancient Chinese life. The windows are adorned with ornately carved natural wooden latticework, and the lead glass panes are embedded with geometric designs.

Lao Du Yi Chu originally opened in 1929, according to Yang Yin Sheng, the present manager, and its dumplings have been enjoyed by customers from all over the world. One can choose from three different levels of dumpling meals. The "first-class meal" contains twenty-five different types of dumplings as well as an assortment of ten hot dishes, at a cost of approximately 100 yuan per person. For a "second-class meal," containing twenty types of dumplings and eight hot dishes, the cost is approximately 80 yuan per person; and the "third-class meal" offers ten types of dumplings and six hot dishes at a cost of 60 yuan per person. Some of the best dumpling fillings are steamed black mushroom, dried tiger lily bud, and sesame paste with meat. Most are steamed, but for the full banquet, boiled and pan-fried varieties also are presented.

All meals begin with a sampling of the smoked specialties of the house, including chicken, pork, tripe, sausage, and fish, and a refreshing cold tossed salad. The smoked chicken and sausage are especially tasty.

Reservations usually should be made about two to three days in advance (on occasion, they may bend the rules and be more flexible). During the Ice Festival, however, pandemonium reigns, and tables are booked about a month ahead.

MA DIAN FANDIAN (MODERN RESTAURANT)

■

129 Zhongyang Jie
Tel.: 45846
Hours: 10:00 A.M.–8:00 P.M.

The Modern Restaurant, which specializes in assorted classic Russian and western dishes, is an institution in Harbin. It is worth a visit if for nothing else than to experience the slightly old-world atmosphere, beginning with the funky decor (heavy burgundy velveteen drapes, and sparkly ceiling globes giving off a subdued light). And then there's a dismaying sight of Chinese families and couples downing cabbage and tomato soup or stuffed cabbage rolls au gratin, potato salad, and side dishes of pickled cucumbers and green tomatoes.

The simpler dishes are by far the best here: the cabbage soup, although undersalted, was hearty and piquant, with a generous dash of cayenne and a fat dollop of sour cream. The pickled musk melon was crisp but needed a bit more pickling time (a problem I've even encountered with the half-sour pickles at the Carnegie Delicatessen in New York City). Deep-fried chicken, pork fillet, and fried pawns are all consistently good.

This restaurant might be considered more expensive than some of the smaller Chinese eateries, but one can easily eat heartily here for about 50 to 60 yuan per person. And the menu is in Chinese and English.

MA DIAN LENG YIN (MODERN BAKERY)

▬

Located next to the Modern
Restaurant
Tel.: 45846 Ext. 286
Hours: 10:00 A.M.–9:30 P.M.

On the corner of one of the busiest streets in Harbin is the Modern Hotel, a testament to the ornate architecture left by the Soviets. Fully restored, it now stands proudly, its glass and brass fittings gleaming.

At the corner of the hotel is a concession with about ten to twelve tables and walk-up service windows. It is a popular meeting place for locals: young and old alike come at all hours of the day to sip cocoa and sample ice cream and assorted pastries and cakes. During the winter, according to a local resident, hot dogs and hamburgers are added to the menu.

It is a wonderful place for people-watching. There are old women gossiping as they nurse their lukewarm cups of cocoa and young children gulping down helpings of ice cream, which, to be frank, tastes more like ice milk with imitation vanilla flavoring.

The pastries, however, are quite good, particularly the layered egg cake with custard filling. There's also toasted, sliced egg bread, a heavy egg roll, and bowls of yogurt with generous spoonfuls of sugar sprinkled on top—a dish that is a rarity in China.

Like the dining room of the Modern Hotel, the ambience is somewhat rundown and old world. In the front, rosy-cheeked Chinese women wearing light blue dresses, their hair restrained under white kerchiefs, dispense the breads and foods cheerfully. Through the glassed-in case you can see the assorted pastries, allowing you to point, if necessary, to your choice. Prices are cheap, and it's a lively place to go for a brief respite from the more banal sites of the city.

BEAR'S PAW

—

Bear's paw is eaten in several different parts of China, but the northerners believe that the best-tasting paw is found in Harbin, where the bear's diet of potatoes gives it a superior flavor.

Because of their dwindling numbers in China, the hunting of bear is strictly supervised by the government. Today, only two northern nationalities are allowed to hunt legally, and their quota is severely limited.

Fall is considered to be the best time to catch the bear, when its paws are full of nutrients before the winter's hibernation. According to Chinese chefs, certain paws are prized more highly than others: the rear paws are meatier, but the two front paws are more nutritious. And the right paw is considered far superior to the left.

The process of preparing bear's paw is lengthy and detailed, accounting for its expense. First the paw is boiled in water over a period of two days to remove the hair, skin, and bones. The remaining flesh is then soaked in clean water overnight. Next the paw is steamed for twelve hours in a chicken broth with seasonings such as ginger, scallions, peppercorns, and garlic. The liquid is discarded, and the paw is again steamed in a similar mixture for six hours to infuse it with flavor. Only then is the paw ready for the final cooking step; it is either braised, steamed, or simmered in an earthenware pot and then presented for eating.

The one time I was privileged to sample bear's paw, it had been red-cooked. The taste was redolent of the rich soy-sauce braising mixture used to cook it to a buttery tenderness, and the overall texture was slightly gelatinous. Certainly it was a dish I will long remember but not rush to order again.

JINAN

Jinan, the capital of Shandong province in northeastern China, is known as the city of springs. Its over one hundred natural bubbling waterholes have been dry on each of my three visits to the city, owing to a drought, yet I have very warm memories of Jinan.

My earliest trip there was in 1984, when I was invited as a guest of the provincial government to teach western cooking to Chinese master chefs. My first two weeks were devoted to preparing for demonstrations, so I had little chance to explore, but once my work was completed, I was left to wander.

I walked around the city, which is fairly modest in size, and saw the now-trickling hot springs and their surrounding parks, all teeming with Chinese tourists. I enjoyed the peaceful serenity of Daming Lake, climbed the Thousand Buddha Mountain, and was rewarded by the stunning view of the city and its surrounding peaks. I also discovered the Shandong Provincial Museum and its impressive collection of bronzes, puzzling over the Chinese titles that had not yet been translated into English.

But the main pleasure of those few days was observing the simple and languorous pace of everyday life. Jinan is a quiet city where a peaceful stroll can be interrupted by the snorting of a donkey hauling a pushcart, transporting hay or crops from the country. And in summer, the city almost comes to a complete stop as its residents disappear every afternoon for an hour's siesta. But the people are warm and generous in a way that is unique in China— even if they are apt to stare, since it may be their first opportunity to see a westerner in the flesh.

JU FENG DE FANDIAN
(JU FENG DE RESTAURANT)
—

Weisi Lu / Jingsan Lu
Tel.: 23753
Hours: 10:00 A.M.–8:00 P.M.

Ju Feng De may look somewhat slick and new, but the restaurant has been in operation for over forty years, and only moved to its present quarters in late 1988. One of the reasons for its tremendous success may be that it was originally opened by eight cooks who had lost their jobs in other restaurants and decided to pool their meager funds and considerable talents to open the Ju Feng De. From the beginning, even the purveyors who sold them their ingredients were sympathetic and allowed them to defer payment until they had enough money.

Today, there are still two cooks from the original group in residence: Wang Xing Nan, who is seventy-six years old, and Cheng Xue Xiang, who is sixty-seven. Both are special-level chefs. Even the manager of the Ju Feng De is a third-level cook, attesting to the restaurant's emphasis on the quality of its food.

The Ju Feng De is renowned for its dim sum—both the sweet and the savory. All are made fresh daily and displayed in a glass case in the front of the restaurant so that customers can even buy off the street. There is a wide selection of sweet of-

(continued)

ferings, such as the flaky sesame rounds with a filling of crushed sesame seeds and a hint of Sichuan peppercorns or the four-pointed stars filled with date paste. Of the savory variety, the *you yuan*, a celebrated Shandong specialty composed of spirals of flaky pastry dotted with bits of minced scallions and flavored with scallion oil, are outstanding. We tasted them hot out of the oven, and they were superb.

The kitchen also delivers some fine stir-fried dishes, and of those sampled, the best were the pieces of chicken and green pepper that were redolent with the flavors of rice wine and the fire *(you bao ji ding)*; a shredded chicken and bamboo shoot dish generously seasoned with fresh coriander *(chao ji si)*; and tender slices of duck liver in sweet bean sauce *(huan men ya gan)*. Shandong produces the best white asparagus in China, and while our stir-fried version had a nice taste, we were disappointed that they were canned. The Ju Feng De also boasts of having the best Peking duck in the city, but we found it to be somewhat fatty. You would do better to wait until Beijing.

As in most other restaurants, reservations for a meal with special dishes should be made twenty-four hours in advance, but the new premises will easily accommodate spontaneous visits —even by foreign customers. Prices are moderate and should vary between 30 to 80 yuan per person depending on the menu and the size of the party.

NANJIAO BINGUAN (NANJIAO HOTEL)

—

2 Ma'anshan Road
Tel.: 613931
Hours:
6:30–8:30 A.M. (breakfast),
11:30 A.M.–1:30 P.M. (lunch),
5:00–8:30 P.M. (dinner)

Most tourists to Jinan may be unfamiliar with the Nanjiao Hotel, a sprawling complex located on the southern side of the city, since hotel policy prohibits groups, and rooms generally are reserved for businessmen and government guests. In fact, the landscaped grounds hold several stunning private guesthouses for heads of state, all preserved in their early 1960s splendor, down to the classic wooden furniture.

The dining room and restaurants are open to the public, however, and food here is consistently good. For lunch or dinner, you can drop into the dining room and partake of the newly installed western-style Chinese buffet, you can order off the menu, or you can feast on a banquet, ordered in advance.

The dining room menu features local Shandong dishes, including red-cooked chicken and boiled dumplings, as well as Sichuanese classics like chicken with peanuts, Ma Po bean curd, and dry-cooked prawns. The buffet offers an extraordinary value of unlimited eating for 15 yuan. On the day we visited, four cold dishes for nibbling were already positioned at each table. The buffet held five to six stir-fried, red-cooked, and fried items as well as a choice of steamed breads, rice, and dumplings. There was also a selection of western and Chinese sweets. The pastry chef, who studied in Beijing and Guangzhou, makes a daily supply of doughnuts, jelly rolls, butter cookies, and pound cake—and he uses real butter.

If you order a meal in advance, some of the dishes you might want to try are the huge prawns split and served with the heads braised in tomato sauce, the middles stir-fried quickly in hot oil, and the ends minced to a mousseline *(louhan daxia)*. The crispy-skin duck *(xiang su ya)* is also excellent. And both the red-cooked eggplant and *guo ta* cucumber squares, a quichelike dish made with eggs and shredded cucumbers, are unusual and filling.

Reservations for a banquet should be made the day before; the price will vary from 50 to 100 yuan depending on the dishes ordered.

PIANYI FANG GUOTIE GUAN (INEXPENSIVE DUMPLING HOUSE)
—

Jing San Lu / Wei Si Lu Kou
Tel.: 33507, 36339
Hours: 9:30 A.M.–8:00 P.M.

The Pianyi Fang is just a hole in the wall where locals sit at formica-topped tables and stools (sometimes still sloppy after the last customer), stuffing themselves with pan-fried dumplings and drinking local beer from plastic mugs. These are hardly the delicate hand-folded variety of dumplings served at a multicourse banquet. The version served here is big, crusty, and maybe even a little greasy, stuffed with a choice of two fillings: dried shrimp with ground pork, or plain ground pork. You may prefer the plain ground pork unless your palate is accustomed to the briny flavor of dried shrimp.

If you are tired of eating ersatz hotel food or partaking of multicourse banquets, or would just like to see everyday life in Jinan while enjoying a cheap, filling meal, you've come to the right place.

YAN XI TANG FANDIAN (YAN XI TANG RESTAURANT)

292 Quan Cheng Road
Tel.: 21703
Hours: 10:00 A.M.–8:00 P.M.

At first glance, the Yan Xi Tang Restaurant, which is situated in the center of downtown Jinan, would certainly receive no accolades for inspiring decor. The first floor, as in most other Chinese eateries, is crowded and noisy and even a bit squalid. But take no notice and instead proceed upstairs to the banquet rooms where all foreigners are seated. Before you go, call ahead and insist on the "red chamber," a room inspired by the celebrated Qing dynasty novel *Dream of the Red Chamber.* The walls are painted with a lovely mural showing graceful Chinese ladies-in-waiting, and the tablecloth, curtains, and napkins are all a deep ruby red.

The kitchen employs some twenty-seven cooks, all under the direction of special first-level master chef Cui Wi Qing. The menu stresses local products that showcase the essence of Jinan cooking. These include three main ingredients, all products of Daming Lake: *pu cai,* a Jerusalem artichoke–like vegetable that is used in soups, stir-fried dishes, and quichelike concoctions; *zhao bai,* which is a form of rice shoot and prepared primarily in soups and stir-fried dishes; and lotus root, which is stuffed, eaten in cold salads, and cooked in soups. Another distinguishing feature of the local cooking style is the clear, fragrant broth found in many of the soups. One of the most delicious dishes sampled at the Yan Xi Tang was an extraordinarily flavorful seafood soup *(qing tang xian mo).* The cold dishes were also excellent.

A simple meal will average about 40 to 50 yuan per person and 60 to 100 yuan for a more formal multicourse banquet.

A NOTE ABOUT SHANDONG COOKING

*A*lthough not as familiar as China's other great regional cuisines, the cooking of Shandong is one of the country's most refined and original styles. In fact, it is considered by many to be its haute cuisine. In imperial times, its chefs were the primary cooks in the palace kitchens, and their culinary expertise influenced the preparation of food throughout China, particularly in the cities of Shanghai and Hangzhou. But then, it is hardly surprising that this regional style was so sophisticated: it was in the small village of Qufu in Shandong province that Confucius was born some 2,500 years ago, and that he established the elevated standards that mark Chinese cuisine to this day.

Shandong, which is a northeastern province bordering the sea, enjoys a temperate climate which, in conjunction with its fertile terrain, makes it a major agricultural area. Wheat, barley, millet, corn, and soybeans are the staple crops. A number of vegetables and fruits, such as pears, apples, grapes, and persimmons, thrive as well. Meat and poultry are plentiful, and the long coastline provides the area with a wealth of seafood. Because of its mild climate, wheat rather than rice is the primary staple crop. Accordingly, flour-based products, such as steamed breads, pancakes, and noodles, grace the tables for everyday meals.

The school of Shandong cooking is generally divided into three regions: Jinan cooking, named after its capital city; Jiaodong dishes, originating from the coastal peninsula of the same name; and Kong Mansion dishes, or Confucian cuisine, centering around the town of Qufu, which is considered by some to be the purest form of classic Chinese cooking.

Sweet-and-sour yellow river carp, candied sweet potatoes, and clear and creamy "rush shoot" soup are three of the dishes most typical of the Jinan style. Cooks from this area are fond of stir-frying, braising, and deep-frying. Jinan cuisine is said to combine a blend of clearness, freshness, crispness, and tenderness. Perhaps more important, it embodies a simplicity that reflects the concern of local cooks, who are intent on preserving and accentuating the natural flavors of the fine products of the region.

Jiaodong dishes are most prevalent in the city of Yantai, located on the Jiaodong Peninsula in eastern Shandong. According to some local sources, it has a history of eight hundred years. Because of Yantai's coastal location, the majority of Jiaodong dishes involve seafood: baked prawns, butterfly-cup goldfish (fashioned from shrimp paste), clear-steamed fish, shark's fin, and sea cucumbers are among the most popular. The preferred methods of cooking are steaming, blanching, and quick-frying— techniques that highlight the fresh, briny taste of the area's ingredients.

The general school of Shandong cooking also includes the broad category of Confucian Mansion specialties, whose main characteristic is meticulous regard for freshness and the inherent flavor of the ingredients. (For further information, see the section on Confucian cooking, page 137.) Qufu, located in southwestern Shandong, is believed to be the birthplace of modern Chinese cuisine, and many of the dishes created by chefs at the Kong Family Mansion have contributed to the impressive repertory of classic northern Chinese dishes.

QUFU

A trip to Qufu takes some effort. Most visitors travel by car from Jinan, a long and rather roundabout six- or seven-hour drive. The journey takes you through the lush Shandong countryside where wheat and rice fields intermingle with grapevines and neat rows of apple and pear trees. The road is rutted and at times seems impassable, but the trip is well worth the obstacles.

Qufu is a tiny town that appears to have been preserved from another century. Cars are rare, and the town center is engulfed by the ornate ancient buildings (most of which are now restored) and series of interconnecting courtyards that make up the Confucius temple and the Kong Family Mansion. The town is rumored to have been inhabited as early as 6000 B.C., and by 2000 B.C. the Yi tribe had settled the area, a fact confirmed by the discovery of bronzes from the period. Confucius was born near or in Qufu around 551 B.C. but spent much of his life traveling throughout China in search of a ruler who would adopt his teachings. Toward the end of his years he returned to his birthplace and began preaching his beliefs to the numerous disciples who had begun to flock to the area. Following his death in 479 B.C., his house was enlarged and transformed into a temple, and over the centuries, it was rebuilt and added on until it became the splendid cluster of buildings and monuments that exists today.

We arrived in Qufu long past sunset after hours of driving aimlessly, lost in a maze of small country lanes. The road leading to the town was lined with stately trees, their boughs overgrown and their branches gnarled with age, forming a natural canopy over the car and blocking out the moon and star-filled sky. We stayed at the Confucian Mansion, the oldest hotel dating back to 1550, where the descendants of Confucius made their home. The quarters are musty and plumbing is antiquated, but some rooms do contain ornate furnishings from the Qing dynasty. The courtyards are peaceful havens where guests can sit at small stone tables and enjoy the serenity of early morning and late evening against a harmonious background of chirping birds. And the kitchen, with the proper arrangements, can prepare an elaborate traditional Confucian feast.

Confucius, it can be argued, was the father of classic Chinese cuisine, for it was he who established the basic tenets upon which modern Chinese cooking is based. In the mansion kitchens, where numerous meals were prepared for Confucius' descendants and visiting imperial rulers, many of the elaborate dishes that the chefs prepare have been relished for centuries. After a leisurely day of exploring the temples, roaming about the Confucius Forest—a peaceful park where members of the Kong (Confucius') family are buried—and steeping yourself in Chinese history, you can dine in splendor just as the imperial rulers did, enjoying such venerable delicacies as Longevity Soup, Dragon-Phoenix Fish, and Imperial Belt Shrimp.

KONG FU FANDIAN
(KONG FAMILY MANSION)
—

1 Donghua Men Jie
Tel.: 985374
Reservations by special
arrangement only

For those interested in Chinese history and culture, a visit to Qufu is a must. And for those fascinated with ancient cuisine, a banquet at the Kong Family Mansion is a rare experience.

Some time after Confucius' death, his three-room house was turned into a temple dedicated to his memory. In 1038, the Confucian Mansion was built next to the temple, initiating a period of construction that would result in the combined mansions and temples covering about thirty-three acres, including gardens, memorial archways, and over 460 halls. In its present form the mansion was built around 1550, and has since been transformed into a hotel. It consists of a series of interconnecting courtyards and bungalows—some exquisitely beautiful with Qing dynasty furnishings, others squalid and dirty. Actually, cleanliness does not rate highly in any of the rooms at the Kong Mansion, and hot water is available only at night. Inconveniences aside, a brief sojourn here is unforgettable.

For guests of the hotel and visiting diners the mansion kitchens cook simple foods but with a special reservation and advance notice will prepare a classic Confucian feast. There are four levels of Confucian feasts, all of which require elaborate ritual and preparation.

The first and highest level is the "imperial banquet." This meal is a replica of one that would have been served to a visiting emperor, royal family, and their relatives, or on the occasion of a memorial ceremony for one of Confucius' sages. These days it is primarily prepared for visiting dignitaries and Japanese wedding parties. The imperial banquet consists of 196 courses, and the cost of the meal for a table of twelve people is approximately U.S. $2,500.

The second level of the Confucius meal is the "guest banquet" for high-ranking guests and relatives. This meal usually features sixty dishes and costs approximately U.S. $2,000.

The third level is the "happiness banquet," which generally includes about thirty courses and costs, for a table of twelve, about U.S. $1,500.

The fourth and lowest level is the "home-style" Confucian meal, with ten to twenty dishes for about U.S. $500 for a table of twelve. The prices are high, but with a full table of people the cost per person is not as daunting.

For our Confucian happiness banquet, huge strings of firecrackers were first set off outside to announce the occasion. The table was set with patterned china, and at each place was a paper-cut double-happiness symbol. In the center of the table was a huge double-happiness symbol made of strawberry Jell-O surrounded by egg flakes spun with sugar. Two women in traditional Chinese dress served the dishes while a massive boom box spewed forth traditional Chinese music.

By far the most impressive part of the meal was the selection of pastries—both sweet and savory—at its conclusion. Ten different varieties were served, including steamed breads in myriad shapes and assorted pastries with sweet bean and date paste.

To make arrangements for a traditional Confucian feast, contact Qian Guangcun, deputy manager of the Kong Family Mansion, about a week in advance.

CONFUCIAN WINE
—

Qufu *is home to one of the oldest distilleries in China. The local "wine," otherwise known as Kong Fu jiu (Confucian wine), is a fiery thirty-eight-proof liqueur made of distilled sorghum, wheat, and yeast. Some foreigners have described the flavor as reminiscent of cheesy socks. It is present at most Confucian gatherings and is rarely found outside Qufu. Originally, the beverage was made as a special product of the family winery of the Confucian Mansion and served to entertain guests and members of the Confucian clan; Confucius himself used to send it as a tribute to the imperial family. King Xuan of Chu in the fourth century* B.C. *judged it to be tasteless, but according to the owner, the flavor and quality have been much improved since then.*

QUELI FANDIAN
(QUELI HOTEL)
▬

1 Queli Lu
Tel.: 411300
Hours:
11:00–1:00 P.M. (lunch),
5:30–8:00 P.M. (dinner)

For those travelers who would like to enjoy the history of Qufu and and would prefer more comfortable lodgings than the Kong Family Mansion, the Queli Hotel is an option. A so-called two-star joint-venture hotel built by a Hong Kong firm, it is conveniently located around the corner from the Confucius Temple and the Kong Mansion.

Since it is a joint venture, the Queli's dining room offers both western and Chinese dishes. The Chinese menu is rather nondescript, but you can, if you prefer, order a classic Confucian feast. There is not the range of dishes, the elaborate ritual according to the ancient customs, or the different levels of feasts to choose that will be found at the Kong Mansion, but several classically trained Confucian chefs are called in for special occasions, and you can confer with the manager and order some of the unique Confucian delicacies. Prices tend to be much higher on a dish-by-dish basis, however, and the quality is not quite in keeping with the Kong Mansion. For making special meal arrangements, contact the main desk or confer with Kong Qing Zheng, who is the manager of the hotel.

CONFUCIAN COOKING

*A*ny visitor to Qufu should, despite the cost, partake of a traditional Confucian Mansion feast. The ritual of this meal and its style of cooking, otherwise known as "Mansion cuisine," are of culinary, historical, and cultural significance. Confucian or Mansion cooking was developed according to the specific guidelines outlined by Confucius, and so many of these dishes might be considered the purest form of classic Chinese cuisine. Needless to say, these dishes have tremendous importance for Chinese culinary historians, who are attempting to trace the development of the country's cooking

Two such scholars are Zhang Lianming, whose pen name is Zhang Zhou and who is one of the foremost authorities on Mansion cooking as well as Shandong cuisine; and Dr. Wan Yu Wei, an associate professor of nutrition at Jining Medical College (Wei heads a team of fourteen editors who for the past four years have been working on a definitive text on Mansion cuisine). Both have spent innumerable hours sifting through the 650 volumes contained in the Confucian Archives, most of which are devoted to the different regulations for meal preparation and to the concoction of the recipes.

According to Zhang Lianming's book titled Famous Dishes at the Kong Mansion, Confucian chefs were strictly and rigorously trained, and of the eight remaining cooks who are skilled in this particular style, two are the descendants of the original master chefs. The dishes made at the mansions were noted for their elaborate preparation, unique seasonings, and the special attention paid to nutritional considerations.

"Apart from the famous and rare delicacies from land and sea, the daily dishes made from local specialties varied in taste, with special attention being paid to lightness of flavor and to the retainment of the original freshness and flavor of the ingredients. And many of the dishes have allusions to Confucius and the history of the Kong family."

The celebrated Confucian Analects, compiled around the end of the fourth century B.C. by Confucius' disciples from his writ-

ings and beliefs, established a number of guidelines for food.

> *When feasting, he thought it necessary to have his clothes brightly clean and made of linen cloth.*
> *He did not eat rice which had been injured by heat or damp and turned sour, nor fish or flesh which was gone. He did not eat what was discolored or what had a bad flavor, nor anything which was ill-cooked or was not in season.*
> *He did not eat meat which was not cut properly, nor what was served without its proper sauce.*

In a recent interview at the Confucian Mansion, Dr. Wan explained that "Confucian cooking can be divided into two categories: banquet and home-style dishes, a repertoire of 196 recipes. In addition, the cuisine features some 64 snack or dim sum specialties, including both sweet and savory pastries. As with Shandong cooking, the banquet dishes are extraordinarily diverse, utilizing seafood, pork, chicken, and duck, as well as costly delicacies such as bear's paw and bird's nest. The chefs maintained meticulous standards concerning the quality of the ingredients."

The cooking methods were many of the same used today, including stir-frying, steaming, and deep-frying, says Dr. Wan, but the preparation of many of the dishes involved unusual and elaborate combinations of these techniques. For the 196 banquet recipes, there were 196 different techniques of preparation.

In her book, **In the Mansion of Confucius' Descendants,** *Kong Demao, one of the last of the direct lineage of Confucius, gives further insight into the elaborate ritual of Confucian cooking, particularly to the meticulous preparations involved in an* *imperial banquet:* "At an imperial banquet, guests sat on three sides of the table while a gaobai, *a decoration made of round, glutinous rice flour pillars over a foot high and as wide as a rice bowl, was placed on the fourth remaining side. On the fruit was a congratulatory message. If the feast celebrated a birthday, it might read 'Longevity Surpassing the South Mountains,' or at a wedding, 'Happiness, Longevity, and Eternal Love.' Using skills as delicate and painstaking as those required for fine embroidery, twelve experienced chefs took forty-eight hours to complete the arrangement of the dried fruit and the creation of the four gaobai."*

The imperial banquet had its own special cutlery and crockery made of porcelain, silver, or tin, all irreplaceable. Each time they were used, especially reliable servants were chosen to look after them. Every serving dish and rice bowl rested in a dish of hot water, which would keep the food warm. The bowls used for soup held only enough for a single mouthful.

The dishes for a full-scale fête were cooked in accordance with a rigid set of regulations. For ordinary feasts, the three most common dishes were sea cucumber, shark's fin, and duck, each of which was accompanied by four cold dishes, four hot dishes, and four dishes to be eaten with rice. Then sweet dishes—cakes, pastries, and fruit, about forty in all—were served.

Eleven emperors of the Han, Wei, Tang, Song, and Qing dynasties visited the Confucian Mansion and partook of the imperial feasts, carrying many of the recipes back to the imperial kitchens. Most of these dishes became part of the classic repertory of imperial palace cuisine, creating a foundation for today's classic Chinese cooking.

CONFUCIAN MANSION
HAPPINESS BANQUET MENU
—

*E*ight Assorted Cold Platters Consisting of Pickled
Vegetables, Sliced Meats, Candied Kumquats, and Fresh Fruits

Mock Carrots Made of Mousseline of Chicken Meat

Imperial Belt Shrimp

Steamed-Egg Money Purses

White Asparagus in Hot Chili Oil

Shrimp Balls Coated with Sesame Seeds

One Egg Broods Double Phoenix

Dragon-Phoenix Fish

Fairy Duck

Steamed Shark's Fin Eggs

"Yi Pin" Pot

Sweet Gingko Nuts in Syrup

Golden Hooks with Silver Bars Bean Sprouts

Top-Class Bean Curd

Longevity Chicken-Turtle Soup

Four Assorted Shapes of Steamed Rolls

Ten Assorted Cakes and Cookies

Fresh Pineapple, Litchis, Mandarin Oranges, and Peaches

YANTAI

Although clearly off the beaten tourist track, Yantai beckons with its sleepy, small-town charm, pristine (or almost) beaches, and locally produced grape and rosepetal wine. It is a place blessed with a mild, sunny climate and fertile soil where apples, pears, peaches, and grapes flourish. Because of its long, calm coastline, Yantai also revels in its wealth of sea products. Prawns, abalone, scallops, fish, and jellyfish are in such generous supply that they are shipped to many parts of China.

With a history of almost 2,200 years Yantai began as a small fishing village. Its original name, Zhifu, was changed to Yantai, which means "smoke terrace," during the Opium Wars, when the Chinese lit fires to warn Chinese ships of approaching British authorities. Yantai's fortunes changed in 1949, when a railroad was built, linking it to the rest of the cities in the Shandong Peninsula. Today, it is one of the most prosperous ports in northern China.

My first visit to Yantai was dreamlike. I flew into the tiny airport in a small prop plane and was taken to the village center, a neighborhood of tiny lanes and old traditional Chinese houses. I also toured the gaudy Fujianese-style temple in the city square, which is dedicated to the goddess of the sea. Its display windows were filled with a potpourri of assorted and sometimes unrelated historical artifacts spanning the period from the Neolithic to the Japanese Occupation. Near the water the cityscape changed dramatically as the cramped paths gave way to spacious boulevards lined with grand whitewashed stucco buildings designed with broad windows and wooden shutters, reminders of the wealthy Europeans who transformed the town into an elegant seaside resort during the nineteenth century.

I was taken to a small restaurant and served a superb lunch of fresh seafood, including prawns steamed in their shells with a light dipping sauce, and scallops chopped to a delicate mousseline, shaped into balls, and served in a delectable soup. After a leisurely and fascinating tour of the oldest grape winery in China with a tasting of some of the vineyard's finest products, and a quick visit to the hillside where the grapes are grown, I bid farewell to this charming place. As the sun set, transforming the sky to a glowing canvas of vibrant colors, I was packed onto a train like a piece of luggage, still warm and content from the day's activities and the lingering effects of the mellow but slightly sweet wine.

DENG SHAN BINGUAN (DENG SHAN GUESTHOUSE)

▬

Deng Jiao
Tel.: 248401
Hours: By appointment only

The best-kept secret about dining in China is its private state guesthouses, many of which, after years of being restricted to government guests and officials, are now opening up on a limited basis to the foreign public. For a foreigner, there is no better deal in China. Guesthouses tend to employ the most talented cooks in the country, so the food is usually superb. And since the kitchens are subsidized by the government, the price of most meals is ridiculously cheap. The only disadvantage is that you must book ahead—a difficulty if you are on a tight traveling schedule.

In Yantai the Deng Shan Binguan is a particularly impressive guesthouse, located on an estate overlooking the sea. Here, in one of the six houses on the beautifully kept grounds, you can dine like a Chinese head of state. In the villa, where foreign customers are allowed, four small dining rooms and three larger ones serve excellent food.

For our meal, a spacious room was set up with two comfortable armchairs pulled up to a small table. The lovely manager, Do Heng Yen, graciously attended to our every need, while the old master chef Liu Wei Xuan puttered about between courses to check on our reactions to the dishes. Liu is a special-first-class cook, the highest level in the Chinese culinary hierarchy, a man who began his apprenticeship as a chef at the age of nineteen at several noted eateries in Beijing. After finishing his training, Liu was designated by the Chinese government to teach Chinese cooking in Shaanxi province, where he remained until 1984, when he returned to his native Shandong to oversee the cooking at the Yantai guesthouse.

Our simple lunch began with individual cold platters artfully arranged with cold smoked chicken, paper-thin slices of beef skin grilled until crisp, and baby corn shoots lightly coated in chili oil. It was followed by eggdrop corn soup, a sole cooked to perfection in a fermented wine rice sauce, and tiny bay scallops stir-fried with green pepper. Accompanying the seafood were flaky cakes, golden brown and crisp. Huge prawns cooked in salt water were served with a spicy sauce and a stir-fried vegetable dish. Each course was beautifully presented on a celadon-colored serving piece. The meal ended with a selection of Chinese pastries. For two, the price was 40 yuan per person; dinner will probably be more. Book forty-eight hours in advance.

A VISIT TO THE OLDEST WINERY IN CHINA

The sun is shining down on a gentle slope of land planted with neat rows of trees heavy with ripening grapes. The sultry air is literally humming with the gentle drone of bees traveling from the fruit to wildflowers nearby. Grapevines seem to go on endlessly to the distant horizon, dropping off abruptly into the blue sea.

In the background are the sounds of workers sharing jokes as they check their precious crop. This is not France or Italy, I have to remind myself, for I am standing in the vineyards of the Chang Yu Pioneer Winery in Yantai.

Little at the entrance of the Chang Yu Pioneer Winery indicates its venerable history, or its success. A somewhat dingy gate with a simple sign proclaiming the name of the winery leads to a group of nondescript stone and brick buildings, making up the head offices of the vineyard.

I am greeted by Wang Shilin, the director of the winery, a youngish-looking man in his mid-forties with a rather gruff voice. As he leads me to the tasting room (which looks like every other reception area for foreign guests in China), he fills me in on some history about the vineyard as well as wine-making in China.

The Chang Yu (formerly known as the Chefoo) Pioneer Winery was founded by Zhang Bishi, an overseas Chinese businessman, who returned to China after making his fortune in Southeast Asia. Zhang settled in Yantai in 1891, and after ascertaining that the growing conditions were favorable, he began the vineyard in 1892. He imported and planted over one hundred different grape varieties from Germany and France; foreign machinery was brought in as well.

Zhang's grapes thrived in the fertile soil and moderate climate. (Yantai is bordered on three sides by the sea and sheltered by mountains to the south.)

The wine-making process has not altered considerably since the vineyard was opened. Grape-picking generally begins in late August and extends to the end of October. The grapes are still individually handpicked by local residents and then crushed by machine. Certain wines, such as cognac and brandy, are aged in huge oak casks imported from Germany. Other varieties, ranging from vermouth to numerous red and white European-style wines to Chinese tonics, are aged in stainless-steel vats.

Once we have dispensed with the formal "introduction" to the winery, Director Wang gives me a sample of the Chang Yu red wine. It is very sweet, reminiscent of Mogen David. Director Wang explains that the wine is made from a blending of the Muscat and Cabernet grapes. "The Chinese credit most wines with specific beneficial effects on the body," he says. "This particular red wine we are tasting is good for enriching the blood and lubricating the stomach, which aids digestion."

Vermouth is one of the winery's most popular wines. Its success, Director Wang claims, is due to a secret formula that incorporates the flavorings of cinnamon and nutmeg. (Wang refuses to divulge exactly how this is done.) "Chang Yu vermouth," Wang says, "is highly nutritious and helps to strengthen the spleen, relax muscles and joints, enrich blood, enhance circulation, and build up the vital power of the kidney." (In fact, there seems to be little that this remarkable wine doesn't do.)

After the tasting and lecture, I am led to the basement where enormous oak casks are filled with the aging vermouth and cognac. The damp coolness of the air combines with the slightly sour but heady scent of fermenting grapes in wood, reviving memories of past visits to vineyards in other countries.

Finally, we are back in the bright sunshine, and after a ten-minute bumpy ride down a dusty road, we arrive at the vineyards. Director Wang looks protectively at fledgling vines and then surveys the vast fields. "There has been a surge recently in popularity for Chinese grape vines," he tells me. "We attribute it to the rise in the national standard of living and to people learning to recognize the nutritional benefits of wine. They now realize that grape wines make people healthy and keep them young."

And with that sales pitch, how can he go wrong!

HUI BIN LOU
(HUI BIN LOU
RESTAURANT)

—

267 Sheng Li Lu
Tel.: 223332
Hours:
11:30 A.M.–2:00 P.M. (lunch),
4:30–8:00 P.M. (dinner)

Across from the picturesque Yantai Museum in the central square of the town is Hui Bin Lou Restaurant, one of the oldest and most respected in the area. Around mealtimes, there's a flurry of activity as the elderly parking attendant furiously gestures in an attempt to coax the customers to park their cars in a somewhat orderly manner. A small crowd often gathers in front of a stand where fried and steamed breads from the restaurant are sold.

The restaurant is divided into several parts. The first floor is a dumpling parlor where bamboo steamers stand stacked and ready for customers. Nearby, cold platters with shredded cucumbers, bean threads, and other fresh shredded vegetables await the onslaught of the crowd. Upstairs are private banquet rooms, and (preferably) a large main dining room with surprisingly clean white tablecloths and calligraphy hangings that pledge longevity and happiness. Each table is graced with vases of psychedelic blue or red and white, which match the chandelier—a master feat of decoration.

It is wisest when ordering to stick to the fresh seafood. Steamed crabs, when fresh, are delectable simply prepared and dipped in vinegar. Steamed clams, smothered with finely shredded gingerroot and scallions, are also excellent. Steer clear of the frogs' legs, but try the clear-steamed fish and red-cooked fish slices. The dumplings, although not on a par with the best in Beijing, are quite good.

Unless you visit Yantai at the height of the tourist season, or have a very large party, visit the Hui Bin Lou at your convenience and order from the menu. Most meals should not be more than 50 to 70 yuan per person.

QINGDAO

My first glimpse of Qingdao was at sunset in late spring, shortly before the summer tourist season. The beaches were empty, and water lapped peacefully at the edges of the shore. A broad causeway that reaches out to the sea, its path leading to a traditional Chinese pagoda, was alive with couples and families leisurely taking an evening stroll. On Qingdao's tree-lined streets, European-style mansions stood proudly, their facades faded and crumbling after years of neglect during the Cultural Revolution; but their red tile roofs, which were still intact, gleamed in the fading light of dusk. It was a charming picture of a seaside resort that had seen better days, and one that could easily have been in Europe.

Several years later, I returned to find a city that was rejuvenated and thriving. Most of the mansions were restored to a former dignity, their broken clapboards replaced and glistening with fresh paint. The main streets were lined with newly opened restaurants, slick department stores, and food shops, all apparently doing a booming business. Crowds clustered in front of store windows gazing at the merchandise, and vendors selling steamed dumplings and freshly cooked scallion pancakes exulted at the long queues.

Qingdao is very much a Chinese city, but its look and feel are still strongly influenced by the Germans who built it after it became a port concession in 1898. The Europeans also dominated the city, confining the Chinese population to selected sections. The Japanese seized control from 1915 until 1922, when the Chinese again regained power. When the Europeans fled, they not only left fine Victorian mansions but also relinquished their rights to the breweries and wineries they had constructed. One such operation, in particular, flourished, and today Qingdao is the home of the most famous brew in China, the Tsingtao brand, which is exported all over the world.

Since Qingdao is a port city, one might expect to sample superb fresh seafood, but oddly enough, although there are fine dishes to be had in a few restaurants, Qingdao can hardly be considered a culinary mecca. When you have had enough of the crowds on the busy streets and on the beaches, escape to the Mount Lao (Laoshan) by car and marvel at the dramatic peaks overlooking the sea. Visit the Taoist temples, bask in a brief moment of serenity, and then line up meekly with the other tourists for a taste of the famous mineral water of Laoshan—cold, clear, slightly salty, but refreshing.

BADAGUAN BINGUAN (BADAGUAN GUESTHOUSE)

---

15 Shanghaiguan Lu
Tel.: 364822 Ext. 556
Hours:
7:30–9:00 A.M. (breakfast),
11:30 A.M.–2:00 P.M. (lunch),
5:30–8:30 P.M. (dinner)

Some foreigners consider this the best hotel to stay at in Qingdao since its recent renovation, and with its big stone gates and slightly overdone lobby, it is quite impressive looking. The dining room continues this theme with sweeping drapes and massive chandeliers. It does, however, have clean linen tablecloths that are changed frequently.

But there are no surprises on the menu here, with choices confined to familiars like spicy chicken with peanuts, mushu pork, and stir-fried noodles with meat shreds. The dumplings are exceptionally flavorful, with a nicely seasoned filling of ground meat and Chinese chives. (We immediately ordered a second round.) If rather unimaginative, the food is consistent and dependable. The cost of dinner should not exceed 50 yuan per person, and lunch will be slightly less.

CHUN HE LOU FANDIAN (CHUN HE LOU RESTAURANT)

---

146 Zhongshan Lu
Tel.: 224436
Hours: 11:00 A.M.–8:30 P.M.

The selection of outstanding restaurants in Qingdao is limited, but according to the locals, one of the best is Chun He Lou, located in the center of the bustling downtown section. In Qingdao, unlike other cities in China, some of the consistently better food is to be found in hotel dining rooms, but the Chun He Lou is an exception. Eating here is a unique experience, if for nothing else than to watch the local Chinese and foreign businessmen enjoying a banquet. Be prepared for a fun, noisy meal.

The eatery has a long history in Qingdao. About eighty years ago, during the last days of the Qing dynasty, a Madame Zhou made a meager living as a street vendor selling her own congee, which she carried around town. She also sold deep-fried crullers, sesame balls, and fried dumplings. Once the business prospered, she opened a small restaurant known as the Guo Tie Pu (Small Dumpling House). At the end of the Qing dynasty, when the Germans arrived in Qingdao, she expanded, renamed her business, and moved to her present location. Madame Zhou also sought to upgrade the menu, importing cooks from Beijing, and soon the restaurant began to establish its present reputation.

Chun He Lou continues to employ special-level cooks, and according to the assistant manager, there are currently eight in the kitchen. We ordered directly from the menu, and the food was good if not exceptional. The abalone, however, stir-fried lightly in a delicate rice-wine sauce, was excellent. Conch was tender though not as flavorful as the abalone. The restaurant offers an extensive list of seafood dishes, so reserve a table and give notice in advance that seafood is what you want. The kitchen can then make the proper arrangements and make certain to have the fresh ingredients on hand. Other recommended dishes include the green beans with dried black mushrooms and straw mushrooms, and the steamed buns, which were fine but skimpy in filling.

The hostess who took our order was not only capable but spoke quite a bit of English and seemed accustomed to dealing with foreigners. Chun He Lou takes Visa, MasterCard, and American Express cards. For a good meal with seafood, the cost should run approximately 100 yuan per person for four to six people. Ideally, reservations should be made forty-eight hours in advance.

HUIQUAN DA FANDIAN (HUIQUAN DYNASTY HOTEL)

—

9 Nanhai Lu
Tel.: 279215
Hours:
7:00–9:30 A.M. (breakfast),
11:30 A.M.–2:00 P.M. (lunch),
5:30–9:00 P.M. (dinner)

This newly renovated joint-venture Chinese–Hong Kong hotel doesn't offer extraordinary dining, but the expansive, airy dining room, with its matching light blue tablecloths, seat covers, and lace curtains offers a clean and cheerful atmosphere—especially in contrast to restaurant dining. The service, as in many restaurants, is uneven, but it's fun to watch the numerous black-coated managers scurrying about looking self-important.

The menu is standard for hotels in this part of the country, offering many of the usual selections, but try the stir-fried bean threads (chao fen si) and crispy-skin chicken (xiang xu ji). The dumplings also had a nice flavor with a generous chopped pork and garlic chive filling. Since the hotel receives supplies of food from Hong Kong, there are treats like fresh milk (sometimes even chocolate), and western pastries, including apple pie and pudding.

Prices are slightly higher here than in restaurants but still quite reasonable. A simple dinner or lunch consisting of a few dishes ordered directly from the menu will probably cost about 40 yuan per person, depending on the selections. (Seafood inevitably will be higher.) Be sure to ask is there is any *fresh* seafood on hand, for much of Qingdao's catch is sent to Beijing and other places in China.

QINGDAO FANDIAN (QINGDAO RESTAURANT)

—

53 Zhongshan Lu
Tel.: 86747
Hours: 11:00 A.M.–8:30 P.M.

Local food authorities regard this as *the* foremost restaurant in Qingdao, and while it does serve some fine dishes, consistency is a problem, and the best offerings are expensive.

Like the Chun He Lou, the Qingdao has a lengthy history. It first opened its doors in 1934 as a coffeehouse serving western food, but in 1949 the Chinese government stepped in and assumed ownership, establishing the type of menu offered today. The predominant style of cooking is Jiaodong, from the Yantai area (see page 146), and the emphasis is on light seasonings and fresh flavors.

The restaurant is massive, with four huge dining halls and an endless succession of private banquet rooms. Approximately three to four hundred customers are fed here each day. Master chef Xu Guo Yuan oversees the immense kitchens. Xu, who is considered one of the most talented chefs in the city, won silver and copper medals at the 1988 National Culinary Competition in Beijing. Xu is only thirty-five years old, but he has been cooking for eighteen years and was sent on government assignment to cook at the embassy in Zambia, attesting to his considerable expertise. But to taste the best here, order a banquet and reserve in advance.

Recommended dishes include the stir-fried chicken with mushrooms, vinegar-pepper fish, braised eggplant with garlic, *shao mai*, Thousand-Layer Bread, and the whole roasted fish. The majority of these specialties must be ordered in advance; if possible, allow forty-eight hours. For a fine meal, with a party of four to six, one should expect to pay at least 80 yuan per person.

TIAN FU JIUJIA
(TIAN FU RESTAURANT—
First Floor Bakery)

210 Zhongshan Lu
Hours: 6:00–8:30 A.M.
(breakfast)

If you'd like to see a fast-food dim sum breakfast place, stop here in the morning and watch a packed house consume sixteen different kinds of sweet and savory pastries. The standard Chinese varieties are available on one side of the room, with some nice-looking western breads and cakes on the other.

ZHANQIAO BINGUAN (ZHANQIAO GUESTHOUSE)

—

31 Taiping Lu
Tel.: 270502 (Main Desk)
Hours:
8:00–9:00 A.M. (breakfast),
12:00–1:00 P.M. (lunch),
6:00–7:00 P.M. (dinner)

Located on the main road facing the ocean, the Zhanqiao Guesthouse captures the eye immediately due to its arresting turn-of-the-century European-style facade. The hotel's delightful dining room offers above-average Chinese hotel fare. There are only sixteen tables, but the hardwood floors and clean white linen tablecloths give this small restaurant a quaint European air.

The lunch and dinner menu offer the usual favorites like fried prawns, sour and peppery fish, oil-soaked *(cong bao)* meat slices, and spicy chicken with peanuts. The stuffed steamed buns were excellent, with a filling of lots of chopped meat and cabbage that tasted German-Chinese, which is hardly surprising, since the recipe came from the old master chef Yin Pin Shan. Yin, who was trained while Germans still occupied the city, still occasionally oversees the kitchen and presides over special banquet meals. The young chef, Yin Shun Chang, is also a special-level cook and will display his expertise for banquet meals, which should be ordered at least a day in advance, and sometimes two.

For a simple but filling lunch or dinner ordered directly from the menu, the cost should be approximately 40 yuan per person. For a banquet with a party of six to eight people, expect to pay about 100 yuan per person. This is a lovely place to stop in—even spontaneously—for a meal.

A VISIT TO THE TSINGTAO (QINGDAO) BREWERY

A quick glance at its drab brick buildings would never lead a visitor to guess that this nondescript site was home to the famous Tsingtao Brewery, producer of the most popular Chinese beer in the country and abroad. But to the right is a newly built fountain attesting to the celebrity of the product: a circle of sizable cement beer glasses with water spewing forth from their tops (perhaps this is supposed to symbolize beer) are grouped around a massive cement beer bottle with its label proclaiming "Tsingtao Beer" in Chinese characters. In front of the buildings, circling the entire driveway leading to and from the factory is an endless line of large trucks and small, waiting patiently to pick up their load of beer. And the air all around is suffused with the heavy, yeasty odor of fermenting hops.

This beverage is so much a favorite worldwide that, except in major hotels and restaurants, it is not available in China outside the city of Qingdao. According to the Director of Public Relations, the demand exceeds the production, and from 60 to 90 percent (depending on whether you are talking to the assistant manager of the company or the director of public relations) of Tsingtao beer is exported abroad. Even local residents have limited access: twice a year, on May first and Chinese New Year, they are issued certificates so that they may buy a case directly from the factory. It is not unusual to see people leaving Qingdao by train loaded down with bags packed with bottles of beer—gifts from their relatives. (Beer was not always so popular a drink in China, and it was really not until the 1960s that beer-drinking caught on.)

The brewery first opened in 1903 as a joint venture between a German and English company and originally catered to the soldiers stationed in the city. In 1916, it was sold to (or taken over by) the Japanese, and finally in 1945, it became a Chinese company under the same government management as today.

Like most other beers, Tsingtao is based on fermented barley and hops. Another component, wheat, is imported not only from northwestern China but from Australia and Canada. But the secret ingredient, what makes it unique in China, is that sacred water from Mount Lao (Laoshan), located about one hour outside the city, is piped in directly to the factory, giving the brew its unusual flavor.

Originally, oak barrels were used for fermentation, but today almost all have been replaced by stainless steel. In fact, much of the machinery is imported from Germany and Italy, and the Chinese are proud of their gleaming machines and mechanical production lines. The brewery's new factory will probably take the mechanized process to an even higher level.

As with most government businesses and schools, a visit here begins with an introduction and debriefing on the product. Your ears will be ringing with the barrage of figures—the hundreds of thousands of tons of beer being produced annually. Next, there will be a tour through the factory, and depending on what department is functioning, you will see some portion of the process. Finally, the highlight of the visit, a beer tasting. On one trip we were allowed to choose a bottle directly from the line. It was still warm from the bottling process, and the rich, warm beer it held had a taste I will savor for the rest of my life.

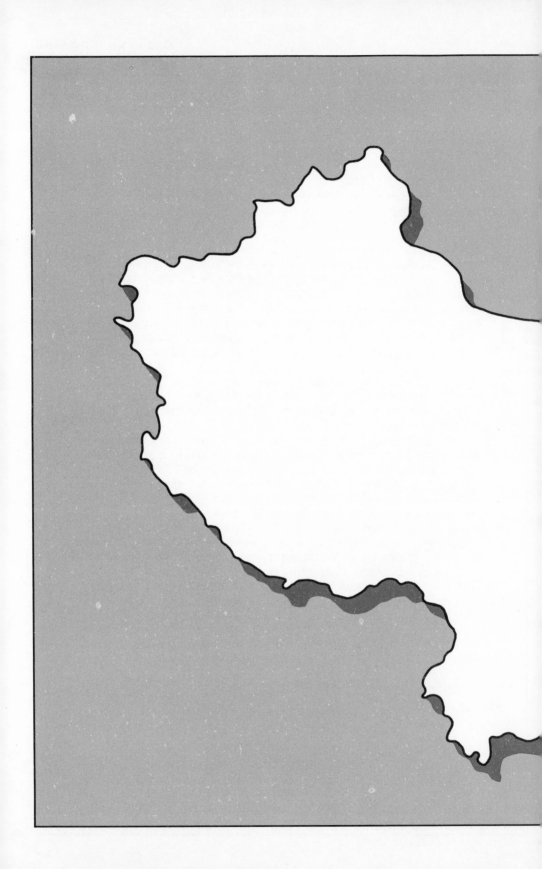

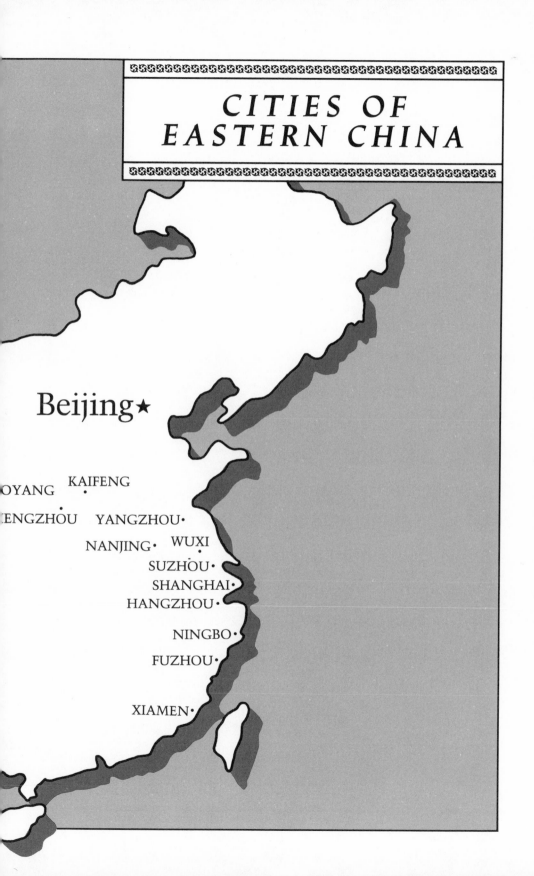

CITIES OF
EASTERN CHINA

Beijing★

OYANG   KAIFENG

ENGZHOU   YANGZHOU·

NANJING·   WUXI

SUZHOU·

SHANGHAI·

HANGZHOU·

NINGBO·

FUZHOU·

XIAMEN·

EASTERN COOKING

⚅

In heaven, there is Paradise.
On earth, we have Suzhou and Hangzhou.

—ANCIENT CHINESE SAYING

Long nicknamed the land of fish and rice, eastern China has always vied with its southern neighbor Guangdong as a major culinary mecca. The reasons are obvious: ingredients are in generous supply; the natives have a great passion for food; and the expertise of many of its chefs is legendary.

Since the climate is lush and humid year round, the area enjoys an uninterrupted growing season, making it one of the richest agricultural regions in China. Rice, wheat, corn, and soybeans all flourish. Vegetables and fruits, in prodigious array, thrive, including numerous varieties of bamboo, cabbage, greens, and gourds, as well as peaches, plums, and grapes. A multitude of salted and fermented pickles are used for seasonings. It is in eastern China that vegetarian cuisine gradually was refined to its present *haute* status.

The area's bounty is not restricted to fruits and vegetables. Duck, pork, and chicken here are considered particularly succulent, while the Yangtze River, plus numerous lakes and ponds, are stocked with a wealth of freshwater products, including shrimp, crab, carp, Mandarin fish, and shad. The sea also offers its share of bounty with fish, oysters, clams, crab, and shrimp.

Since the quality of the ingredients is so extraordinary, the food *has* to be good, and in many cases, chefs will let the products stand on their own, using a light touch with seasonings and sauces to enhance the natural flavors. Crabs—fresh from the water—are steamed and served unadorned with a hammer for cracking the shells. Fresh baby hearts of cabbage are lightly tossed with a smattering of oil and wine over a searing fire, then offered steaming in their own juices. Chicken with a touch of rice wine, ginger, and water is steamed in a closed container to preserve its rich juices, resulting in an intensely flavored clear stock.

In keeping with this obsession for freshness and simplicity, stir-frying, steaming, quick-simmering, and poaching are favored. Since soy sauce is a main product of the area, red-cooking or brais-

ing also is popular. For this technique, the soy sauce–based braising mixture, which is often seasoned with star anise, cinnamon stick, and orange peel, cooks the food to a tender doneness, leaving it a rich, brownish-red color—hence the name *red-cooked.*

There is little to prepare the foreigner for the local specialties in the east. In Hangzhou, one can sample flaky poached West Lake fish and smoky-sweet steamed Jinhua ham. Suzhou offers similar delights, such as stir-fried eels bathed in chopped garlic and ginger, and crisp Squirrel Fish coated with a sweet and sour sauce crowned with golden pine nuts. The rich, hearty specialties of Shanghai include whole red-cooked Eight Treasure duck and luscious steamed fresh crab with red vinegar laced with fine shreds of spring gingerroot. To the east, Fujian provides its share of unforgettable delicacies, among them stir-fried rice vermicelli and deep-fried oyster rolls. All these dishes are typical of the eclectic school of eastern regional cooking, incorporating a broad area that includes the provinces of Zhenjiang, Jiangsu, and Fujian.

One would be remiss in not mentioning the fine array of snack foods offered throughout the area. First and foremost, there are the dumplings, too numerous to be listed individually, though one of the most famous is the steamed *xiao long bao* dumpling, with its pleated top, round middle, and delectable filling of ground meat and "spurt" of juicy liquid. Crusty-bottomed chicken buns, which are first steamed and then pan-fried, also are relished. Spring rolls are filled with myriad vegetables and meat in a thin steamed wrapper, a refreshing departure from the traditional deep-fried variety.

One could go on and on. After sampling only a few of the renowned dishes of eastern China, one can easily understand how this area has earned its nickname of a culinary paradise.

SHANGHAI

My first memories of Shanghai are still shaded by a raw, misty grayness. It was mid-March in 1979, and every day a cold drizzle slowly drenched the city, accentuating its drabness. It was shortly after the end of the Cultural Revolution, and its devastation was evident—particularly in Shanghai, one of the main targets of the ten-year purges that began in the late 1960s.

Shanghai was only beginning to recover, and it still looked like a casualty of a recent war. Its old, once grand European-style buildings were dilapidated. But on our way in from the airport, our tour bus ran head-on into a huge demonstration; masses of people were blocking the street holding signs and silently protesting the repressive measures used during the Cultural Revolution. The solemn procession cheered us all a little on that cold day, giving us a glimpse of the strong spirit of Shanghai and its residents.

On the next morning of that visit we took to the streets exploring, and it was then that I began to fall in love with the city. There are few places in China that are as colorful or as alive as Shanghai, particularly on a Sunday afternoon, when it seems as if the entire Chinese population is out strolling on the mobbed sidewalks of Nanjing Road to see the latest fashions.

Today, Shanghai is the most flourishing commercial city in China. Newly renovated structures and construction sites are everywhere. It is the cultural capital for all China; the center for science and technology; and the main port for foreign trade. I have returned there many times, enjoying its vitality, marveling at its growth, and appreciating its beauty and many moods. There is the city in early morning along the Bund; the bustling harbor in the city central, crowded with a sea of people performing various forms of exercise, with the more traditional practitioners of Chinese shadow dancing *(tai ji quan)* standing next to the modern lovers of disco; and the Old City, where the small alleys are packed with purveyors hawking fresh fruits and vegetables. Nearby are small stands where cooks stand diligently all day, every day, cooking endless batches of crusty pot-stickers, which are sold by the pound. Just around the corner is the entrance of the Yuyuan Park where stone and flower gardens, a small pond filled with fat goldfish, and majestic pagodas lend a surreal peacefulness to the urban landscape.

And then, of course, there is the food. Since Shanghai is the culinary center for eastern cuisine, its many restaurants offer a host of regional classics, including traditional delicacies like stir-fried eels with garlic and braised Eight Treasure, and delicate dumplings. In spring, fresh shad is doused with a sprinkling of black vinegar, and steamed hairy crabs are served in their shells with a ginger-vinegar dipping sauce for their sweet meat.

Shanghai is also famous for its refined vegetarian fare, and both Buddhist temples and vegetarian eateries have cultivated an extraordinary repertoire of delectable meatless dishes. Here you can partake of a sumptuous twelve- or twenty-four-course banquet and never even suspect or regret the absence of meat.

True to its traditional role in China as a cosmopolitan port, Shanghai also offers an eclectic selection of styles. The city's gastronomes have adventurous palates, and their chefs are as well-versed in preparing the spicy flavors of Sichuan-Hunan as they are at producing delicate Cantonese entrees and dim sum. For those visitors hungering for the comforting flavors of home, you can even enjoy a flaky croissant or gratify your sweet tooth with confections like New York–style cheesecake and a chocolaty Black Forest torte.

JESSICA MARKET
JINJIANG HOTEL
—

59 Maoming Lu
Hours: 8:30 A.M.–10:00 P.M.

If you find yourself with a craving for Sara Lee chocolate or Sultana pound cake, Evian water, Kellogg's Frosted Flakes, V-8 juice, or Kraft cheese, then a visit to the Jessica Market is in order. The shop is around the corner from the reception area of the older section of the Jinjiang Hotel and down the alley from Food Street, next to the post office.

The Jessica is like a 7-Eleven convenience store stocked with all types of liquor, wine, crackers, cookies, cakes, candy, and other snack items, plus a few rather tired-looking vegetables. It can be very convenient, particularly if you need high-quality batteries for your camera or you are gift-searching for a Chinese friend, relative, or tour guide. (It's also great if you're in the mood for some western junk food.)

Local residents like to wander the aisles gazing at the unfamiliar goods, while foreigners walk around in a daze, soaking up the friendly reminders of their western world and trying to make a decision as to what they want and if they really want it badly enough to pay the inflated prices. All items (even the Chinese products) are imported from Hong Kong and are an eclectic mix of commodities from America, Japan, France, and China. As in shops in major hotels, only Foreign Exchange Certificates are accepted.

JING AN MIAN BAO DIAN (JING AN BAKERY)

▬

370 Hua San Lu
Tel.: 2551888
Hours: 7:00 A.M.–8:00 P.M.

When this shop first opened in April 1985, word spread quickly of the city's first French bakery. Within days, lines were so long that the shop couldn't possibly meet the demand, and all items were sold out earlier than anyone would have ever anticipated. At the time, it seemed that everyone was talking about the croissants from the Jing An Bakery.

The Jing An, which is a cooperative effort between a French company and the Chinese-owned Jing An Hotel, was riding the crest of joint-venture businesses, which soon deluged the city. But even today, despite the opening of other bakeries as well as pastry shops at the Hua Ting Sheraton and Hilton Hotel, business is still brisk. Lines continue to form, and the bakery continues to enjoy an excellent reputation. But it's hardly surprising that the croissants are fresh and flaky (if a little doughy) with a full-bodied, buttery flavor.

The Jing An claims that it makes thirty different varieties of breads, but don't expect to find more than five or six on any given day. Among the most popular varieties are the French baguettes and coconut-filled rolls. Prices are reasonable—about 1 yuan per croissant—and the baked goods are perfect for a long train ride, picnic, or any excursion.

If you are using Foreign Exchange Certificates, make certain to avoid the lines and use the entrance to the right. The lines to the left are for local currency only.

JINJIANG FANDIAN–SICHUAN FANGUAN (JINJIANG HOTEL—SICHUAN RESTAURANT)

—

59 Mao Ming Lu
Tel.: 2582582
Hours:
11:30 A.M.–2:30 P.M. (lunch),
5:30–10:00 P.M. (dinner)

If you order a banquet at the Jinjiang Hotel, Yang Li Jun, the Food and Beverage Manager, may offer, in her dignified, no-nonsense manner, suggestions about what to order. Miss Yang will probably recommend the crispy-skin duck with steamed lotus buns (which must be ordered at least twenty-four hours in advance), the spicy lotus-wrapped rice powder chicken served in miniature bamboo steamers, and the shredded ham and bean curd soup, which arrives in individual porcelain egg cups. Heed her advice, and you are guaranteed to have a wonderful meal.

The Jinjiang is one of the most distinguished hotels in Shanghai; its rooms are often reserved for high-ranking foreign visitors and heads of state. Its kitchen has an equally impeccable reputation, and while dining in private restaurants is usually preferable in any city, the Jinjiang is a wise choice for those who are wary of adventuring in the private eateries. If its prices are higher, service, presentation, and the decor at the Jinjiang are above reproach. And since its new quarters opened, customers have a choice: for banquets, select the beautiful bamboo-decorated private rooms in the old building; for ordering directly from the menu, opt for the new building's restaurant.

Like Mei Long Zhen, the Jinjiang Hotel offers a more refined version of Sichuan cooking as well as a number of eastern regional specialties. There are spicy dry-cooked green beans and exquisite, nearly pencil-thin fried spring rolls. The appetizer cold platter offers delectable renditions of spicy sesame *beng beng* chicken, sliced pork with garlic sauce, jellyfish in a light sesame oil dressing, and cold-tossed duck. The sweet and savory dim sum, which are served throughout a banquet, should definitely be sampled: flaky turnip cakes, sweet lotus seed buns, and steamed juicy buns are all memorable. All major credit cards are accepted including American Express, Visa, and MasterCard.

MEI LONG ZHEN JIUJIA (MEI LONG ZHEN RESTAURANT)

1081 Nanjing Xi Lu
Tel.: 2562718
Hours:
11:00 A.M.–1:30 P.M. (lunch),
5:00–8:00 P.M. (dinner)

When you enter Mei Long Zhen, a distinguished-looking Chinese man with spectacles, a gentle demeanor, and an excellent command of the English language will probably greet you. He is Wang Linchao, who is on staff to aid foreign customers by ordering and making them feel comfortable. Mr. Wang, in his courtly and gracious manner, does just that. You will probably be shown upstairs—where most foreigners are seated—to a rather charming dining room where plastic grapevines adorn the ceiling, lending a festive air.

The Mei Long Zhen was established in 1938 by a group of filmmakers, actors, playwrights, and authors. Today, although owned by the government, this eatery still maintains an impeccable reputation. The food could be classified as Sichuanese, although it is not quite so spicy as that found in Chengdu, nor is it the messy stuff one finds in this country. It is, rather, a Shanghai version prepared with refined and subtle seasonings and superb local ingredients. And unlike many restaurants where ordering in advance is de rigueur, at Mei Long Zhen you can order directly from the menu upon arrival.

Traditional Sichuanese dishes at Mei Long Zhen include crispy-skin duck with steamed lotus buns, fish-flavored eggplant, dry-cooked prawns, and stir-fried chicken with bean sprouts. In the Shanghai vein, there are superb stir-fried eels and Lion's Head casserole with baby hearts of cabbage. River shrimp, stir-fried with jasmine tea leaves, is a unique specialty of the kitchen. The Mei Long Zhen's steamed buns shouldn't be missed.

Reservations should be made at least several hours in advance; for a filling meal, the price will be about 40–60 yuan per person.

NANXIANG MANTOU DIAN (NANXIANG STEAMED BREAD SHOP)

Yuyuan Garden (Old City)
Hours: 8:00 A.M.–5:00 P.M.

About forty-five minutes by car from the city of Shanghai is Nanxiang, a town that has become famous for its steamed dumplings. For those who wish to sample this local specialty but don't have the time or the inclination to travel, visit the charming Nanxiang Steamed Bread Shop, which is housed in one of the small buildings clustered inside the Yuyuan Garden, all of which offer some of Shanghai's famous snacks. The Nanxiang is at the foot of the zigzagging path leading to the Midlake Pavilion, and you will probably be able to recognize it by the long queue waiting in front of it.

The premises are quite simple, with eight to ten small tables with accompanying stools on each of the two floors. The menu is equally basic: fresh steamed dumplings and soup served with a vibrant dipping sauce of black vinegar with fine shreds of gingerroot. As you wait you can look into the kitchen and watch the workers deftly rolling out skins, stuffing them with a ground meat filling, and arranging them in steamers.

Dumplings are ordered by the steamer layer *(leng)*, and eight to ten sell for a little over 2 yuan, which is quite a bargain for a food that is legendary in Shanghai.

SAN JIAO DI CAI SHICHANG (SAN JIAO FOOD MARKET)

Han Yang Lu, Sanjiao Di
Hours: 5:30 A.M.–7:00 P.M.

Like any large city, Shanghai has innumerable markets. The San Jiao Food Market, located in the center of town, is one of the largest, hosting both private purveyors selling "free" goods and government-regulated shopkeepers.

Not long ago, Chinese markets were rather depressing affairs, even in this colorful city. Dark, dirty, with a few limp-looking products, they were hardly worth a detour from a day of sightseeing. But that has changed with economic reform. Today, customers have money to spend on all types of products, and both enterprising farmers and shopkeepers are more than willing to cater to the demand. At one stand you might see a butcher pasting ration coupons onto pieces of paper, while next door, a farmer selling green peppers, huge bamboo shoots, and other fresh vegetables from his garden bargains with customers and counts his yuan. The market offers almost every conceivable form of food—fresh, dried, and preserved.

The San Jiao Market is bright and airy, bordering on cavernous. Cathedral ceilings with huge windows provide space and light. During the summer and fall seasons the market nearly bursts with produce, but even in winter, there is a decent supply of potatoes, cabbage, celery, bamboo shoots, black fungus, and cauliflower. Other regular items include seafood—fresh shrimp, squid, and several varieties of fish—plus bean curd, eggs, chickens, pork, and beef. Purveyors are friendly, and even welcome pictures.

The best times to visit are the busiest, starting at seven to eight-thirty in the morning and five to six-thirty at night.

SHANGHAI LAO FANDIAN (OLD SHANGHAI RESTAURANT)

242 Fuyou Lu
Tel.: 3282782
Hours:
11:00 A.M.–1:00 P.M. (lunch),
5:00–8:00 P.M. (dinner)

Shanghai Lao Fandian or Old Shanghai Restaurant is situated in the heart of the oldest sector of the city, near the Yu Garden. The front glass window looks more like that of a restaurant in Japan than of one in China, for it contains lifelike plastic models of a number of the restaurant's specialties: red-cooked Eight Treasure duck and braised chub's head in earthen pot are captured for posterity under a clear polyurethane finish.

The restaurant was first opened during the Qing dynasty, when it established a reputation for its home-style cooking. Later, the menu was expanded to include more refined banquet dishes, and today, both are offered. Don't be put off by the somewhat drab interior, for the Lao Fandian serves some of the best local food in the city. The best meals here are those ordered twenty-four hours in advance, rather than impromptu affairs. At a banquet there we had a superb rendition of a popular Shanghai dish, stir-fried baby river shrimp. Since it was spring, there were excellent seasonal offerings, such as mountains of shredded green peppers and river bamboo shoots and steamed Helsa herring with ham. Other specialties of the restaurant worth sampling are whole steamed Mandarin fish with black mushrooms, turtle soup, and steamed shredded meats (a brothy dish made with threads of shredded ham, bamboo shoots, and bean curd). The restaurant also makes a most unusual dish that should be sampled: a huge sea cucumber cooked until butter-tender in a rich stock and served dotted with dried shrimp roe.

Since the restaurant is very popular among the locals, banquet reservations should be made several days in advance. For a party of four to six, the price of a multicourse meal will be about 80 to 100 yuan per person.

SHANGHAI NAN GUO JIUJIA (SHANGHAI SOUTHLAND RESTAURANT)

---

813 Beijing Dong Lu
Tel.: 3220480, 3220020
Hours:
6:30–10:00 A.M. (dim sum),
11:00 A.M.–1:30 P.M. (lunch)
5:00–7:30 P.M. (dinner)

My first introduction to the Shanghai Southland Restaurant was via Shanghai Culinary Institute, which is housed upstairs. The steamed open-face dumplings that the students prepared in honor of our visit there in 1982 were memorable. Several years later, the restaurant opened on the first and second floors and it was not long before the Southland acquired a devoted following in the city. Even today the Southland employs top graduates from the institute.

Southland's entrées are highly rated, but it is the morning dim sum that most customers clamor for. Ethereal barbecued pork buns, garlic-laden spareribs in black bean sauce, and crisp slices of turnip cake are among the many snacks offered here. (At a recent visit, the steamed dumplings were still quite good.) During peak hours, you can pick and choose from the rolling carts, which are filled to overflowing with freshly cooked pastries, hot from the kitchen. At other times, you just order directly from the menu.

Generally dim sum is a leisurely ritual, and the Southland encourages this tradition. Cushy booths line one side of the first floor, and classical music plays sedately in the background. On a recent visit we watched several businessmen amiably thrashing out some type of contract and a father patiently hand-feeding his small child some noodles until our own dim sum arrived, steaming and sizzling from the fire. Reservations are advised for lunch or dinner, but it's a first-come, first-served policy for the morning dim sum. The busiest time is from seven-thirty to nine A.M., and usually a short wait is necessary.

SHANGHAI SHENYANG FANDIAN (SHANGHAI SHENYANG RESTAURANT)

1321–1327 Yuyuan Lu
Tel.: 2520229
Hours:
11:00 A.M.–1:30 P.M. (lunch),
4:30–8:00 P.M. (dinner)

The Shanghai Shenyang Restaurant is not yet listed in major guide books, but it is such a jewel that in the four years that it has been open, word of its quality has spread among local residents, Japanese delegations, and selected westerners, making it a very popular eatery.

The restaurant is the creation of the manager Cai Liang Chao, whose novel touch is everywhere. Before opening the small eatery, Cai studied interior design in his spare time and combed through foreign magazines looking for inspiration for his dining room plan. The main dining room, designed by Cai, is arranged on three different levels, a layout that gives each of the five tables the semblance of privacy. Stuffed sofas and easy chairs are arranged near the tables, creating a relaxed and somewhat homey feeling. Fresh flowers gathered in simple but elegant arrangements are centerpieces, a simple touch that further reflects Cai Liang Chao's concern for aesthetics.

Since Cai is a third-level chef who has worked at a number of noted restaurants in Shanghai, he was also intent on fashioning a personal repertoire of dishes. The classic dish deep-fried Hundred Corner shrimp balls is given a new twist with a burst of hot broth in the center. Minuscule cubes of fresh fish are stir-fried with pine nuts, coated in a delicate sauce, and served wrapped in lettuce leaves. Perfectly formed stuffed dumplings are served individually to customers in miniature bamboo steamers. Everything we sampled was superb, and waitresses were helpful and efficient.

Given the excellent quality of the dishes and the elegant presentation one might expect the prices to be high, but in fact, the cost is quite reasonable, with the average price for a filling meal 50 yuan per person. The menu is in Chinese and English, which is a help, but Manager Cai is more often than not available with suggestions. Reservations should be made twenty-four hours in advance, especially for a large party.

SHANGHAI XINYA YUECAIGUAN (SHANGHAI XINYA GUANGZHOU RESTAURANT)

—

719 Nanjing Dong Lu
Tel.: 3224393
Hours:
6:30–10:00 A.M. (dim sum),
11:00 A.M.–1:30 P.M. (lunch),
5:00–7:30 P.M. (dinner)

Shanghai has long hosted a number of noted Cantonese eateries, a trend that has further increased with the influx of Hong Kong joint-venture businesses. One of the oldest and most established of the group is the Xinya Guangzhou Restaurant, on bustling Nanjing Dong Road. Established in 1926, the restaurant is so popular that many locals book the entire eatery for a family wedding, making reservations difficult to come by—even though the three-story building easily seats six hundred customers at one time.

The first floor features traditional-style dim sum and western pastries and cakes, while on the second and third floors, diners can indulge in their passion for Cantonese entrées. Foreigners are generally shown to the third-floor dining room, where there are two main dining areas as well as about twenty private rooms for banquets. The decor is pleasant, although undistinguished, and for special dinners, clean linen napkins are neatly folded into whimsical animal shapes.

The menu features over 150 dishes—many of which are the traditional Cantonese specialties one comes to expect from any good southern Chinese restaurant. Abalone, bird's nest, and shark's fin are in great supply. Avoid these costly items and order smoked pomfret, shrimp cooked in two ways, Mandarin fish rolls, fragrant scallion-oil chicken, and if you're in the mood, sweet-and-sour pork (one of the restaurant's signature dishes). Steamed dumplings are also quite good.

One or two of the waiters are holdouts from pre-Liberation days, and with their aggressive manner and fine command of the English language, they provide a certain charm. Hold firm to your own preferences, be adventurous, and don't allow them to railroad you into ordering the stereotypical dishes they think all foreigners eat.

Banquets can be expensive, with the cost running 100 yuan or more per person, depending on the number of delicacies ordered. Simpler meals ordered from the menu are much cheaper and average about 60 yuan per person. Whatever the case, reservations are essential and should be made several days in advance. If the day is auspicious and appropriate for a Chinese wedding, be prepared to eat elsewhere.

SICHUAN FANDIAN
(SICHUAN RESTAURANT)
—

457 Nanjing Dong Lu
Tel.: 322247
Hours:
10:30 A.M.–1:30 P.M. (lunch),
4:30–7:30 P.M. (dinner)

Don't expect to be greeted with open arms at this popular Shanghai eatery. Despite our reservations, we were ferried from one dining room to the next until someone finally located a table, and even then the waiters were less than very helpful. And by the time we ordered, the kitchen had run out of some of the dishes we coveted. Still, once we were organized and had relaxed with several glassfuls of cold beer, the food arrived promptly.

The two dining rooms reserved for foreigners, the Chongqing and Chengdu Halls, are pleasant with bamboo wallpaper. Linen tablecloths are slightly dingy, and at peak hours, the roar of conversation can be overwhelming, but these are two common features one finds at popular restaurants in China. The menu is classic Sichuanese: traditional western Chinese specialties like crispy duck, chicken with chili oil, hot-and-sour soup, chicken with peanuts, fish-flavored meat shreds, and Ma Po bean curd are all featured items. Our food was nicely seasoned with just the right proportion of hot chili pepper, ginger, and garlic. Dishes were a trifle oily, but this is often the case with Sichuanese food. *Shao mai* were plump and fragrant with ginger. The crispy-skin duck was deliciously crisp on the outside and tender and meaty underneath. Braised fish in a *douban* sauce was flaky but a trifle bony. The pungent sauce was especially good over steamed rice.

Established in 1951, the Sichuan has a fine reputation among foreigners and locals, and although we were somewhat disappointed by our meal, which was ordered directly from the menu, the kitchen staff can produce excellent food if given advance notice. When booking a banquet, steer the manager away from sea cucumbers and bird's nest, and concentrate on the classic specialties of this restaurant. The cost for a table of ten to twelve people is approximately 400 to 500 yuan, depending on the number of courses. Since the eatery is so popular, reservations are essential: for a banquet, book several days in advance, whereas for a smaller party, the day before is sufficient. If you do plan to order from the menu, go early, before the crowds arrive. Expect to pay about 40 to 50 yuan per person.

SHANGHAI'S HAIRY CRABS

Before crabs are in season, I always save up money to await their advent. My family used to tease me about my obsession with crab, saying crabs are my life. So I called the money thus saved for buying crabs "life-buying money."

—Li Yu, a seventeenth-century dramatist and poet.

For centuries, Chinese gastronomes have relished the sweet flavor of crabmeat and the rich delicacy of crab roe. One of the most highly prized varieties is the hairy crab, a freshwater species from eastern China, which appears for a month from mid-September to mid-October. The crab gets its name from its "hairy" claws. It is still available in Shanghai during the season in the city's best restaurants. The meat is occasionally served stir-fried with black mushrooms and water chestnuts, and often the roe is used to flavor dumpling fillings and stir-fried dishes. But most contend that the best way to savor this delicacy is steamed whole, with a black vinegar and gingerroot dipping sauce.

WU XING TING (HEART OF THE LAKE TEAHOUSE)

━

Yuyuan Garden (Old City)
Hours, First Floor:
5:30 A.M.–12:00 P.M.,
1:30–4:30 P.M.
Hours, Second Floor:
8:00–11:00 A.M. (breakfast),
12:30–4:30 P.M. (lunch)

Sitting tranquilly on the lake in the middle of the Yuyuan Garden is the Heart of the Lake Teahouse, a welcome contrast to the bedlam of the crowded garden. The only path to the island is via a zigzagging bridge, which was constructed this way to deter evil spirits. (An ancient Chinese belief holds that devils can cross water only in a straight line.) With its classic sloping roofs and pagoda-like design, the teahouse, built over one hundred years ago, offers a stunning reminder of the beauty and grace of traditional Chinese architecture.

At the entrance a woman sells tickets for tea and snacks for the two floors. Prices are modest: green tea sells for 1 yuan downstairs and 4 yuan above, while a pot of black tea is offered at 80 cents on the first floor and 3 yuan on the second. (The second floor offers a better view of the lake and a finer quality of tea.) The price includes peanuts and melon seeds.

At a glance, it seems little has changed since the teahouse first opened. The dark wooden tables and stools are shiny but grooved from countless customers. The windows are flung open, shutters secured back, so that the tables afford a clear view of the lake and surrounding paths of the garden. Customers contentedly sip tea, gnawing on melon seeds and flinging the empty skins to the floor below. Even if you don't have time for a cup of tea, take a brief walk through the teahouse for a glimpse of an age-old tradition.

YANGZHOU FANDIAN (YANGZHOU RESTAURANT)

308 Nanjing Dong Lu
Tel.: 322779
Hours:
10:30 A.M.–1:00 P.M. (lunch),
5:00–8:30 P.M. (dinner)

Visitors to the Yangzhou Restaurant might be put off slightly by the decor in the small mandatory guest dining rooms. The wallpaper is a busy olive green pattern, and the red velvet draperies have seen better days. But this eatery is considered one of the finest in the city, and on a good day the kitchen is capable of achieving greatness in its preparation of Shanghai and Yangzhou regional dishes. In fact, the chef is so highly regarded in China that he regularly travels to Singapore for guest stints in restaurants and for demonstrations.

Eastern cooks are renowned for their dexterity in slicing ingredients. You can view this skill firsthand by ordering the delicate stir-fried pine nuts and cubed fish or the dried bean curd shreds and ham cooked in soup. In each dish, the foods are meticulously cut into minute squares and slivers.

For a fall delicacy try steamed crabmeat served in its shell. The meat, roe, and fat from the "yellow crab," a famous variety, is removed and steamed in the shell with spices and black mushrooms. The platter is garnished with carrots, cucumbers, and *daikon* radish in the shape of chrysanthemum flowers in honor of the crab and chrysanthemum season. Other dishes worth trying are the steamed shad (spring), olive-shaped yams cooked in a sugar syrup (winter), boiled shrimp caught from Ding Shan Lake, and the Lion's Head casserole with hearts of cabbage.

Meals at the Yangzhou are not inexpensive: for a large banquet, the cost could easily be 100 yuan per person, even with eight people or more, but the quality and presentation here are extraordinarily fine. Since the private dining area is so limited, reservations for a banquet require several days' notice.

YOUYI JIUJIA (FRIENDSHIP RESTAURANT)

100 Yenan Chung Lu
Tel.: 2534078
Hours:
8:00 A.M.–2:00 P.M. (dim sum and lunch),
5:00–9:00 P.M. (dinner)

For a number of years, the Friendship Restaurant, which sits atop the Shanghai Exhibition Center, was a subject of some controversy. Some reports were good, others bad, but everyone agreed that it was worth the trip if only for a seat on its terrace and a grand view of the city's skyline. I can happily state that a visit is most definitely worth making for the food as well as the view. For excellent Cantonese fare, there is none better in the city.

In 1986 the Friendship owners teamed up with a Hong Kong firm to establish a joint venture. They redecorated the dining room, bringing in waiters from Hong Kong to train the staff. Today, the soft green, art deco–style dining room is spacious and inviting. Windows line all sides of the restaurant, affording a stunning view of Shanghai, and service is solicitous and efficient.

The menu, which is available in English, is varied, but traditionally Cantonese. There are pages of shark's fin, abalone, and sea cucumber dishes, in addition to a wide variety of seafood specialties. Some of the more noteworthy items to try are steamed fish, baked chicken with salt, stir-fried scallops, and steamed crab. Every dish that we tried was excellent: the hot-cold appetizer of roast suckling pig and tossed jellyfish was outstanding. The pig was lean, tender, and crisp on the outside. Whole fried shrimp were incredibly fresh and flavorful—the skin so beautifully crisp, you could eat it like candy. The corn soup was subtly seasoned, with whole kernels and creamed corn in its rich chicken-broth base. And steamed *shao mai* were meaty and nicely crisp, with chopped water chestnuts and chopped fresh gingerroot—a reliable indication that the morning dim sum would definitely be worth trying.

This restaurant is not inexpensive: customers should expect to pay about 100 yuan per person (and occasionally more if ordering shark's fin, bird's nest, or abalone), but it is still worth a visit. Reservations are advisable, particularly for a banquet, but seats are usually available for smaller parties. Diner's Club credit cards are accepted.

YU FO SI SUCAI GUAN (JADE BUDDHA TEMPLE VEGETARIAN RESTAURANT)
—

170 Anyuan Lu
Tel.: 4335745
Hours:
11:00 A.M.–1:00 P.M. (lunch),
5:30–8:00 P.M. (dinner)

Anyone who has never sampled Chinese vegetarian cooking is in for a wonderful surprise. Chinese meatless cooking, far from being bland, is redolent with flavors like sesame oil, scallions, and smoky black mushrooms, and many dishes are artful mock re-creations of their meat, fish, and seafood counterparts. Stir-fried crabmeat with vegetables is an excellent example of such a preparation. Minced carrots, black mushrooms, water chestnuts, fresh coriander, and mashed potatoes are stir-fried with seasonings in a hot pan and served with a garnish of black mushrooms cut in the shape of crabs. This dish is light and delicately seasoned. Mock stir-fried eels are made from Chinese black mushrooms, and a delicious deep-fried fish made of mashed taro with minced carrots and water chestnuts is served in a sweet-and-sour sauce. Also excellent are *luohan cai,* the Cantonese vegetarian classic, and mock sea cucumber and shark's fin. Mock duck and chicken are made from bean milk skin seasoned with stock and soy sauce, wrapped into loaflike shapes to be steamed, and then served cold sliced or deep-fried. Even hard-core meat lovers will be content.

For a sumptuous banquet, the cost will be about 80 to 100 yuan per person, providing there are at least four people. Reservations should be made at least twenty-four hours ahead, and three or four days for a banquet of special dishes that require advance preparation.

PAN-FRIED CHICKEN BUNS
▬

*P*an-fried chicken buns are a popular Shanghai specialty served year round. For this snack a dough circle is stuffed with diced chicken, pork, and flavored with gingerroot, scallions, and sesame oil. Then, according to an old recipe book, "the dough is gathered into fifteen little pleats," creating a neat little bun. The top is then sprinkled with minced scallions and sesame seeds.

The buns are then arranged on a grill and their bottoms pan-fried until crisp and golden brown. Water is added, and the buns are steamed until done. The resulting bun is deliciously crisp on the bottom and soft on top. Pan-fried chicken buns are served hot from the pan with a dipping sauce of soy sauce or black vinegar. The Xinya restaurant serves superb pan-fried chicken buns; there is also a stall in the Yu Garden near the wading pool where some of the best in the city are available.

SUZHOU

With its lush gardens and quaint canals, Suzhou is considered one of the most beautiful cities in China, and after my first visit there in 1979, I could only agree with that assessment. The city was peaceful in contrast to the urban chaos of Shanghai, an hour away, yet bustled with a smalltown energy. Its canals lent an Old World, romantic charm, and each garden possessed its own serene appeal. Some were ornate in their layout and design; others were simple and understated.

On recent trips to Suzhou, I have been less enchanted. The gardens are still beautiful, but you now have to search to find a peaceful corner. Most are packed with tourists and echo with the drone of repetitious speeches announced over loudspeakers by tour leaders. The Suzhou of the past prevails in a few untouched areas, but the downtown section is messy with construction as new stores and shops are being built. The slick, new Friendship shop is filled with floors of overpriced antiques and kitschy handicraft items. It seems Suzhou may be on the verge of being transformed into a tasteless tourist trap.

Despite its aggressive modernization Suzhou is still a city enshrouded in history. It was settled over three thousand years ago, but its first claim to prominence was as the capital of the Kingdom of Wu in 518 B.C. Even then, the city was famous for its canals. During the Tang (618–907) and Song (960–1279) dynasties, Suzhou prospered, becoming a significant trade center and establishing a reputation for its fine textiles, particularly silk. The first gardens were planted as early as the tenth century, and were built upon successively throughout the Song, Yuan, Ming, and Qing dynasties.

Suzhou natives are considered to be especially gracious and gentle, an opinion that is connected to the softness of their native Wu dialect. We certainly found this to be the case at a recent dinner at the Suzhou Garden Restaurant, when one of the oldest and most highly respected cooks in the city was determined to show us why Suzhou's eateries have delighted the palates of gastronomes for centuries. Because of traffic, we were over half an hour late for our meal. Nonetheless, he greeted us warmly and courteously, bowing formally at the waist as we entered. He then insisted that we toast our arrival with a special local wine that was made in very limited quantity from sweet rice. The flavor was sweet, yet mellow, reminiscent of fine sherry.

We dined superbly that evening, enjoying some of the city's specialties, including crisp sweet-and-sour fish with pine nuts, succulent stir-fried eels with ginger and garlic, delicate shrimp with tea leaves, and fresh steamed cracked crab. We had to eat more quickly than we would have liked, attempting to savor the fine flavors but determined not to miss our train. But as we left, he pressed upon us a bottle of the priceless wine, entreating us to return again. Aboard the train, as the crowded streets disappeared in the distance, we cradled our gift and forgot all but the pleasurable memories of this ancient city.

CAIZHIZHAI TANGGUO DIAN (CAIZHIZHAI CONFECTIONERY STORE)

▬

91 Guanqian Jie
Tel.: 23388
Hours: 8:00 A.M.–8:30 P.M.

Suzhou is known for its candies, sweet and savory pastries, and confections, and one of its most famous sweetshops is the Caizhizhai, located on the main street downtown. You will undoubtedly encounter crowds here, for almost every Chinese visitor considers a visit to the store a mandatory stop on the Suzhou itinerary. Although it's just a small place, Caizhizhai is chock full of all kinds of cookies, cakes, and a vast selection of savory items, including tinned preserved vegetables and smoked ham.

Among its specialties is the famous Suzhou pine nut candy, a square of caramel embedded with pine nuts. There are two varieties—one is brittle and the other slightly chewy—but both are buttery and rich with the flavor of the roasted nuts. Variations of this candy are made with walnuts, sesame seeds, and melon seeds. All are sold by weight and will keep refrigerated indefinitely.

CUIHUAYUAN CAIGUAN (CUIHUAYUAN RESTAURANT)

▬

23 Jingde Lu
Tel.: 21042
Hours:
10:30 A.M.–1:00 P.M. (lunch),
4:45–7:00 P.M. (dinner)

A recent addition to the roster of fine restaurants in Suzhou is the Cuihuayuan. Though it only opened in 1986, this eatery has already acquired a reputation as one of the best in the city. One of the reasons for its popularity may be its ties to the Suzhou Culinary Training Institute. The school is housed in the same building, with the three lowest floors devoted to classrooms and training kitchens, and the two highest levels allocated for the restaurant.

Don't be discouraged by the grim walk up the dingy stairway. The main dining rooms of the restaurant are pleasant, and the three small private rooms, each with its own theme decor, are lovely. The prettiest of the lot is the "boat room" decorated with handsome wooden paneling and stained glass screens. Along the walls are bright blue glass squares simulating windows, which look out on a large painted mural of a peaceful river scene.

The help here is very sweet but slightly giggly and gangly, since they are young students who have completed their year and a half of study in the school. (After working for another year and a half, they are placed in jobs in other restaurants and hotels.) Service is a bit slow, but the food, when it finally arrives, is excellent. (You can almost imagine eager young chefs agonizing over their creations before they come out of the kitchen.)

The menu, which is in Chinese and English, is seasonal; some of the recommended dishes available year-round are sweet-and-sour Squirrel Fish, crispy-skin duck stuffed with shrimp *(cui pi xiang ya)*, Ma Po bean curd, and steamed soft-shell turtle *(qing zheng jiayu)*.

One might assume that prices would be lower since the restaurant is a training kitchen, but unfortunately, this is not the case. For a filling meal, expect to pay about 40 to 50 yuan per person; for a banquet, the cost could easily reach 100 yuan per person, depending on the delicacies ordered. Since service is slow, you might do well to book tables in advance, establishing a cost per person and suggesting several dishes at the same time. The restaurant will plan the rest of the menu.

HUANGTIANYUAN DUMPLING SHOP

—

88 Guanqian Jie
Hours: 7:00 A.M.–8:00 P.M.

With a two-hundred-year history, the Huang-tingyuan has become a landmark in Suzhou. Although its name may lead one to think the Huangtianyuan produces only dumplings, its main products are in fact Chinese cakes and pastries. The kitchen is reputed to draw from a repertoire of 160 different varieties, many of which start with a base of glutinous rice powder and continue with the addition of pine nuts, walnuts, sesame seeds, preserved fruit, red bean paste, and pumpkin seed. For many foreigners, the pastries may look sloppy, and taste somewhat cloying, but a visit to this legendary shop is still worth making.

SONGHELOU (PINE AND CRANE RESTAURANT)

—

141 Guanqian Jie
Tel.: 22066, 21859
Hours:
10:30 A.M.–1:00 P.M. (lunch),
5:00–7:30 P.M. (dinner)

Few restaurants outside of the Fangshan in Beijing have achieved the national reputation of Songhelou in Suzhou. With a 210-year history, it is an eatery that first came to prominence during the Qing dynasty, when it was reputed to have been the favored dining place of the Emperor Qianlong (1736–1796). The first time I ate at the Songhelou several years ago, I was extremely disappointed. The setting was grim, and the food was almost inedible, but the the restaurant has recently moved to two new buildings, and the kitchen seems to have hit its stride.

The main dining hall, which is situated on the main street of Suzhou, is plain but pleasant. Large windows line the wall overlooking the street, giving life to the room. In the Songhelou's second building, located in an alley in back of the main restaurant, banquet rooms are splendid. The entire banquet area is decorated with one magnificent black lacquer and gold screen painted with a continuous row of serene Tang dynasty maidens in traditional Chinese dress bearing fruit and other delicacies. Inside the rooms, the reverse side of the screen is no less enchanting, with lively scenes from a Tang dynasty village.

The Songhelou offers all the standard Suzhou favorites and then some. Squirrel Fish with sweet-and-sour sauce is beautifully presented with its scored sides, crisp outer coating, and pungent sauce. Stir-fried eels *(chao shanyu)* are delicious and redolent of sesame oil, garlic, and pepper. Watermelon chicken soup *(xigua ji zhuang)* is magnificent and delicate with tender chicken pieces steamed in a small watermelon. Braised duck *(mu you ao ya)* in a hearty soy sauce–based glaze is so tender, the entire bird (available in winter only) can be divided and eaten with chopsticks. And snacks like open-face shrimp dumplings *(xia ren shao mai)* and steamed dumplings *(xiao long bao)* are artfully shaped and delectable.

The kitchen employs six special-level chefs; the master chef in charge, Liu Xue Jia, has been working at the restaurant for over fifty years. Liu often travels abroad to demonstrate, and he has received awards of achievement from his colleagues in China.

If you have the time and money, a banquet at Songhelou is a memorable experience. Reservations should be made two days in advance, and the cost can reach 100 yuan per person. You also can walk in off the street to the main dining hall and order from the menu. A filling meal will cost about 30 yuan per person. The restaurant accepts Visa, MasterCard, and American Express credit cards.

SUZHOU YUANWAILOU FANDIAN (SUZHOU GARDEN HOTEL)

▬

99 Liu Yuan Lu
Tel.: 331013 Ext. 570
Hours:
11:00 A.M.–1:00 P.M. (lunch),
4:30–7:30 P.M. (dinner)

Suzhou is famous for its gardens, and it is in their spirit that the owners of the Suzhou Garden Hotel have designed its dining room. Serene and meticulously fashioned, the enchanting restaurant, which opened in 1987, resembles a bamboo garden with bamboo-carved wooden tables and chairs and a rear glass wall that looks out on a simulated bamboo grove planted with live bamboo stalks.

The first time we visited, the room was dimly lit, accentuating the tranquil garden. Since it was before mealtime, the room was empty save for the serving people setting up the tables for dinner. Waitresses, outfitted in black skirts and sweaters with starched white collars and carrying straw baskets laden with chopsticks, waltzed around the tables, methodically arranging the chopsticks at each place. It was a scene lifted from a Chinese novel.

The kitchen is under the capable administration of Shao Rong Gen, a celebrated sixty-eight-year-old master chef. After working for nineteen years at the Nanlin Hotel, Shao taught in the local culinary institute for twelve years. He also

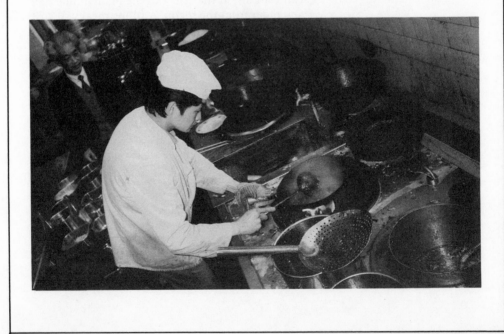

taught in Japan on an official invitation, and he is as familiar with good food as he is skilled in the special dishes of Suzhou. With Shao's supervision young chefs turn out excellent food. Squirrel Fish is fried until crisp and bathed in a pungent sweet-and-sour sauce. Steamed shad is delicate with a light dousing of tart black vinegar. Stir-fried shrimp with tea leaves *(bi lun cha ye)* is fresh and unusual, with its sprinkling of jasmine leaves, and chicken with sweet wine rice sauce *(cun xiang jiu men ji)* is deliciously tender and fragrant. The restaurant also prepares excellent dim sum.

Since the Suzhou Garden is very popular and as yet does not have an English menu; twenty-four hours' advance reservations are advised. You can specify the amount of money per person that you would like to spend, recommending any dishes you prefer, and the manager will plan the rest of the menu. For a filling and memorable meal, plan on spending about 50–80 yuan per person with a party of four to six.

SUZHOU SHANGTANG CAICHANG (SUZHOU SHANGTANG MARKET)

Shangtang Jie
Hours: 7:00 A.M.–7:30 P.M.

Directly off Guanqian street is a small but colorful street market whose stalls brim with dried provisions such as rings of skewered chili peppers, pork sausages, red beans, and black wood ears. Interspersed among the purveyors of dried ingredients are stalls where freshly picked vegetables are arranged in neat piles. Along the way, you may also see cooks swinging noodles and stacking bamboo layers of steamed dumplings. On the opposite side of the street stands a larger indoor market with a sign proclaiming "Fresh Meat." This is not the largest market in Suzhou, but it is colorful and conveniently located for those who would like the chance to experience a bit of everyday life in this lovely city.

WUXI

I had not expected to like Wuxi, and apart from its famous spareribs, there seemed little to attract me in the way of food. Furthermore, friends who had been to the city some years before returned with stories of an unattractive industrial metropolis and complaints about mediocre hotel fare.

On paper, the 3,000-year-old city certainly seemed worth a visit. Even in olden times, it was an important trade center: silk production is believed to have originated in Wuxi some fifteen hundred years ago, and by the middle of the eighteenth century, it had become one of the four largest rice markets in China. Its location in the heart of lush Jiangsu province, bordering Lake Taihu, one of the largest freshwater bodies in China, also added to its appeal. And from my reading I learned that Wuxi was endowed with numerous beautiful gardens, as well as what is believed to be the oldest park in China.

Despite my skepticism, I went, determined to find the best while expecting the worst. Wuxi captivated me immediately. The city was large, but not overwhelming, and hummed with the excitement and vitality of a place finally coming into its own. A number of joint-venture high-rise hotels were in the process of being completed, and restaurants, which we had been warned were unfit for foreigners, welcomed and seduced us with superb food.

At first, we stayed away from the center of the city and its tourists, enjoying instead the tranquil serenity of Liyuan Garden. It was early spring, and the garden was ablaze with trees heavy with plum blossoms at the peak of bloom. Nearby, at locations marked "Angling Spots" on the city map, local people struggled with fishing rods straining with plump carp.

On a trip into the city, we strolled through the busy streets, exploring the local markets, which were overflowing with vegetables and freshwater fish. We wandered into an old dumpling shop where customers sat at beautiful carved wooden booths, their heads down, faces intent, as they shoveled slippery dumplings into their mouths. Nearby, at a famous vegetarian restaurant, while workers at the next table gossiped and snipped caps off black mushrooms, we tasted exquisitely seasoned sweet-and-sour mock eels and puffy buns stuffed with fragrant chopped smoky mushrooms and cabbage, seasoned with ground ginger.

As the day progressed, it only seemed to get better. At the Wuxi China Hotel, we giggled with delight as four aging Dixieland musicians labored over several songs, playing their off-key notes with an earnestness that was endearing. And finally, we sampled the famous Wuxi spareribs: the meat was tender as butter, barely hanging on to the bones. The sauce was rich and infused with the flavor of the reduced braising mixture, redolent of soy sauce, rice wine, and star anise. Even in my fondest dreams, I never expected the dish to taste so good.

GONGDELIN SUCAI GUAN (GONGDELIN VEGETARIAN RESTAURANT)

—

182 Renmin Zhong Lu
Tel.: 227069
Hours:
5:30–9:00 A.M. (dim sum),
10:30 A.M.–1:00 P.M. (lunch),
4:30–7:30 P.M. (dinner)

Gongdelin is a name that in China has become synonymous with vegetarian cooking, since so many cities boast a Gongdelin vegetarian eatery. Each one operates independently, but if all were like the Gongdelin in Wuxi, they would be recommended stops for hungry travelers on any itinerary.

A tiny, wooden doorway and creaky stairs lead up to the second-floor dining rooms of the Wuxi Gongdelin, which is over one hundred years old. Rather than having one large central area, the restaurant is made up of a series of small rooms, each with a different and charming decor. For the past several years, the eatery has been in the process of renovation, but even the oldest room is quaint and appealing, with old-fashioned, diamond-shaped leaded glass windows with black trim, and wicker chairs. Although the staff doesn't speak English, they are very friendly, and many have been working at the restaurant for a number of years.

Until 1986, the menu was strictly vegetarian. Now the Gongdelin offers a number of meat dishes, but you would be wise to ignore these items and stick to the meatless choices. Mock chicken stuffed with bamboo shoots, black mushrooms, and peppers (juan tong ji) is memorable. The vegetarian buns (sucai bao) are filled with pickled cabbage, bean curd, and gingerroot, and mock eel (su shanyu) is excellent with its gingery sweet-and-sour caramelized sauce contrasted with the crisp pieces of fried black mushroom. Ingredients are very fresh, and most of the stock vegetarian classics are also available, such as mock crab, whole yellow fish in a sweet-and-sour sauce, mock shrimp, and mock Peking duck.

Since the restaurant, for reasons that are unclear, is hesitant to relinquish its menu to foreigners, it might be wise to call twenty-four hours ahead to book a table and designate the amount per person you want to spend. For 60 yuan per person, the Gongdelin will prepare six courses and a soup. You may prefer to make some suggestions of your own and negotiate a price.

HUBIN FANDIAN
(HUBIN HOTEL)

Liyuan Garden
Tel.: 668812
Hours:
6:00–9:00 A.M. (breakfast),
11:15 A.M.–2:00 P.M. (lunch),
4:30–8:00 P.M. (dinner)

About twenty-five minutes outside Wuxi, on the edge of the Liyuan Garden, is the Hubin Hotel, a perfect place for a lunch or dinner of local specialties. Hotel food in China tends to be disappointing, but the Hubin has a top-notch restaurant; both food and service are above reproach.

The dining room, like that in many hotels, is somewhat overwhelming. At first glance it appears to be a large, antiseptic hall, but the large tile mural on the back wall lends warmth and color, and starched linen tablecloths and napkins add another nice touch.

Although the restaurant had been highly recommended, any apprehensions we may still have had disappeared after we were seated and happened to watch the waiters and waitresses preparing the dining room for dinner. Each one meticulously polished silverware and inspected glasses, leaving all tables set with unusual care. Our own waiter was almost overly solicitous as

(continued)

he took our order after offering recommendations from the Chinese-English menu. Furthermore, all dishes arrived promptly, still sizzling from the fire.

Lake Tai shrimp, reportedly caught just outside the door on the adjoining Lake Taihu, are tiny and wonderfully sweet. They are stir-fried quickly and served simply, full of their own fresh juices. Simple steamed fish is also superb, served whole with a light seasoning of scallion and ginger. Wuxi spareribs are tender, meaty, and rich with their anise-flavored sauce, and gluten cooked with bamboo shoots and black mushrooms (another Wuxi specialty) is plump with soy sauce and the smoky flavor of the mushrooms.

Dishes that require advance booking but are recommended are the braised chicken in bamboo leaves, Beggar's Chicken, and crispy-skin duck. Several snacks are also worth trying: wontons stuffed with a meaty pork and shrimp filling float in a clear chicken broth; and steamed dumplings with perfect pleats are bursting with juice and ground meat filling.

Reservations are unnecessary unless you would like to order dishes that require advance preparation. For a filling meal, prices should be no more than 30 to 40 yuan per person.

JIANGNAN CAIGUAN (JIANGNAN RESTAURANT)

—

435 Zhongshan Lu
Tel.: 27483
Hours:
10:00 A.M.–1:00 P.M. (lunch),
4:00–9:00 P.M. (dinner)

The Jiangnan kitchen produces some very fine dishes, and its prices are modest, making it a favorite choice for local residents and Chinese visitors. But don't come here for a serene meal: during peak dining hours it is a very rowdy place, every one of its tables crowded with talkative Chinese families and friends who are especially exuberant after a few toasts of Maotai wine.

Opened some twenty years ago, the Jiangnan has only recently welcomed foreigners to mingle with locals. The three main dining rooms, with their dingy bamboo-relief wallpaper, are quite simple with large banquet tables that seat twelve. Interspersed throughout each room are a few small tables for accommodating parties with fewer people. Service is slow and somewhat haphazard, but there is one waiter who does speak surprisingly good English, and he is automatically sent to wait on any foreign customers.

The restaurant offers all of the usual Wuxi specialties such as Wuxi spareribs, fried whitebait, stir-fried eels, and steamed dumplings. Mushroom soup with sizzling rice crusts is delicious with a delicately seasoned broth and crisp rice cakes. And steamed fish is very fresh, albeit a bit bony.

To be certain of a seat, you should make reservations several hours in advance. If you order a banquet, expect to pay about 60 yuan or more per person; if ordering from the menu, the cost will be much lower.

WAN XING JI HUNTUN DIAN (WAN XING JI WONTON RESTAURANT)

391 Zhongshan Lu
Tel.: 2484
Hours:
6:00 A.M.–1:00 P.M. (lunch),
2:00–6:00 P.M. (dinner)

For those adventurous souls who would like to sample a taste of local Wuxi snacks, the Wan Xing Ji Wonton Restaurant is conveniently located on one of the major streets downtown. It's a small, charming place with an outer room set with simple stools and wooden tables where customers, faces hidden in their bowls, busily sip away at a quick meal of wonton soup.

Through a doorway in another room a more leisurely pace is set. The atmosphere is homey and inviting with beautiful wooden booths. Here one can sit and savor local snacks such as wontons served fried or in soup, or steamed dumplings.

Prices are extraordinarily cheap (four steamed dumplings cost under 1 yuan and a bowl of soup with five wontons is 50 cents). Needless to say, reservations are unnecessary, and seats are available on a first-come, first-served basis.

FRIED GLUTEN

■

*G*luten is eaten all over China, but it is especially popular in the city of Wuxi, where it has become a local specialty. Almost every restaurant in the city offers fried gluten in some form. Gluten is made by rinsing a flour and water dough under running water, leaving a spongey mass of protein. After it is shaped into balls, the gluten is deep-fried briefly in hot oil so that it resembles a hollow fried ball. It may then be stuffed and braised, or left empty and served in soups and meat or vegetable dishes. In Wuxi, one of the most popular forms of fried gluten is simmered in soy sauce with black mushrooms and bamboo shoots. The cooked gluten becomes plump and juicy with the taste of dried mushrooms and soy sauce.

WUXI ZHONGGUO FANDIAN (WUXI CHINA HOTEL)

—

81 Han Chang Lu
Tel.: 220041, 227454
Hours:
7:00 A.M.–12:30 P.M. (dim sum),
10:30 A.M.–1:00 P.M. (lunch)
5:00–8:30 P.M. (dinner)

If you were to ask anyone in Wuxi for the name of the best restaurant in town, the inevitable response would be the China Hotel. Since its opening in 1947, this eatery has striven to maintain a standard that is laudably high. Its general manager, Gao Hao Xing, who is a first-level chef, runs the dining rooms and kitchens with meticulous precision. The kitchen staff includes five special-level chefs, fifteen first-level cooks, eighteen third-level cooks, and thirty third-level chefs. Manager chef Gao is also a gold medal recipient, one of four chefs from Jiangsu province participating in the 1983 National Culinary Competition.

The restaurant itself is sizable, with over one hundred tables, including eight private banquet rooms and two huge dining rooms. The first floor is mainly reserved for eating snacks. On the second floor, in a cavernous dining room, a sleepy band with four aging musicians grinds out Dixieland tunes at lunch and dinner. There are tables for dining here, but the noise is deafening. The inner dining rooms, with their comfortable bur-

gundy chairs, impeccably clean linen, and graceful flower arrangements are far more appealing.
(Although once the tables are filled, the conversational roar can be almost as loud as the music.)

The food is exceptional. The classic specialty,
Wuxi spareribs, *(Wuxi paigu)* are meaty and rich
with the braising sauce seasoned with soy and
star anise. The meat is so tender that it falls away
from the bone with little prodding. Fried whitebait cakes *(Tai Hu yinyu bing)* are crisp and delicate with a taste reminiscent of potato latkes
with minced scallions. Bean curd stuffed with
ground pork, shrimp, and black mushrooms *(jin
xiang doufu)* is succulent, as are the steamed
buns. Even the wontons are exceptional. Floating
in a mellow chicken broth, they are stuffed liberally with ground meat seasoned with dried
shrimp. If you are in the mood for a sweet finish,
you must try the almond soup with sweet peanut
balls *(xingren fen bao)*.

Reservations are recommended, but you may
call several hours in advance. Rather than take
the chance of missing any dishes, you might
want to pre-order some foods and book the remainder of your choices when you arrive. For a
filling meal, the cost will be about 50 yuan per
person.

HANGZHOU

Hangzhou charms even the most jaded tourist. With its traditional teahouses, the serene, often misty beauty of West Lake, and its bustling but still small-scale city center, Hangzhou is a city that has captivated visitors for centuries—including Marco Polo, who was one of the first foreigners to discover its beauties. After a visit in the thirteenth century, he was reduced to a state of rapture, proclaiming it "one of the most splendid and magnificent cities in the world."

The major attraction of Hangzhou is West Lake, whose different moods are shaped by the time of day and weather. In the early morning, mist hangs suspended in the still air, obscuring its surface and rendering it mysterious. Ghostly figures around the lake, some solitary, some in groups, practice shadow-boxing, their bodies slowly moving in a fluid, primal dance.

As the sun rises and boats appear on the water filled with laughing groups of visitors, the lake brightens, dappled with sunshine. At night, as the waters darken and become reflecting pools for the pale shadows cast by the moon, the lake becomes romantic and serene, a haven for lovers and those in search of a tranquil sanctuary.

The weather has never cooperated fully during my visits to Hangzhou, remaining raw and gray for most of my sojourns. But even on a gloomy day, Hangzhou is beguiling, and it has been consistent for some of the most delectable and unusual dishes I have enjoyed in China.

Hangzhou was founded over 2,200 years ago, and from its earliest days it prospered not only as a leading port for trading but also as a cultural mecca, attracting scores of painters, poets, scholars, and officials of the imperial courts. Its silks and handicrafts were revered, and its cuisine was highly sophisticated, catering to the tastes of the refined audience. Local chefs had the advantage of access to an extraordinary variety of meat, seafood, vegetables and fruits, a legacy that continues to this day.

Like other gastronomes before me, I have sought out the local specialties on my visits, relishing dishes such as whole poached fish in a spicy hot-and-sour sauce and steamed honey ham as I sat on a balcony overlooking the lake. In a city renowned for its vegetarian cuisine, I have enjoyed a whole stuffed mock chicken redolent with the flavor of black mushrooms and five-spice powder and a magnificent fish shaped out of taro and stuffed with a sumptuous Eight Treasure filling. I marveled at the presentation of Beggar's Chicken, a whole chicken wrapped in a lotus leaf and packed and baked in mud. Then I watched as it was smashed open by a chef with a sure hand and unwrapped, exposing one of the most succulent chickens I had ever tasted. And I delighted in the pastries and dumplings served all over the city, many molded into delicate and appealing shapes with rich fillings. Like most visitors to Hangzhou, I was thoroughly captivated by the scenery and the culinary delights, and I long to return.

CHENGDU JIUJIA
(CHENGDU RESTAURANT)
—

44 Yan'an Lu
Tel.: 22756
Hours: 7:00 A.M.–10 P.M.

According to reliable local sources, no Sichuan-style eateries were to be found in Hangzhou before 1984. Recognizing this lack, the city's catering company took action and established a joint-venture restaurant with the catering company of Chengdu, Sichuan province's capital. One usually thinks of plush, grandiose hotels when talking about joint-venture projects, but the Chengdu Restaurant is definitely a modest "people's" eatery, with an informal, family-style atmosphere.

Chopsticks are disposable and tablecloths are obviously not replaced after each meal, but ignore the surroundings and concentrate on the food. The chefs, who are imported from Sichuan province, do a masterful job of preparing authentic (even down to the amount of oil, which is *very* generous) western regional classics. Dishes such as fish-flavored pork *(yu xiang rou si)*, Ma Po bean curd *(Ma Po doufu)*, and spicy braised fish *(douban yu)* are all deliciously seasoned with spicy blasts of hot chili pepper mingled with intermittent accents of black vinegar, ginger, and garlic.

Reservations are not necessary, but there may be a short wait until a table becomes free. Prices are reasonable; a very filling meal for four to six people can be had for 30 to 40 yuan per person.

HANGZHOU QINGZHEN FENGHUANGLOU (FENGHUANGLOU RESTAURANT)

—

93 Renhe Lu
Tel.: 23860
Hours:
6:00–10:00 A.M. (dim sum),
10:00 A.M.–9:00 P.M. (lunch and dinner)

In marked contrast to the refined tenderness of Hangzhou cuisine are the robust flavorings and meaty entrées of Muslim cooking. Fenghuanglou, a wonderful Muslim-style eatery, offers dishes that can be described as a combination of the two styles: the heavy, spicy dishes that Muslims crave are produced here with a slightly lighter hand and an eye for presentation that Hangzhou cooks have become famous for.

The restaurant is hidden on a small side street and except for the Near Eastern flavor of the exterior, one would hardly guess that it is the foremost Muslim eatery in the city, catering to a community of over four thousand Muslim residents. The manager, Su Xiang Sheng, the original master chef, is head of the Muslim Association as well as a member of the People's Congress, and while Fenghuanglou appears to be a small, modest restaurant, its list of past customers includes the king of Nepal, Zhou Enlai, and Chairman Mao himself.

Proceed up the stairs to the second-floor private dining room, which is simple but clean with pink walls and red velvet chairs. Although no one speaks English, the waiters and cooks could not be friendlier or more helpful.

All the dishes we sampled here, ordered directly from the menu, were delicious. Red-cooked lamb in a Yunan pot *(chi guo niurou)* was redolent of soy sauce and seasonings. Flavorful deep-fried beef rolls *(juan teng niurou)* had a crisp bread crumb coating and scallion heart center. Grilled shashlik *(kao yangrou juan)* was exceptional, pungent with garlic, cumin, and ginger. The dim sum we tasted, including the lamb *shao mai (yangrou shao mai)* and lamb dumplings *(yangrou shui jiao)*, are recommended. In the autumn roasted baby lamb also is available.

Service tends to be a little slow, so it would be wise to call in advance, making reservations and ordering some of the dishes you would like to try. Bookings should be made one day ahead. For a full meal, prices range from 50 to 100 yuan per person.

LINGYIN TEMPLE
VEGETARIAN RESTAURANT
▬

Lingyin Temple
Tel.: 26378
Hours: 9:00 A.M.–1:30 P.M.
(by reservation only)

At the foot of the Northern Peak, near the Yue Lake area of West Lake, is the Lingyin Temple, one of the most popular tourist attractions in Hangzhou and one of the most famous Buddhist temples in China. Be prepared for the crowds, for local Chinese tourists are as compelled to visit this historic place as foreigners.

The name "Lingyin" means "Souls Retreat," and it was thus christened some sixteen hundred years ago by the Buddhist monk Hui Li, who had emigrated here from India. Throughout its history, the temple has been intermittently destroyed and rebuilt, and today it is resplendently restored with a bright yellow painted facade and magnificent gold Buddha statues.

While the temple has long drawn a stream of visitors to pay homage to the Buddha, it is only in the past fifty years that its restaurant has been open to the public and has gained renown as a fine vegetarian eatery. Hangzhou is recognized as a culinary mecca for outstanding vegetarian cuisine, and many of the most skilled of these meatless chefs were trained at the Lingyin temple.

The dining room facilities at Lingyin are simple, bordering on primitive. The larger private dining room (still small by most standards) has large wooden tables and tall-backed bamboo chairs, with white plastic tablecloths and paper napkins. Specialties include mock shark's fin, mock West Lake fish, vegetarian whole duck, mock chicken with chestnuts, and a variety of sweet and savory pastries including vegetarian mooncakes, Longevity Peach Buns, sesame cakes, and Buddha's Hands (a fried dough pastry faintly resembling a hand).

Prices for a full meal or multicourse banquet can range from 30 to 100 yuan, depending on the quality and number of dishes ordered. Unless otherwise specified, the temple will decide on the menu. Reservations for all meals should be made at least twenty-four hours in advance.

LOU WAI LOU
(HALL BEYOND HALLS
RESTAURANT)

—

30 Outer West Lake
Tel.: 21654
Hours:
10:30 A.M.–1:30 P.M. (lunch),
4:30–7:30 P.M. (dinner)

Because Hangzhou is so richly endowed with fine eateries, naming the best is no easy task, but most natives would probably settle for the Lou Wai Lou. For over 140 years this restaurant has been synonymous with great food. The dishes may be a little pricey, but with a fine meal under your belt, you may find the expense easy to forgive.

As well as superb dining, the Lou Wai Lou offers a splendid view of the lake through the expansive glass windows of its second-floor dining room. You can relax in your chair and see, off in the distance, steep mountains shrouded in mist. Peeking through graceful trees that line the banks, you can watch small boats gliding serenely across the peaceful waters. If the second-floor dining room, with its simple decor and worn-looking green drapes, seems cavernous, you may prefer one of the banquet rooms, lavishly decorated with carved bamboo panels and ornate wooden sculptures.

The restaurant was expanded in 1980 according to the recorded personal wishes of the late Zhou Enlai. Today, with its ten banquet rooms and four dining rooms, it can seat over one thousand people at one time. Despite the size, waitresses, dressed in Chinese-style red and green shirts with black velvet skirts, are efficient and provide prompt service.

The Lou Wai Lou menu, which is conveniently written in Chinese and English, does boast an extensive selection of special dishes, but the kitchen excels in preparing the traditional regional specialties. West Lake fish *(Xi Hu cuyu)*, although slightly bony, has a delicious sauce with a perfect blending of fragrant black vinegar and finely shredded ginger. Steamed honey ham *(mi zhi hou fang)* is exquisite: the meat is tender, and the fine smoky flavor of the Jinhua ham contrasts nicely with its sweet sauce. Madame Sao soup *(Song Sao yu geng)*, a dish with a seven-hundred-year history, is memorable, with its hot-and-sour seasonings and flecks of sweet fish. And

(continued)

the stir-fried shrimp with green tea leaves *(long-jing xiaren)* is wonderfully subtle and refined. We were lucky enough to be enjoying the very first picking around Qing Ming, a festival in mid-spring when the leaves are most tender.

Reservations for banquets should be made a day in advance, but for smaller parties, half a day's notice is adequate. When ordering from the menu, expect to pay 60 to 80 yuan per person, depending on the dishes ordered. For full-scale banquets, add an additional 20 to 30 yuan per person.

WEST LAKE FISH

One of the most famous specialties of West Lake is a dish of freshly caught grass carp poached until flaky and doused with a hot-and-sour sauce made of black vinegar, finely shredded gingerroot, and red peppers. After the fish is caught, it is usually kept in a freshwater tank for a few days to flush the mud out of its system. Once cleaned, the gutted fish is butterflied but left joined in the center. It is then poached slowly in a wok until just flaky. Served in its pungent sauce, it is said by some critics to have the flavor of crabmeat.

Zhou Enlai was said to be particularly fond of this dish, and returned repeatedly to the Louwailou restaurant to sample this delicacy. Today, West Lake fish is found on the menus of restaurants all over China, but nowhere is it as delicious as in Hangzhou, the city of its origin.

SUCHUNZHAI GUAN (SUCHUNZHAI RESTAURANT)

—

30 Yan'an Lu
Tel.: 23235, 25239
Hours: 7:00 A.M.–8 P.M.

Along with the Linglin Temple, the Suchunzhai Restaurant is Hangzhou's best vegetarian eatery. Originally opened in 1919, it combined with two other vegetarian eateries in 1949, firmly establishing it as the foremost restaurant of its kind within the city limits. At first glance it might appear that the restaurant's decor hasn't changed much since then. The green tiles on the second-floor dining room walls are cracked, and slightly soiled calligraphy hangings add to the general drabness. The food, however, makes up for these imperfections.

The restaurant boasts a repertory of over two hundred meatless specialties, many offered according to seasonal availability. Some of the most outstanding dishes are the red-cooked mock chicken rolls *(hong shao juan ji)*, where bamboo shoot is substituted for the chicken; dry-cooked quail, fashioned from soybean milk sheets; and five-flavor fried chicken *(wu xiang yazi)*, resembling a whole chicken and stuffed with glutinous rice and numerous vegetables. Almost every dish is artfully presented and fragrant with pungent seasonings like ginger, garlic, sesame oil, and black mushrooms.

One of the most unusual signature dishes of the restaurant are its miniature mock Chinese hams *(su hou tui)* made from bean milk skins that have been braised, smoked, and pressed into delicious duplicates of the traditional Chinese ham shape. Suchunzhai also prepares vegetarian buns *(sucai bao)*, said to be the best in the city. Lines form at five o'clock every morning to buy them for breakfast or lunch, and so brisk is the demand that the restaurant sells out its daily production of five thousand by lunchtime.

Reservations should be made twenty-four hours in advance to allow preparation time for some of the special dishes. Meals run anywhere from 50 to 100 yuan per person, depending on the menu.

TAI HE YUAN JIUJIA (TAI HE YUAN RESTAURANT)

67 Renhelu
Tel.: 25193, 28250
Hours:
10:30 A.M.–1:30 P.M. (lunch),
4:00–7:30 P.M. (dinner)

Hangzhou has an interesting custom: the name of each restaurant is branded in shiny brass lettering across the steps of each stairwell on all floors of the eateries. So even though "Tai He Yuan" is not readily translated into English, after walking up the three flights of stairs to the second-floor dining room, the name may be permanently etched in your mind. But after sampling the fine food served here, you may agree that it *should* be.

The Tai He Yuan has been serving Hangzhou specialties for over one hundred years, and with a recent renovation, the second-floor dining areas have been transformed into lovely banquet rooms with artfully crafted wall bamboo sculptures. (The first floor is reserved for customers without reservations.) We discovered, to our surprise, that the newly decorated rooms as well as all recent renovations were the work of the manager Lu Kui De, a modest and gifted individual who has won awards for his vegetable carvings and *garde-manger* dishes. Lu began cooking in 1974 and quickly gained a reputation in the city as a master carver. Although on special occasions, he still wields a cleaver, he has capably managed the Tai He Yuan for the past ten years.

Under the name Xing Hu Caiguan the Tai He Yuan was originally situated on the shores of West Lake outside the city center. An imperial official who visited likened the design of the restaurant to a hall in the Summer Palace, renaming the eatery "Tai He Yuan" after the building in Beijing. During the Cultural Revolution, the restaurant was closed, and it finally reopened in its present location in 1985, quickly recapturing its outstanding reputation.

Like many restaurants in Hangzhou, the menu is seasonal, but the several noteworthy items on hand year round include Tai He duck, which is baked to a succulent tenderness. Xin Xin braised eel *(Xin Xin shan yu)* is a delectable stew that contains ham, spring bamboo shoot, and bean curd. (Both dishes must be ordered several hours in advance.) Paper-wrapped fish slices *(bo li yu pian)* are wonderful and unusual in their clear-wrapped cellophane that seals in the fresh fish juices. Stuffed peppers with shrimp and stir-fried peas with morsels of Jinhua ham also are commendable.

Reservations are necessary for this popular restaurant and should be made twenty-four hours in advance, particularly for a banquet. For a filling yet modest meal for four to six, expect to spend 50 to 80 yuan per person, but for a special banquet, the price per person might be closer to 100 yuan.

BEGGAR'S CHICKEN

The story of the origin of Beggar's Chicken has been told countless times, and perhaps embellished with new details at each retelling. According to legend, a highway robber was happily roasting a chicken, which he had just poached from a local farmer, over an open pit. Hearing footsteps in the distance and fearing the authorities, he quickly wrapped it in some leaves and buried it under the coals. After being interrogated and dismissed, he returned to his campsite, unearthed the package, opened it, and sampled its contents. The chicken had cooked to a succulent tenderness.

The modern-day version of Beggar's Chicken has been refined considerably. A whole chicken is stuffed with bits of meat, black mushrooms, and pickled vegetable, which provide considerable flavor. The bird is wrapped in lotus leaves, and then packed in a coating of mud. Baked for several hours, it is presented in its hardened clay casing accompanied by a hammer that is used to crack open the outer shell. The lotus leaves also are then removed, leaving an extraordinarily succulent chicken.

TIANWAITIAN
(HEAVEN BEYOND HEAVEN
RESTAURANT)
—

2 Tianzhu Lu
Tel.: 775450, 23001
Hours:
6:30–10:00 A.M. (dim sum),
10:00 A.M.–2:00 P.M. (lunch)
5:30–8:30 P.M. (dinner)

Directly at the foot of the path leading to the Lingyin Temple gates is the Tianwaitian Restaurant, where many foreigners stop, if only because it is the sole eatery in the area that can accommodate them. Don't expect a sedate meal here. The Tianwaitian is usually awesomely crowded, both in its large, rather appealing but plain dining room for local customers and in the smaller, attractively decorated banquet rooms. It's not unusual for a steady stream of small children and adults to stray into your private room throughout the meal.

If you are part of a tour group and arrangements have been made for a set lunch, you may be in for a disappointment: expect palatable but simple food. But if you do give the restaurant some advance notice and allow a little more money for the meal, you may see a vast improvement. The Tianwaitian, which first opened in 1911, does have a justified reputation for serving fine food, and as in many eateries in Hangzhou, the best dishes are the regional classics.

Deep-fried sweet-and-sour Squirrel Fish is excellent—the crisp, batter-coated whole fish bathed in a flavorful sauce. Deep-fried mock quail made with bean milk skins wrapped around shreds of bean curd, bamboo shoots, and black mushroom *(cui zha shuang que)* are superb. Dry-cooked fresh bamboo shoots *(you men chun sun)*, which are available in spring and summer only, are tender and fragrant in a light soy sauce–based dressing that accentuates the freshness of the vegetable. Chestnut chicken *(li zi chao zi ji)* is also worth sampling.

If you have a choice, try to dine on the upper floors (there are three), or at least take a peek at the small terrace on the second floor, which overlooks the paths leading to the temple. The third-floor extravaganza banquet room, with its dragon-motif relief ceiling, mirrored panel walls, and colorful ceiling disco lights, is a must-see. All rooms have been refurbished and redesigned in the past three years under the capable direction of Zhang Gen Xing, who is a third-level chef himself and whose late father was one of the most skilled cooks in the city of Hangzhou.

Because of the immense volume of the temple crowds, reservations for lunch are advised. If you are planning a special banquet for dinner, book about twenty-four hours ahead. Multicourse banquets will run approximately 80 to 100 yuan per person, with meals ordered from a menu generally costing about 40 to 60 yuan per person.

WEST LAKE WATER SHIELD SOUP

Water shield is the edible stem of a perennial water plant that grows in several lakes in China, but the best in the country is held to be that found in Hangzhou. It is prized for its unusual texture (the plant itself is covered with a clear, slippery skin) and is believed to be highly nutritious. Water shield is also prescribed for ailments of the lungs and stomach.

One of the most traditional versions of the soup is made with shredded ham and chicken. Other ingredients frequently used include fish and pork.

DONGPO PORK

—

The famed poet and statesman of the Song dynasty, Su Dongpo, was also quite a gourmand. He held office in Hangzhou and was respected and loved by his constituency, thanks to his successful efforts to clear West Lake and to build a dike. In gratitude, people brought Su gifts of pork, since it was rumored that he especially loved this meat. Su developed a special recipe and forever immortalized the dish by writing a poem that also served as a recipe:

> Over a slow fire,
> With a little water,
> Simmer till soft
> A very good taste.*

The same recipe is used today. The pork is braised in a covered clay pot for hours with soy sauce and seasonings. The finished meat is shaded a dark, brownish red and is tender as soft bean curd.

* *Su Tung Po*, translated by Burton Watson (Columbia University Press, 1965)

TIANXIANGLOU (HEAVENLY FLAVOR TOWER RESTAURANT)

—

166 Jiefang Lu
Tel.: 22038, 24538
Hours:
6:30–9:00 A.M. (dim sum),
10:30 A.M.–1:30 P.M. (lunch),
4:30–7:30 P.M. (dinner)

Located in the middle of Hangzhou, with six floors and four private banquet rooms, and the capacity to seat one thousand customers at one time, the Tianxianglou is one of the largest restaurants in the city. And plans for expansion are under way yet again, with new rooms to be added at the end of 1989.

As in many Chinese restaurants, the decor leaves something to be desired. One banquet room offers a rather bad attempt at French Provincial, with alternating yellow and rust paneling and crystal chandeliers. The bamboo motif of the "Penglui Fairyland" room is more appealing, with carved bamboo wall screens to separate the private parties from the rest of the customers.

Ambience aside, the Tianxianglou has built a solid reputation since its opening in 1927, as offering consistently good Hangzhou cooking. Special-first-level master chef Chen Shang Chang commands a full kitchen of first- and second-level cooks, and in the service department, the staff is equally impressive. Of the six first-level waitresses in the city, the Tianxianglou employs two. Several are even skilled enough to speak a fractured English and will recite the history of the more famous dishes. Fortunately, an English-Chinese menu is available with full-color pictures of the noted banquet specialties.

The outstanding dishes include many of the standard Hangzhou classics: West Lake fish, honeyed ham, shrimp with Longjing tea, stir-fried peas and Jinhua ham, and West Lake water shield with shredded chicken and ham. Beggar's Chicken here is particularly delicious—tender and rich with star anise and garlic. Su Dongpo pork is like butter (and almost as fatty) and nicely presented in individual small clay pots. The Four Treasure *shao mai* also are memorable.

For a party of six to eight people, a filling meal will average about 50 to 80 yuan per person. Tianxianglou also offers a special West Lake ten-course banquet extravaganza for 200 yuan per person. Reservations for all meals should be made twenty-four hours in advance.

XI'AN JIAOZI GUAN
(XI'AN DUMPLING HOUSE)
—

119 Yan'an Lu
Tel.: 23341
Hours:
6:30–8:00 A.M. (breakfast),
10:00 A.M.–1:00 P.M. (lunch),
4:00–7:30 P.M. (dinner)

If you have never had the indescribably spectacular experience of partaking of a dumpling banquet in Xi'an and you find yourself in Hangzhou, be sure to make reservations at the Xi'an Dumpling House. Opened in 1987, this restaurant is a joint venture between the Xi'an and Hangzhou catering companies. And judging from the meal sampled, the Hangzhou branch may even surpass its Xi'an cousin in terms of the variety and quality of the dumplings.

Don't be put off by the crowds in the downstairs dining rooms, and ignore the soiled carpet on the stairs. Instead, turn your attention to the framed hanging where many of the different dumplings are pictured and meticulously labeled. The repertory of dumplings number over one hundred, and the chefs rotate the varieties every ten days.

Although the second-floor dining room is not much more appealing, there is, under lock and key, one very attractive banquet room with two tables and mirrored mosaic and wooden walls. If you have made advance reservations, this is probably where you will be seated. (Don't be surprised if another party is seated in the room at the other table.)

The restaurant offers several levels of dumpling banquets. With a large party from ten to twelve, for 40 yuan per person, you can enjoy the 17 courses of dumplings; for 50 yuan per person, there are 20 different courses; and for 60 yuan, there is the grand imperial banquet with 23 different types of dumplings. If you have a group smaller than a full table, you may negotiate with the management concerning the price.

Some of the best dumplings sampled were the five-flavor dumplings, with a fragrant five-spice-powder-based filling; the black rice stuffed dumplings; the miniature fish dumplings, shaped like their name and filled with garlic chives and eels; the Buddha Opened His Mouth dumplings, with a vegetarian stuffing of garlic chives and eggs; and crystal steamed dumplings with sweet, sugary filling. Each dumpling is fashioned into different shapes and served in a massive bamboo steamer. The meal ends with a fiery finish: the last course of every banquet, even the least expensive, is a firepot served in an ornate, Sterno-fueled brass pot that contains boiling broth and is accompanied by seafood and vegetables. The diner dips the ingredients in the pot briefly to cook.

Service is excellent, and our charming waitress did speak enough English to recite several stories concerning the dumplings. Once reservations are made at least twenty-four hours in advance, the restaurant will automatically select and prepare the proper number of dumpling courses.

STIR-FRIED SHRIMP WITH LONGJING TEA

It is thought that the Chinese began planting Longjing, or Dragon Well, tea near Hangzhou as early as one thousand years ago. Then as now it was considered one of the finest varieties of green tea in the entire country. Of its sixteen grades, the best is picked before the Festival of Pure Brightness, Qingning, in late March and early April, shortly after the first leaves appear.

Many Chinese cooks also believe that early spring is the best season for lake shrimp, and the timing of these two factors probably provided for the inspiration for creating the classic dish of stir-fried shrimp with Longjing tea.

Only the highest grade of male shrimp is used. They are lightly marinated and stir-fried over a searing fire to bring out their inherent flavor and crisp texture, then lightly sprinkled with the first picking of the green tea leaves. The dish is masterfully simple yet delicate.

NINGBO

After an exhausting eleven-hour train ride on a dark and gloomy day, we reached Ningbo. By the time we arrived at our hotel, the sky had opened and the rain washed down in endless sheets. An hour later, the showers had abated briefly, enough to tour the city, which was small and seemed relatively undistinguished.

After a brief nap, however, things looked up. The skies cleared and we were taken to the largest free market in the city, a huge flea-market affair with stalls overburdened with every conceivable object one could imagine. Piles of stone-washed denim jeans and jackets greeted us at the entrance, but not far back, tables were filled with a colorful selection of vegetables: bundles of leafy greens, huge winter bamboo shoots together with tender spring

shoots, the first of the season, and piles of cultivated and wild mushrooms. Nearby, whole fish, their eyes still clear and bulging, glistened on tables, surrounded by massive piles of five different varieties of shrimps. Fresh scallops, squid, cuttlefish, and clams were all in abundant supply.

It is hardly surprising that Ningbo's markets are brimming with seafood, since it is surrounded by water. Situated at the meeting point of three rivers, two of which empty into the East China Sea, it has been a prominent port since ancient times. Because of its subtropical climate and lush surrounding countryside, the land yields plentiful supplies of rice, tea, and numerous varieties of produce.

Like that of its neighbors Shanghai and Hangzhou, Ningbo's cuisine is typical of eastern regional cooking. Dishes are subtle and delicate, and light sauces and mild seasonings serve to accentuate the flavor of the high-quality, fresh ingredients. Seafood—including eel, croaker, crab, turtle, and razor clams—dominates the menus at most restaurants, but chicken and pork, often steamed, stir-fried, or red-cooked, are also popular.

As in Shanghai, plump steamed dumplings bursting with flavorful juice, and thin, crisp spring rolls are relished. Ningbo is also famous for its rice dumplings *(yuan xiao)*, which are filled with ground sesame seeds and sugar and served in a simple sweet soup. The people of Ningbo believe that the dumplings endow the diner with good luck, and so they are always eaten at Chinese New Year.

I tasted the famous dumplings of Ningbo in a tiny dumpling shop in the center of town. Their exterior was smooth, soft, and slightly gummy, as sweet rice-powder skins tend to be. The filling was nutty and sweet, rich with the flavor of roasted sesame seeds. My research assistant and I had two bowls apiece; we ate one for luck in the coming year and another extra serving in hopes of good luck for all the years to come.

NINGBO FANDIAN
(NINGBO HOTEL)

—

65 Ma Yuan Lu
Tel.: 66334
Hours:
7:15–9:00 A.M. (breakfast),
11:00 A.M.–2:00 P.M. (lunch),
5:30–10:00 P.M. (dinner)

In the small city of Ningbo, some of the most consistently good food happens to be found in hotels.

The dining room at the Ningbo Hotel may be slightly cavernous with a nondescript decor, and at peak times, the service may be sluggish, but the kitchen can rise above these drawbacks and produce some excellent dishes. The hotel offers the usual local specialties such as sugar-crystal turtle, deep-fried croaker coated with algae, stir-fried eels, scallion-oil squid, and egg soup with clams. Spicy Ma Po bean curd and stir-fried vegetable hearts lightly dressed with sesame oil also are worth trying. Unfortunately the steamed dumplings were doughy and dry, and you should alert the chef if possible to avoid using any MSG. (They will still use a small amount, but at least your food will be edible.)

We ordered directly from the Chinese-English menu, and prices were quite reasonable, averaging about 15 to 20 yuan per person. No reservations are necessary. Banquets are said to be quite good, but expect to pay about 80 yuan or higher per person. Reservations should be made twenty-four hours in advance. Visa, Diner's Club, MasterCard, and American Express are all accepted.

NINGBO HUAQIAO FANDIAN (NINGBO HUAQIAO HOTEL)

---

130 Liuting Jie
Tel.: 63175
Hours:
7:00–9:00 A.M. (breakfast),
11:00 A.M.–2:00 P.M. (lunch),
5:30–10:00 P.M. (dinner)

Some thirty years ago the Ningbo Huaqiao opened to great fanfare as what was then the largest hotel in the city. Today, foreign visitors may prefer to stay at the Ningbo Hotel or the new Asia Garden, but the Ningbo Huaqiao is still rated as the number-one restaurant in the city, and it is the choice of the local resident and knowledgeable visitor alike as the place to go for a fine banquet.

Although not overly large, the dining room has a preserved wooden trim and an elegant, charming fifties feel. Waitresses in high-necked burgundy blouses and slim black skirts are sweet and helpful, as well as being prompt and efficient. Assistant Manager Li Yi, who in a former life was a chef, is often seen running about the dining room, recommending special dishes to customers, overseeing the service, and keeping an eye on the food preparation in the kitchen. As a result, the Huaqiao is a very well-run place.

The food is no less exemplary. Spring rolls are pencil thin, crisp, and chock full of shredded pork and garlic chives. Seafood here is fresh and well prepared. Steamed crabs are outstanding, as is the yellow croaker with bean curd skin *(fu pi bao huang yu)* and the fish-flavored fresh scallops *(yu xiang xian bei)*. Although not considered a Ningbo specialty, diced chicken with chili sauce and peanuts *(geng bao zhi ding)* is tender and saucy with just the right amount of spiciness. Pan-fried dumplings shouldn't be missed.

Since the dining room is rather small, reservations are recommended. They should be made at least the morning before if ordering from the menu, and the day before for a banquet. Expect to spend about 40 to 60 yuan for a simple meal and 80 to 100 yuan for a full-scale banquet, especially if you are ordering the Ningbo specialties of turtle and eel. Most dishes on the menu are available in several sizes, with corresponding prices depending on the size of the party. The menu is available in Chinese and English.

NINGBO JIAOZI GUAN (NINGBO DUMPLING SHOP)

—

37 Zhong Shan Lu
Tel.: 64514
Hours: 6:30 A.M.–10:30 P.M.

The sweet rice dumplings of Ningbo, with their crushed sesame filling and clear syrup broth, are famous throughout China, and have a history as impressive as their reputation. Culinary experts estimate that sweet rice dumplings *(tang yuan)* were first eaten in the Tang dynasty, some fourteen hundred years ago. Today, you can find these dumplings all over the country, but many (even nonresidents) will contend that nowhere is the flavor of the filling (and the soup) so fine as in Ningbo. And if you are in the mood for an adventure, the place to try *tang yuan* is at the Ningbo Dumpling Shop on the main boulevard of Zhong Shan Road.

The shop is quite small, consisting of two dining rooms. To the right, conditions are primitive: simple tables with wooden stools are arranged haphazardly in a small, rather gray area. Customers hunch contentedly over their soup, unceremoniously spooning the contents into their mouths. Steamed dumplings in large bamboo steamers and sweet glutinous rice soup are also offered. To the left, in the other room, customers relax in worn wooden booths. Coffee, fried noodles, soupy noodles, and a limited selection of basic local dishes are sold. According to the manager, during peak dining hours, reservations are often necessary for this room.

Probably the best idea is to go at a nonpeak time, settle yourself into one of the wooden booths, and order a bowl of the sweet dumplings with sesame filling. The price per bowl is under 1 yuan.

NINGBO JIUJIA (NINGBO GREAT RESTAURANT)

—

82 Zhong Shan Dong Lu
Tel.: 66020
Hours:
7:00–9:00 A.M. (breakfast),
10:30 A.M.–1:30 P.M. (lunch),
4:30–7:30 P.M. (dinner)

Sitting squarely in the downtown section of Ningbo on one of the main boulevards is the Ningbo Great Restaurant, a highly regarded eatery in this small city. The first floor has a small dining room off to the right with attractive wooden tables and bamboo chairs, but as a foreigner, you will most likely be turned away and directed up the stairs to the third floor, through the doorway with the impressive sign reading

"Local Flavor Dining Room" (Fengwei Canting).

With its six tables the room is clean but rather plain, a marked contrast to the tall, regal-looking upright chairs covered in burgundy velvet. The starched linen tablecloths have a fleur-de-lis pattern, and a broad window along one wall affords customers a murky view of the street activities. But appearances aside, the Jiujia offers impeccably prepared local dishes, a feat it has been accomplishing since its opening in 1958.

For our first visit, we found other customers in the dining room, so after studying their selections, consulting with the waitresses, and badgering a local culinary historian for information, we made our choices. Although crystal sugar mud turtle was strongly recommended, we demurred, especially after discovering that advance reservations were necessary. All the dishes we did order arrived quite promptly, were steaming hot, and above reproach in the flavor department. The stir-fried eels were among the best we had ever tasted—fresh, tender, and redolent of garlic and ginger. Deep-fried croaker with a light batter sprinkled with algae was flaky and light. The algae had a very pleasant, slightly briny flavor. The sweet meat from the steamed baby crabs was bursting with flavor, although it required some patience to extract the meat from the shell. Other recommended dishes are the stir-fried crab with eggs, algae-coated pork cubes, and black mushrooms with vegetable hearts.

Reservations for small parties are usually unnecessary, whereas banquets should be booked twenty-four hours in advance. Prices for a banquet should run about 50 to 80 yuan per person, and if ordering directly from the menu, they should be about 40 to 60 yuan for a party of four to six.

WANG HU QIAO CAI SHICHANG
(WANG HU QIAO MARKET)
—

There are markets and there are markets. In one of the most unlikely of locations in China, one can find a huge combination free market–flea market filled with clothing, sundry items, and all types of food. The market, which opened in 1987, is so impressive and unexpected in this small city that it was included in the schedule for the official visit in 1987 of Zhao Ziyang, the former Premier of China.

At the entrance of the formidable tunnellike structure (constructed of a plastic material that creates an open, airy effect) are stall after stall of virtually every item you could think of, plus a few more. One table is devoted just to zippers, holding every conceivable color, shape, size, and weight. And all shopkeepers seem to welcome—if not expect—bargaining, so you can have a good time and possibly get a decent price on some items.

Farther on, in the middle of the market, are the vegetable and fruit vendors, interspersed with seafood and meat counters. The produce tables are piled high with the fresh offerings of the season: spring and summer offer huge bouquets of leafy greens. Bright purple eggplants vie with green gourds, fresh mushrooms, and tender bamboo stalks. The fruit is equally varied and colorful. Since Ningbo borders the sea, there is no lack of variety in the sea products: fresh and hard-shell crabs energetically wave their claws and scurry about in woven baskets. Three or four varieties of fresh shrimp are arranged in piles next to tin tubs of swimming eels and sluggish turtles. There also are tables covered with huge piles of dried shrimp, each with four or five varieties arranged according to weight and quality.

Still farther on are cages of live chickens, cackling away, and next to them are rows of freshly slaughtered cuts of pork, each arranged artistically to show it to best advantage.

The market aisles are fairly clean (though they might be muddy if there has been any rain), and purveyors are curious but friendly. In short, there's almost something for everyone, and the sheer quantity of items is a testament to the growing economy and lush climate of this eastern seaport.

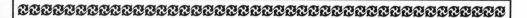

NANJING

Although situated picturesquely along the southern banks of the Yangtze River with a colorful backdrop of the Purple Mountains (Zijin) towering to the east, Nanjing may not be a place that impresses you immediately. Certainly it does not have the stunning beauty of Hangzhou or the frenzied energy of Shanghai. It is a city that seduces its visitors only gradually. The broad tree-lined avenues with their carefully manicured parks, the warm, generous attitude of its people, and the unhurried pace of this city will quietly win you over. All combine to create a relaxed, gracious atmosphere.

Nanjing is located squarely in Jiangsu province in southeastern China, an area that was inhabited as early as six thousand years ago. It first became prominent in A.D. 220, when it became the capital of China, a position it sustained for over 350 years. In addition to its political importance, Nanjing was an economic stronghold, owing to its prime location as a trade center linking it to the South Seas. The city also boasted ten steel foundries, including the first in China. And artistically and culturally the city offered handicrafts (particularly pottery and weaving), which became one of its trademarks, and a large group of poets, writers, and painters.

After a turbulent period when civil unrest prevailed and the capital was moved, Nanjing again was reinstated briefly as the center of power during the beginning of the Ming dynasty (1368–1644) as an "adjunct capital" to Beijing. It was at this time that the city was first named Nanjing (which means southern capital) and designed with the dimensions of its inner city outlined by the Ming walls, which still stand today.

In 1911, Nanjing played a vital role in modern Chinese history when it became the site of the election of Sun Yatsen as president of the Republic of China at the end of the Qing dynasty. Since then the city has seen its share of hardship. In 1927, Chiang Kaishek established the Guomindang provisional government in Nanjing, where it remained until 1938. Although Chiang anticipated a Japanese attack and moved his troops, the Japanese devastated the city, raping its citizens and looting their property, and occupied Nanjing until 1945. It took years for the city to recover from the war, but today it is thriving.

Nanjing's cuisine reflects the strong influences of the eastern regional school. Seasonings are light. Because of its mild climate and proximity to the Yangtze River and other bodies of water, all types of fish, eel, shrimp, and turtle are abundant and are most often lightly stir-fried or steamed to highlight their freshness. Pressed, salted duck and steamed crab are local specialties.

Chefs also are well versed at making elaborate and delectable dim sum: at the Yongheyuan Jiulou (Everlasting Peace Restaurant) in the heart of the Old City, in a traditional teahouse setting complete with smoked glass lanterns and bold-brush calligraphy hangings, customers giggle with delight as they consume puffy steamed buns filled with pork, chicken, and bamboo, jade-colored open-face dumplings, and flaky sesame cakes. But few are too full to leave any drops of the last course, another classic Nanjing delicacy: bowls filled with a fragrant chicken soup garnished with threads of shredded bean curd and bits of chopped shrimp.

BAIYUAN CANTING
(BAIYUAN RESTAURANT)
—

Liangzhou Isle, Xuanwu Lake
Tel.: 632745, 631903
Hours: 10:00 A.M.–8:00 P.M.

One of most scenic settings in Nanjing for a meal is the Baiyuan Restaurant, located on Xuanwu Lake in People's Park. Formerly an imperial preserve, the park was first opened to the public in 1911. The large lake, which measures about seven miles in circumference, is dotted with five islets, many of which are now connected by stone bridges or causeways. On the Liangzhou Isle, set apart in a sheltered corner of the park, is the Baiyuan. Until 1955 customers reached the restaurant by boat, but now a road runs to its entrance, making travel slightly easier.

The first floor of the restaurant is a combination snack bar–cafeteria. During most of the day, chaos reigns as sightseers with small children and grandparents in tow gather at the tables to partake of picnic lunches they may have prepared at home or snacks purchased on the premises. The food offered is not worth mentioning, and one would do far better to set down a blanket outside and enjoy the serenity of the lake.

Upstairs on the second floor, the atmosphere changes dramatically in the rambling private dining rooms with broad balconies that overlook the water. Each room has floor-to-ceiling windows with doors leading out to a terrace so that diners may stroll out and view the scenery while dining. The banquet tables are placed in the center of the room and surrounded on most sides by sofas and overstuffed chairs for relaxing before or after the meal. While the decor is slightly funky, a sense of formality remains, perhaps a legacy of the state functions held here since the fifties.

Although the service could stand improvement, the Baiyuan earns high marks for its food. According to the manager the kitchen employs five first-level master cooks, one second-level chef, and twenty third-level cooks—an impressive number for any restaurant. And the seafood, which is featured prominently on the menu, is very fresh and treated with a subtle hand. Stir-fried eel (chao shanyu) is excellent, as are the fish fillets with a spicy chili topping (douban bai yu).

Other noted dishes include the sweet-and-sour whole fish *(tang cu huo li yu)*, dry-cooked fish *(gan shao zhi yu)*, stir-fried scallops with vegetables *(bai zhi xian bei)*, and a fresh "milky" fish soup *(nai zhi jiyu tang)*.

Reservations are essential and should be made twenty-four hours in advance. The restaurant prefers to plan the menu, on the basis of the available ingredients, but customers can make suggestions. For a party of six to eight, plan on spending about 60 to 80 yuan per person.

JIANGSU JIUJIA
(JIANGSU RESTAURANT)

—

126 Jiankang Lu
Tel.: 623698, 625632
Hours: 6:00 A.M.–7:30 P.M.

Local culinary authorities recommend the Jiangsu as the best restaurant in town serving Nanjing specialties, and since its opening some forty years ago, this restaurant has employed a roster of cooks who have been celebrated in the city for their expertise. The Jiangsu is owned and operated by the city's catering company, which also runs a chef's training school, from which it plucks the best graduates to work in the kitchens.

The restaurant is huge, with a seating capacity of one thousand customers. Walking through the mazelike series of interconnecting dining rooms, you can easily lose your way, and during the peak dining hours, the atmosphere is best described as chaotic. Every room is mobbed, children run free, and at times, the cigarette smoke is as thick as fog. The private dining rooms for foreigners are much more sedate and quite pleasant, so make certain to book in advance.

In keeping with many of the basic tenets of the Nanjing style, the Jiangsu offers excellent roast duck *(jing lin kao ya)* that is dramatically presented on a pitchfork-type skewer, baked to a burnished bronze color. The skin is crisp and, like Peking duck, it is eaten in Mandarin pancakes with a smear of sweet bean sauce. The meat is served in another dish shredded and stir-fried with bamboo shoots, fresh garlic, and gingerroot. We were told that the different parts of the duck can be used in one hundred different dishes. Braised eel also is superb, served in a fanlike shape with sweet, whole garlic cloves, also cooked in the braise. On the more delicate side, a mousseline of fish with bits of black mushroom shaped into a lotus leaf *(he lian yi jia)* is fragrant and refined. The snacks, vegetarian dumplings *(su jiaozi)* and sweet buns filled with apple *(ping-guo bao)*, are beautifully seasoned and light.

Bookings should be made twenty-four hours in advance, and it would be wise to pre-order certain dishes at the same time. The cost of a filling meal for six to eight people will be about 40 to 60 yuan per person.

LULIUJU SUCAI GUAN (GREEN WILLOW VEGETARIAN RESTAURANT)

248 Taiping Nan Lu
Tel.: 643644
Hours:
10:30 A.M.–1:30 P.M. (lunch),
5:00–7:30 P.M. (dinner)

In 1911, when the Luliuju Vegetarian Restaurant first opened in a temple, few took notice. But after 1927, when Nanjing became the capital city of the Guomindang government, word began to spread that the kitchen was capable of producing mock meat creations that were even more flavorful than the originals. In 1962, the restaurant moved to its present location, where master chef Chen Bing Yu reigned for ten years, reestablishing its premier standing. Today, Chef Chen's legacy continues as the kitchen employs one first-level chef and four second-level cooks, but there is a new dimension to the menu: because of many Muslim customers, Luliuju has added an impressive number of Muslim dishes. Still, you would do well to stick to the meatless menu, since the kitchen has a reputation for using very fresh ingredients, one of the keys to fine vegetarian cooking.

Luliuju is small and quite plain, but it is clean. The second-floor dining room has simple wooden paneling with 1960s flavor. Waitresses are warm and try to be helpful even though they do not speak English. Although it offers the usual vegetarian Chinese favorites, some are particularly outstanding: the mock eels (su shanyu), meatless ham (su huotui), and vegetarian buns (sucai bao) are all excellent. Also recommended are vegetarian whole fish (su dao yu), mixed vegetables (luohan cai), and mock Eight Treasure duck (Ba Bao ya).

For those desiring a completely vegetarian meal, reservations are mandatory, but since space is limited, make them for any type of meal. Calls should be made twenty-four hours in advance. Prices are very reasonable: for a filling vegetarian banquet, the cost will be about 50–60 yuan per person for a party of four to six.

MAXIANGXING CAIGUAN (MAXIANGXING MUSLIM RESTAURANT)
—

5 Zhongshan Bei Lu
Tel.: 305807
Hours:
10:30 A.M.–1:30 P.M. (lunch),
4:30–7:30 P.M. (dinner)

According to local culinary experts, there is a major difference between southern Muslim cooking and its northern counterpart, and that is the heavy use of beef rather than lamb. This leaning is especially evident on the menu of Maxiangxing, which has been a fixture in Nanjing for 150 years. Originally, the restaurant began humbly as a small stand selling noodles and vegetables over rice. Today, the menu offers traditional Muslim-style dishes as well as regional recipes featuring chicken, seafood, and eggs.

The Maxiangxing is a bustling, smoky place. During most meals, the rooms are packed with customers, and often tables are even added in the hallway along the stairs. You've probably never seen anything like the decor: it's not often that shocking pink and turquoise are combined to grace the walls of a restaurant. Private rooms off the main room are labeled with Islamic names, a reminder of the restaurant's roots.

Specialties include main entrees and dim sum. Sweet-and-sour Mandarin fish (songshu yu) is nicely filleted, scored, and presented in a tart sauce. Egg shao mai, or open-face dumplings, are almost a meal in themselves with their fragrant filling. Fried beef (xiang gu niurou) turned out to be a tasty but heavy meatloaf-type affair with an egg stuffing, dotted with tomato sauce. The vegetarian ham (su huotui) is also recommended. For dim sum, there are Ten Treasure vegetarian buns (shi jin sucai bao), steamed beef buns (niurou bao), and steamed shrimp dumplings (xiarou zheng jiao).

Since the place is so popular and to allow the restaurant appropriate time to prepare some of its best dishes, reservations should be made about twenty-four hours in advance. Most meals will cost approximately 40–50 yuan per person for a party of six to eight.

NANJING FANDIAN
(NANJING HOTEL)

—

259 Zhongshan Bei Lu
Tel.: 34121
Hours:
11:00 A.M.–1:30 P.M. (lunch),
5:30–9:30 P.M. (dinner)

With its spacious grounds and walled-garden lawn, the Nanjing Hotel is another attractive option for dining. Almost in spite of its rather grand but somber Soviet-style architecture, it has become an institution, and its restaurant has built a consistent reputation for serving fine food.

A new restaurant building has been under construction for some years; the old dining hall is a rambling affair set on two floors. The decor is simple, but attractive with lovely wooden paneling and muted Chinese watercolor paintings.

The menu, in Chinese and English, is quite varied. Featured are the traditional Nanjing specialties of roast duck, Nanjing salt duck, baked shad, and flattened eel, accompanied by a number of dishes from other regions such as Squirrel Fish, crispy-skin duck, stir-fried chicken in chili sauce with peanuts, and Ma Po bean curd. The pan-fried dumplings are recommended and fried noodles—crisp on the outside and tender inside —with mushrooms and vegetables also are quite flavorful. Most dishes are available in different sizes depending on the size of the party.

Service is efficient, and several of the waiters speak passable English. Reservations are unnecessary unless you are ordering a banquet in advance, which will cost approximately 80 to 100 yuan per person. For those ordering from the menu, prices are much cheaper and average about 40 to 50 yuan per person.

SICHUAN JIUJIA
(SICHUAN RESTAURANT)
—

171 Taiping Nan Lu
Tel.: 646651
Hours:
11:00 A.M.–1:30 P.M. (lunch),
5:00–7:00 P.M. (dinner)

One would hardly expect to find superb Sichuanese fare in Nanjing, but that is the case at the Sichuan Restaurant, one of the city's most popular eateries. A testament to the success of the business is the construction going on in back of the restaurant. If building goes according to plan, the Sichuan will become the largest restaurant in Jiangsu province, with six floors.

Recognizing the lack of a Sichuanese eatery, the Nanjing Catering Company, which oversees most of the city's restaurants, decided to do something about it. In 1959 it contacted the Chengdu Catering Company and established a joint-venture project. Selected Nanjing chefs were then sent to Sichuan province for training. Once their schooling was complete, they returned armed with native seasonings and opened the restaurant.

Given the refinement and discreet seasoning of eastern regional cooking, one might assume that the chefs would tone down the flavoring to suit their local clientele. But it appears that Nanjing residents like spicy seasonings as much as the Sichuanese: the dishes we tasted hardly lacked fire. All the traditional Sichuan specialties are offered here: *ma la* beef *(ma la niurou)*, Ma Po bean curd *(Ma Po doufu)*, dry-cooked carp *(gan shao guiyu)*, and stir-fried chicken with peanuts *(gong bo ji hua)* are highly recommended. The crisp-fried duck *(xiang su ya)*, and snacks such as chili oil dumplings *(hong you shuijiao)* and *dan dan* noodles *(dan dan mian)* also are memorable.

Since the restaurant is so popuular, it is wise to book a table in advance—at least several hours before the meal. This is one restaurant where you won't be disappointed in the food by ordering directly from the menu. For a filling meal, the price will be approximately 40 to 50 yuan for a party of four to six. Banquets tend to run about 80 to 90 yuan per person.

NANJING PRESSED SALT DUCK

*T*hrough the years pressed salt duck has become synonymous with the city of Nanjing. Ducks are preserved throughout China, but nowhere is their flavor as fine as in Nanjing. The city's streets are dotted with shops and stalls offering this specialty because no Chinese tourist would think of leaving without a plump, pressed duck or two to take back home as a souvenir.

With a history of at least three hundred years, Nanjing ducks were called tribute ducks during the Qing dynasty, since each year local officials would cull the finest specimens from the first batch of ducks preserved to present as a tribute to the imperial household.

For traditional Nanjing pressed duck, birds raised between early winter and midspring are used exclusively. They are then salted, pressed, and dried completely. In this form the duck will keep almost indefinitely. The traditional method for preparing the duckling for eating calls for the duck first to be soaked in cold water for four to six hours to remove the salt. The duck is then placed in a pot of cold water with seasonings such as scallion, gingerroot, and star anise and simmered for at least 1½ hours, with the water and seasonings discarded and replenished two or three times during this period. Finally, once cooled, the duck is cut and served cold or at room temperature as an appetizer.

YONGHEYUAN JIULOU (EVERLASTING PEACE RESTAURANT)

122 Gong Yuan Jie (Fuzimiao)
Tel.: 623863, 629206
Hours: 6:30 A.M.–8:00 P.M.

Set amid the grandeur of the recently restored Old City section of Nanjing is the stately Yongheyuan Restaurant. Several years ago, like its neighbors, the restaurant was refurbished to resemble a traditional Chinese teahouse. The wooden parquet floors now gleam, charming wooden lanterns with smoked glass hang from the ceilings, and bold-brush calligraphy hangings grace the walls. It is, in short, a stunning setting for any meal.

Founded in the 1930s under the original name of Xueyuan, or Snow Garden, the restaurant had its name changed briefly to Nanyuan (Southern Garden). In 1941 it was closed, until in 1949 it finally reopened under its present name, though its menu was restricted to teas and a variety of snacks. Today, although the Yongheyuan has broadened its menu with main dishes from Beijing and Yangzhou, it is still primarily the snacks

that draw customers from all over the country and abroad.

Nanjing dim sum share some common characteristics with snacks from other parts of China. The traditional puffy, light steamed buns are filled here with chicken, pork, and bamboo, or a variety of vegetarian fillings. Jade *shao mai* are stuffed with chopped leafy vegetables and eggs. Baked cakes *(bing)*, with their flaky crust and dusting of sesame seeds, are both sweet and savory: barbecued pork, chinese sausage, red bean paste, and chopped sesame seeds with sugar are among the choices for fillings. The Yongheyuan also makes a delicious rendition of the Nanjing salt duck, a local specialty that is boiled in salted water until tender. Also memorable is their chicken soup, garnished with shreds of bean curd and bits of dried shrimp.

With twenty-four hours' notice, a customer can partake of a dim sum banquet. With a full table of twelve people, for 8 to 10 yuan, you can sample nine different kinds of dim sum plus four cold dishes. (If you have a smaller number of people, the restaurant probably will negotiate on the price.) The types of snacks prepared depend on what is seasonally available. For those who would just prefer to sample off the menu, reservations are not absolutely necessary, but be prepared to settle for whatever the kitchen has on hand.

YANGZHOU

Do not expect too much excitement on a visit to Yangzhou. It is a calm little place whose beauty is understated, a city that has existed for 2,400 years and is famous for its gardens and pavilions. I had been lured to Yangzhou by the seductive descriptions in guidebooks. Since it lies at the meeting point of the Yangtze and Hua rivers, it is "an especially charming" town—so the books said —that attracted a host of rhapsodizing Tang dynasty poets. I was also curious about the town where Marco Polo had served as mayor from 1282 to 1285.

Yangzhou was smaller than I had expected, and its gardens were overgrown with weeds, and the walls of the pavilions were faded and crumbling. They were crowded with Chinese and Japanese tourists and had faded and slightly seedy looking fixtures. But I spent a relaxing and somewhat lazy two days there, browsing in the small shops that offered a fine selection of locally produced jade carvings and lacquered screens, and traveling happily by pedicab along the tiny lanes that crisscross the city.

I followed a tip from a local and ate at one of the city's best-known restaurants, an unpretentious but comfortable eatery that specializes in stuffed dumplings and buns. We were forewarned that half the town ate there for breakfast, which made eating next to impossible. So we arrived slightly later and watched the kitchen prepare for lunch: dozens of workers at different stations skillfully shaped blobs of dough, stuffing, folding and steaming until the dough was transformed into scores of perfectly pleated fluffy buns with sweet and savory fillings. We ordered a selection and ate to our hearts' content, dipping the savory varieties in pungent Zhenjiang black vinegar, a product made in a neighboring city and famous throughout China.

The next day, we traveled by ferry to Zhenjiang, enjoying a peaceful, sunny ride across the murky river. At the railroad station, the stalls were filled with the usual foods available for snacking on trains, but among the packages of peanuts and watermelon seeds were bottles of the famous Zhenjiang black vinegar for visitors to buy as a souvenir of their visit to the area. As the arrival of the departing train was announced, we watched as hundreds of passengers struggled with heavy bags and suitcases, but each one carefully carried what appeared to be a more precious cargo: a six-pack of the mellow Zhenjiang vinegar.

FUCHUN CHASHI (FUCHUN TEAHOUSE)

---

35 Deshengqiao
Tel.: 22314, 24326
Hours:
6:00–11:00 A.M. (dim sum),
11:00 A.M.–2:30 P.M. (lunch),
4:00–9:00 P.M. (dinner)

The Fuchun Chashi is not the easiest restaurant to locate, even in a city as small as Yangzhou. You must turn off the main road downtown, and walk a distance down a meandering alley filled with knife vendors and cookware stalls until you see a set of crumbling gates with the name in Chinese and English emblazoned in bright red letters on top. Finally, you have arrived at the most famous restaurant in the city.

As you walk through the gates, you may have to avoid one or two chickens wandering about looking for food, but just down the path is the outdoor dim sum area where customers gather to enjoy noodles and steamed buns. The Fuchun Chashi serves a full range of entrees, but it is the three-dice steamed buns *(san ding baozi)* filled with chicken, bamboo shoots, and diced pork that draws customers from all over the country, as well as Japan and Europe. The kitchen also produces five-dice steamed buns *(wu ding bao)*, glutinous *shao mai (nuomi shao mai)*, Thousand Layer Cake *(qian ceng gao)* and open-face jade dumplings *(fei cui shao mai)*.

So great is the business generated by these snacks that the downstairs kitchen has become a veritable *baozi* factory with dozens of employees who begin preparing the day's supply between three o'clock and four-thirty in the morning, depending on the season. If you walk into the restaurant, you can see them at work rolling out the dough and stuffing and pleating the buns. The rows of stacked bamboo steamers are mountainous, and workers move them on and off the fire with nimble speed and dexterity.

The Fuchun opened over a century ago as a teahouse, offering its own special brand of tea, which is served to this day. For the drink, Fuchun Chashi brews a unique blend of Longjing tea from Hangzhou, Kuizhen tea from Anhui province, and *zhulan* blossoms picked from trees located near the restaurant. Customers would come for a cup of this refreshing drink as well as a taste of the *tang gan si*, finely shredded bean curd served in a light broth and garnished with minced ham and dried shrimp. A few years later steamed buns were added to the menu, and the restaurant began to achieve its current fame.

Since business is brisk at dinner, many customers like to reserve tables for large parties and order a banquet in advance. The banquet dining room is plain but appealing with tall-backed chairs, somber burgundy drapes, clean linen tablecloths, and a large sign that sternly orders "No Litter." The regular main dining room is plainer still, with cement floors and slightly soiled tablecloths. Service is somewhat haphazard, but the help is friendly and accommodating.

Dinner reservations should be made twenty-four hours ahead and a banquet meal (which will include a mixture of main dishes and snacks) will cost about 50 yuan per person. If you just want to sample some of the dim sum, go early and order directly from the menu. The whole meal, with five or six dishes, shouldn't cost more than 30 yuan per person for a party of four to six.

LION'S HEAD

Lion's Head is a hearty soup consisting of ground pork meatballs and cabbage leaves. It is slow-cooked in a covered earthenware pot so that the flavors mingle, resulting in a rich stock. Today, it is a dish found in restaurants all over China, but it was invented in Yangzhou. The large meatballs are thought to look like a lion's head, and the cabbage leaves, which become wilted and slightly browned in the cooking process, suggest a lion's mane.

LIU YANG CUN JIULOU (LIU YANG CUN RESTAURANT)

—

34 Shan Yuan Lu
Tel.: 41767, 41198
Hours:
6:00–9:30 A.M. (breakfast),
11:30 A.M.–1:00 P.M. (lunch),
5:30–7:00 P.M. (dinner)

Reservations are not necessary at this no-frills restaurant located off one of the main streets in downtown Yangzhou. On the first floor, customers line up at the service desk located near the entrance, consult the handwritten menus posted on the wall behind, and order their meal, paying in advance. They then take a seat in the simple, plain dining room with wooden chairs and tables. Across the hall is a somewhat faded ballroom with red velvet drapes framing the stage and fold-up chairs for the band that plays there in the evening.

The second-floor private dining room for banquets and large parties is almost less attractive than the lower area, and each party must pay a 12-yuan fee to cover the service, but it does have one huge advantage: you don't have to stand in line fighting the crowds to order dishes. Waitresses will (after a while) come to serve you. Also, the upstairs menu is much more diverse, offering dishes such as fish head in earthenware pot *(shaguo yu tou)*; Lion's Head *(Shizi Tou)*, and hot-and-sour whole fish *(cu liu guiyu)*. All require advance ordering.

For an impromptu meal, try a flavorful dish like stir-fried chicken *(chao ji ding)*, which is nicely spiced with chili paste, garlic, and ginger. The restaurant's personal version of shredded bean curd *(tang gan si)*, which is found in almost all Yangzhou eateries, is excellent. Shrimp, wood ears, and bamboo shoots mingle with the finely shredded bean curd in a light sauce. Vegetables are fresh and seasonal, so you will have to consult to order what is available. A simple lunch or dinner for four to six will average about 30 yuan per person.

XIYUAN FANDIAN
(XIYUAN HOTEL)

■

1 Fengle Shang Jie
Tel.: 43511
Hours:
11:00 A.M.–2:00 P.M. (lunch),
5:00–9:00 P.M. (dinner)

Like many other large hotel dining rooms, the Xiyuan lacks any character in its decor, but the food can be quite good, and for foreigners who are in town briefly (most of the prominent sites of Yangzhou can be seen in a day or two), it is a convenient spot to sample some of Yangzhou's specialties. The menu is in Chinese and English; seats are almost always available; and the waitresses speak some English. Standard Yangzhou items include the three-dice steamed buns (tasty and filling, but slightly doughy); Lion's Head soup, a rich, cabbagey flavor; bean curd shreds; and crispy cakes *(xiang su bing)*. Other dishes worth sampling are the mushrooms with rice crust *(denggu guo ba)*, crispy-skin duck, and noodles with three delicacies.

For those desiring a banquet with dishes that require advance preparation, bookings should be made a day before. Expect to pay 30 to 40 yuan for a filling meal ordered directly from the menu and about 60 to 80 yuan for banquet dishes.

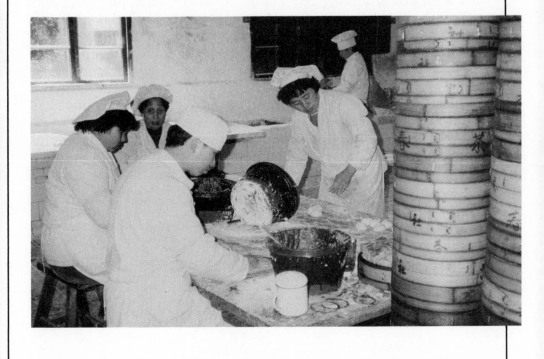

KAIFENG

Kaifeng was once an elegant and prosperous city, its streets alive with merchants and traders from all parts of China who flocked to the then-booming metropolis for the city's famous silks, textiles, and porcelain. It was the capital of China under the Wei (220–265), Five Dynasties (907–960), Later Liang (907–923), Later Jin (936–946), and Later Zhou (951–960), and finally reached its greatest glory in the Northern Song period (960–1127). But in 1126, Jurched tribes invaded the city, destroying its grand buildings and reducing it to ruins.

Today, little remains of Kaifeng's splendor, although the Chinese government is making an attempt to restore some of its former color by refurbishing the few remaining pagodas and building a replica of a Song city complete with inhabitants in period costumes. It is a small town, somewhat sedate, which does retain a flavor suggestive of ancient China, a flavor that is heightened by the ancient city walls, which still stand. The streets in the inner city are narrow and dusty and overshadowed by the tiny faded wood and stone buildings that were built many years earlier.

I had gone to Kaifeng curious to see the remnants of a city that in its heyday had once been described as a place that "combined the bustle and excitement of a great commercial city with the majesty which attended the residence of the Son of Heaven." *
And I had endured a long and bumpy ride to sample some authentic Song dynasty cooking, which was supposedly prepared as it had been some thousand years ago.

I did not find any great commercial city, but on a short, two-day trip I did meet with one of China's foremost authorities on Song dynasty cooking and as he wove his tales of delicacies that were

---

* From an essay on Song dynasty cooking by Michael Freeman quoted in K. C. Chang, *Food in Chinese Culture* (New Haven: Yale University Press, 1977).

prepared centuries earlier, we sampled some dishes that were true to their Song roots. We devoured a whole fish that had been rubbed with pungent seasonings and grilled until flaky over an open fire, and in a tiny dumpling shop, we gorged ourselves on scores of ornately folded dumplings, each one filled with a different sweet or savory center. It was several days before I had any desire ever to eat again.

DIYILU BAOZI GUAN (FIRST STREET DUMPLING HOUSE)

—

88 Xiang Guoa Si Hou Jie
Tel.: 24328
Hours: 10:00 A.M.–8:00 P.M.

The main street of Kaifeng is a bustling place. Shoppers linger on sidewalks gawking at the latest Chinese electronic gadgets and remnants of last year's fashions, the slick merchandise in sharp contrast to the old stone buildings that house the stores. In the center of town is a calligraphy shop with a window display of bold Chinese hangings, graceful brushes, and inkstones that creates a mood far more in keeping with the general tone of history pervading the city.

Next to the calligraphy store is a small dumpling house, modest by any standards, where the local people go for bamboo steamers bursting with pork dumplings. There is sawdust on the floor, and it isn't the cleanest place, but the dumplings are good, hot, and filling. And it's a chance to mingle with the local people who come here in droves.

Upstairs, there are two tiny "banquet" rooms (barely large enough to hold tables) where you can pre-order a dumpling banquet for 100 yuan per table. The meal consists of ten hot dishes with ten varieties of steamed dumplings—among them shrimp, chicken, garlic chives, bamboo shoot, sea cucumber, and water chestnuts. The most unusual and delicious filling is made with minced pork and hawthorn, a tart fruit with a somewhat cranberrylike flavor, though without the bitterness. The dumpling skins are thin, and the filling properly explodes with juiciness in your mouth.

YOU YI XIN FANZHUANG (ANOTHER VILLAGE RESTAURANT)

—

16 Gu Lou Jie
Tel.: 24986
Hours: 6:00 A.M.–9:00 P.M.

If you are visiting Kaifeng for a day and would like to sample a taste of Song dynasty cooking, be sure to visit You Yi Xin, one of the oldest restaurants in the city. First opened in 1912 under the name Zuo Shang Chun, by 1945 You Yi Xin was firmly established under its present name. Don't be put off by the rather ramshackle entrance, for this restaurant has produced a long line of noted master chefs, and if you make the proper arrangements, the kitchen can produce lovely food.

The majority of dishes offered here are regional Henan province and Song dynasty. Avoid, if possible, the main dining room, and head upstairs to the private room with the leaded glass windows and waitresses who don traditional costumes to serve you in the style befitting the food. One of the more unusual Song specialties offered here is a thin sheet made from the clear starch of the mung bean and filled with seafood, fish, or meat. At a recent meal, our cake was stuffed with sea cucumbers, minced black mushrooms, and shrimp. Whole fish also are prepared in the Song manner, rubbed with spices and grilled over a hot fire. The meat is tender, flaky, and redolent with the flavors of gingerroot and rice wine. Pork fillets are also delicious pounded until butter-tender and fried in sesame oil.

For special dishes, orders should be made twenty-four hours in advance. The cost for special dishes will be approximately 75 to 100 yuan per person, but the experience of tasting them is well worth the expense.

SONG DYNASTY COOKING:
AN INTERVIEW WITH SENG SHI ZHENG
▬

*F*orty-eight-year-old Seng Shi Zheng hardly looks the role of a culinary historian. His teeth are yellow and decayed, perhaps as a result of the endless stream of cigarettes that he chain-smokes daily. He is painfully thin, even though food is his passion and he is acknowledged as the foremost authority in Kaifeng—if not in China—on Song dynasty cooking.

Seng conducts his research from Kaifeng, because it is here, in this somewhat decayed city, that the Song dynasty reached its glorious peak some eight hundred years ago. Here, Seng picks among the remains, seeking out the clues of past times and dishes.

Seng began his career in food as a chef after graduating from middle school. He first worked at the celebrated You Yi Xin, the foremost restaurant in the city, in 1960, before moving on to other eateries, but it wasn't until 1972 that he began to research the Song style. Today he regularly consults with You Yi Xin, adapting authentic Song dishes for its menu, and also conducts some classes at the Kaifeng Eating Research Institute. He spends most of his time, however, in research, compiling information and recipes for what he hopes will soon be published in a book.

Seng is well versed on the glories of the Song period, an era that, in many historians' eyes, represented the Renaissance Age in China. "Abundance is the word that comes to mind when speaking of the foods of the Song," he says. "Pork, lamb, chicken, and beef as well as wild game were all widely available. Everyone also ate fish and all types of seafood, including scallops, clams, mussels, shrimp, and crab. And shark's fin, which is such a delicacy now, first became popular during this time. Vegetables too, of all varieties, were common ingredients, and fruit—fresh, dried, and preserved in sugar and honey—was a treasured food of the time.

"The primary condiments were soy sauce, vinegar, sugar, and honey, but the adventurous cooks of the period also used cumin, coriander, and other spices from the Middle East. Another Near Eastern import, cakes and pastries, also was a popular staple. Actually, all types of wheat-based products, including noodles, dumplings, and steamed breads, were in demand."

The city of Kaifeng, according to Seng, teemed with activity. Restaurants, teahouses, noodle shops all thrived, catering to a sophisticated and appreciative audience. Markets and all types of food stores were also bustling, packed with ingredients from all over China. There were few provisions that the Chinese gourmand lacked.

Seng also points out that, apart from some foods like the thick blood soups that were then relished, many of the Song dishes resemble eastern specialties prepared today, thus confirming the theory that the cooks of this time were the major influence in establishing the sophisticated style of eastern cooking that prevails to this day.

LUOYANG

Like Kaifeng, Luoyang is a city with a glorious past. But unlike its sister city to the west, which never regained its former prosperity, Luoyang is on the move, transformed by vitality and growth. Surrounded by fertile rolling hills, the city is immersed in construction, but the old town in the center still maintains a quaint, ancient facade with some houses and shops that have been standing as far back as the Ming (1271) and Yuan (1644) dynasties.

Luoyang, which literally translated means "north of the River Luo," has a history as old as Chinese civilization itself. It is believed to have been inhabited during Neolithic times (circa 6000 to 5000 B.C.), and like Kaifeng, the city has suffered through a turbulent past. It was the capital during the Eastern Han, Wei, Western Jin, and Northern Wei dynasties, enjoying its height of prominence during the latter periods, when it became a Buddhist center with over thirteen hundred temples.

The city was devastated, during the Sui dynasty (581–618) but was quickly rebuilt, with the addition of two major canals running through it, one linking it to Beijing and the other to Hangzhou. From this period through the Tang dynasty, Luoyang prospered as an educational and cultural center, attracting scholars and poets who were drawn to its famous imperial library. Ironically, as Kaifeng prospered in 937 during the Five Dynasties, Luoyang began a decline, which continued until the city almost completely disappeared. After Liberation the city began a period of revival and growth, and today it is not only an important industrial and agricultural center but also a popular stop on tourist itineraries.

One of its chief attractions are the Longmen, or Dragon Gate Caves, which are situated south of the city. Here, carved directly in stone on the sides of mountains and on the walls of over one thousand caves and grottoes are exquisitely detailed Buddhist images whose scope and splendor are absolutely breathtaking. I visited the grottoes on a lazy, hot afternoon when the sun beat mercilessly down, making the caves a cool haven. Like those around me, I forgot the outside world and was transported to the past by the vivid and lifelike figures, which had endured through hundreds of years.

I stepped back into the present with a jolt and I was then taken to a newly opened joint-venture eatery established with a Hong Kong firm. The slightly gaudy decor included gold chandeliers and a mosaic of mirrored panels covering several walls. Petite waitresses in short dresses wheeled carts, laden with hot Cantonese dim sum, and soon the tables were strewn with empty plates and cans of Coca-Cola.

A later meal brought me back to Luoyang's ancient past when I dined at one of the city's oldest restaurants and enjoyed a local specialty known as the "water dinner," which was the favorite meal of Empress Wu Ze Tian, who ruled from 684 to 705. We sampled some twenty-four dishes, each one more exquisite and flavorful than the last. Like the figures in the Dragon Gate Caves, these recipes have endured as a vital testament to Luoyang's remarkable history.

GUANGZHOU JIUJIA (GUANGZHOU RESTAURANT)

—

7 Jing Hua Lu
Tel.: 231123
Hours: 8:30 A.M.–8:30 P.M.

Before the arrival of Ya Xiang Lou, the Guangzhou was the premier Cantonese restaurant in Luoyang, and even now, many locals and foreigners still prefer this eatery. Recently, however, there have been rumors of unevenness. In order to give the Guangzhou a fair chance, it is imperative that you call several hours in advance, discuss the menu, select recommended dishes, and pay 70 to 90 yuan per person.

The makings for great food are certainly here. In its thirty-year history, the Guangzhou Restaurant has always enjoyed an excellent reputation, and its kitchen employs three first-level, two second-level, and more than twenty third-level chefs. Master chefs were imported from Canton to train the local cooks, and many are still in residence. And the kitchen can justly boast that the young woman who is in charge of the cold dishes is the number one cook in her field in Henan province.

Some of the suggested items to try are the salt-baked chicken, whole braised duck, seasonal stir-fried vegetables, and for those who are adventurous, the bamboo shoot, chicken, black mushroom, and snake soup. For those ordering special dishes, the cost should be about 70 to 100 yuan per person.

YA XIANG LOU (YA XIANG LOU RESTAURANT)

—

1 Anhui Lu
Tel.: 21997
Hours:
6:30–9:30 A.M. (dim sum),
11:30 A.M.–2:30 P.M. (lunch),
5:30–9:00 P.M. (dinner)

If you have been dreaming of a fluffy barbecued pork bun, hungering for a mouthful of steamed spareribs in black bean sauce, or craving some simple, honest Cantonese fare, look no further than around the corner from the Friendship Hotel to the Ya Xiang Lou. During the morning hours, the place bustles downstairs as locals enjoy drinking tea and partaking of dim sum.

Don't worry if there are no tables available when you arrive; rather than keeping you standing, the waiters will just go to a pile of rounds sitting in a corner, screw in some legs, and drag out a few chairs to accommodate you. The service here is quite efficient and friendly. Some even understood a bit of English.

This joint-venture eatery opened in the spring of 1988, and its original twelve head chefs were imported from Canton. They, in turn, trained the kitchen staff of local Chinese cooks. Today, some of the original crew still remains, and ingredients are flown in once a week from Canton.

For lunch and dinner, the menu changes to classic Cantonese dishes. There's fresh steamed fish and crab (in season), sesame chicken with oyster sauce, grilled pork, and Four Treasure braised duck. For those interested in some classic Cantonese delicacies, the menu features a full list of shark's fin and bird's nest.

A filling dim sum breakfast will cost about 8 to 10 yuan per person. Lunch or dinner with a group of four to six persons could easily run as high as 70 or 80 yuan, depending on the dishes ordered. The restaurant will accommodate customers on a walk-in basis, but it's probably wise to call several hours in advance to book a table, especially if you would like to order special dishes.

YOUYI BINGUAN (FRIENDSHIP HOTEL)

—

6 Xiyuan Lu
Tel.: 22159, 22049
Hours:
6:30–9:00 A.M. (breakfast),
11:00 A.M.–1:30 P.M. (lunch),
5:30–8:30 P.M. (dinner)

While hotel restaurant food is hardly the best fare to sample in any country, in China, it can be worse. For the most part, meals vary from mediocre to inedible. There are, however, a handful of places that provide consistently excellent food, and the Friendship Hotel is one of them (a welcome option in Luoyang, where your choices are quite limited). The Friendship is generally *the* hotel where all—or most—foreigners stay. With the completion of the new wing last year, guests are now given a choice of a chic room with all the modern conveniences or one of the old-fashioned, slightly run-down, but clean rooms in the original section. Everyone, however, still eats in the old dining room. The hotel employs six first-level cooks, and the Friendship is one of the most popular places in the city for business banquets.

If you are staying at the hotel with a group, you will be given a set-price meal with simple meat and vegetable entrées. You can also order

(continued)

from the menu, which offers the standard selections one finds on most hotel menus *(geng bao* chicken, crispy-skin chicken wings, black mushrooms with vegetables, and tomato sauce prawns). These dishes can be quite good, and you can upgrade the quality further by ordering some dishes in advance. Among the suggested local specialties, which require advance notice and may cost 80 to 100 yuan per person, are the braised monkey brain mushrooms, *yancai* soup, peony soup (originally named by Zhou Enlai on a trip to Luoyang), fried river carp in wine, and Spun Thread sweet potatoes.

When ordering special dishes, allow twenty-four hours. Otherwise, no reservations are necessary.

ZHEN BU TONG FANDIAN (ZHEN BU TONG RESTAURANT)

▬

359 Zhong Zhou Dong Lu
Tel.: 52338
Hours: 9:00 A.M.–8:30 P.M.

Zhen Bu Tong is, as its Chinese name implies, "like no other," for it is the only eatery in Luoyang where you can partake of the unusual regional specialty known as the "water dinner." While the restaurant has been in existence for only some sixty years, the water dinner is a ritual with a thousand-year history.

The origin of this unique meal is related to the geography and climate of the city: Louyang rests in a basin, bordered by mountains, and although the Yellow River flows south of the city, traditionally, the area is quite dry. To offset the aridity local chefs developed a meal consisting of sixteen hot dishes and eight cold dishes. Each of the sixteen entrées is made with a great deal of broth or liquid. Many are soups—hence the name —and the overriding flavors are hot and sour in some form.

The ingredients of each dish vary, depending on the season and the chef, but their serving follows a basic formula. Of the eight cold dishes that open the meal, four are made with meat and four are vegetarian. Of the sixteen main dishes that make up the bulk of the meal, four are very substantial, eight are "middle dishes" or less substantial, and four are considered "end dishes" or light fare that appropriately concludes the meal. Generally, each time a large platter is served, it will be followed by two smaller ones.

One of the most refreshing aspects of the water dinner (particularly if you have been sampling endless formal banquets) is its focus on fresh, common ingredients rather than on exclusive delicacies. Mock sea cucumbers are fashioned from mung bean starch sheets of vermicelli, and turnip is transformed into bird's nest. The flavor is delicious, and each course becomes an adventure.

Among the memorable dishes served recently for the water dinner at the Zhen Bu Tong were the following:

- *Luoyang yen cai*—a colorful soup pot containing a melange of meat, seafood, and vegetables including beef slices, squid, bamboo shoot, egg strips, and vermicelli noodles.
- *Luoyang ben di rou pian*—a soup made with shredded pork stomach, peas, black fungus, and bamboo shoots.
- *Suan xiang yu*—a whole clear-steamed fish smothered with shredded ginger and scallions and doused with tart vinegar.
- *Lao zi ji*—a small chicken steamed with star anise and soy sauce until tender and served in a rich chicken broth garnished with bamboo shoots and vegetables.

Since the cost of the water dinner is quite high (for foreigners, the price may vary from 500 to 1,000 yuan per table of twelve), most locals reserve it for a special occasion such as a birthday or wedding, or for the Spring Festival. Many even prepare the dinner themselves at home. Reservations should be made twenty-four hours in advance.

ZHENGZHOU

Zhengzhou is the picture of China's present. A booming metropolis located in the center of Henan province, Zhengzhou is significant to the tourist mainly because it is the midway point between the ancient cities of Kaifeng and Luoyang. And for those interested in martial arts, Zhengzhou is a relatively short distance from the Shaolin Monastery where monks become masters of these disciplines. An industrial center and important link in the country's transportation system, Zhengzou nevertheless does not have an especially unique character.

Zhengzhou has been described as one of the oldest and newest towns in China. Surrounded by the earliest settlements of Chinese civilization, Zhengzhou was one of the first cities to be built some 3,500 years ago during the Shang dynasty. But after an auspicious beginning, Zhengzhou barely progressed. Some argue that its backwardness was due to its close proximity to Kaifeng and Luoyang. The city experienced little significant growth until it was linked to the Beijing–Guangzhou railroad in 1923, and it was not until the 1950s that it began the upward curve that characterizes it today.

Like many travelers en route to other places who may find themselves in Zhengzhou, I spent several days there, relaxing and not really expecting much in the way of fine dining. But like their municipal leaders who are intent on growth and recognition for their city, Zhengzhou's chefs are also eager to establish culinary credibility. At a rather rundown restaurant that was in the process of renovation (and should never have been open to customers), we feasted on cold shredded chicken poached in its own juices and delicately seasoned with sesame oil, gingerroot, and scallions.

There were also sweet, tiny fried scallops lightly coated in a crisp batter. Finally, his face barely concealing his delight and excitement, our chef unveiled his masterpiece: a mousseline of bean curd shaped and steamed to resemble a South Sea Island paradise, complete with palm trees. It seems that even in the heart of China, culinary innovation is thriving.

JIU HUA YUAN (JIU HUA YUAN RESTAURANT)

■

Zhengzhou Huochezhan
(across from the train station)
Tel.: 26420
Hours: 8:30 A.M.–8:00 P.M.

Surprises often come in strange packages. Judging by appearances, one would hardly expect to sample a superb meal at Jiu Hua Yuan. Situated in a mini–restaurant complex, the restaurant is entered through a dingy stairway, but even that hardly prepared us for the construction within. A gaping hole lay open in the floor of the eatery, and random electrical wires lay about in snake-like clumps. We were led through the debris to the banquet room, which looked delightful—even with its sickly pea-green motif—but this reaction was only in contrast to the squalor in the dining room.

Despite these problems (which should be cleared up by the time this book is published), the food managed to overcome our initial despair. The Jiu Hua Yuan's head chef is in fact a member of the prestigious People's Congress committee, as well as one of the judges of the National Culinary Competition in Beijing. If you do go to this restaurant, by all means make reservations twenty-four hours in advance and discuss the menu. Insist on trying the *xian weir ji*, an unusual appetizer made with lightly poached chicken whose meat is shredded by hand into delicate strings and tossed in a light marinade of rice wine, scallions, gingerroot, and sesame oil. Also ask for the *qing zheng yu*, clear-steamed fish with a vinegar-pepper sauce poured on top. Our fish was fresh, flaky, and perfectly cooked—an ideal contrast to the light, sour sauce. The tiny fried bay scallops on skewers, *(xian bei feng wei xia)* and baby shrimp are also a good choice, as is the vegetarian *shao mai* (open-face dumplings.) The chef also makes a very delicate and unusual dish of steamed egg whites in the shape of palm trees with an accompanying vinegar-pepper serving sauce.

The banquet prices should be 80 to 100 yuan per person for six people, and reservations should be made at least twenty-four hours before the meal.

PLAZA REGENT HOTEL

—

Jin Shui Dadao Dong Lu
Tel.: 28046
Hours:
6:30–8:00 A.M. (breakfast),
11:00–1:30 P.M. (lunch),
5:00–8:00 P.M. (dinner)

Perhaps the poshest eatery in Zhengzhou is situated in the Plaza Regent Hotel, where you can expect all the amenities of a Hong Kong–style restaurant—well, almost all. To get to the restaurant, you must first pass through the Friendship store, beyond the pool hall, and up the stairs past the coffee shop, the Cantonese and Henanese restaurant on the second floor, and the western restaurant before coming to the private banquet rooms where advance parties are booked and served. For meals ordered on a walk-in basis, go directly to the second-floor restaurant.

The Plaza Regent Restaurant is a joint-venture operation between a Hong Kong company and the Henan International Travel Company. Its decor is slightly garish, and its prices are higher than at other local eateries. (Banquet dinners can easily cost 100 yuan per person.) Few natives venture here, but it is a popular spot for high-level government banquets. One night, our neighbors in the next banquet room were the president of Henan province and his invited guests.

There's every reason to expect the kitchen to produce great food. Master chef Chen Jin Chang, who oversees the kitchen, has a list of formidable credits. He has worked at the Great Hall of the People and the prestigious Fang Shan restaurant in Beijing. In May of 1986 he garnered gold and copper medals at the national culinary competition. Unfortunately, the food just did not meet our high expectations. Dishes were flavorful but not outstanding. One of the best tasting was a local dish made with rice and a sweet potato filling. Service is polished, and hygiene is better here than at most other local eateries. Book a table twenty-four hours in advance and encourage the chef to prepare less elaborate local specialties.

SHAOLIN CAIGUAN
(SHAOLIN RESTAURANT)

▬

Jinshui Dadao Dong Duan
Tel.: 52541
Hours: 8:30 A.M.–8:00 P.M.

For centuries, the Chinese have been regaled by tales of the Shaolin Temple, a mystical place about two hours by car from Zhengzhou where priests observe their sacred vows and practice the martial arts. To fuel their bodies for their rigorous training, they, unlike most other monks, eat meat. (Supposedly, permission for this indulgence was given to them by Li Shi Min, the second emperor of the Tang dynasty, who ruled A.D. 627–649.)

The Shaolin Restaurant in Zhengzhou takes its name and inspiration from this famous temple. Opened in 1981, it has become one of the most popular eateries in the city. The kitchen employs three special-level chefs and five second-class cooks, attesting to its potential.

Unfortunately, banquet dishes tend to be disappointing, emphasizing technique and appearance over flavor. The most successful dishes are the local specialties like the *min zhuan xiao chi*, a thin pancake garnished with Chinese chives, bean threads, chopped eggs, and flecks of fresh fennel. The flaky cakes with egg *(jidan bing)* also are unusual, and the steamed vegetarian *shao mai* are delicious.

Prices are quite reasonable (30 to 40 yuan per person for a full meal ordered from the menu, 80 to 90 for a full-scale banquet). Reservations should be made at least two hours in advance, and insist on some local specialties for the menu.

A NOTE ABOUT HENAN COOKING
■

A quick glimpse at a map of China will provide the first clue as to why most foreigners are unfamiliar with Henan and its cuisine. It is a small land-locked province, bordering seven other neighbors, and its location isn't exactly north, south, east, or west. It's definitely central, but. . . .

Describing the cuisine is just as difficult. When asked to list its predominant characteristics, a chef from the capital city of Zhengzhou replied: "Northern food is salty, the south is sweet, eastern cooking is sour, and the west is spicy, but here we are in the middle of the country, so the flavor is suitable to all tastes."

Henan cooking might best be described as a melting pot of Beijing, Cantonese, and Sichuanese, combining their ingredients and offering signature dishes from all three areas. Since the climate is moderate, like that of Beijing, wheat, peanuts, and corn thrive, and wheat-based products like steamed breads, noodles, and pancakes are staples for everyday meals. Despite its being land-locked, freshwater fish and other products are widely available and popular. Frozen saltwater seafood such as shrimp and scallops are shipped from the coast and play a vital role, but they tend to be expensive and less desirable than at the source. Vegetables thrive and are lightly cooked, as in the Cantonese style, to preserve flavor, color, and texture.

ZHENGZHOU BINGUAN (ZHENGZHOU GUESTHOUSE)

—

115 Deng Duan
Tel.: 22944
Hours:
7–8:30 A.M., (breakfast),
11 A.M.–1:00 P.M. (lunch),
5:00–7:30 P.M. (dinner)

At first glance, it will be apparent that the Zhengzhou has seen better days. The once glorious lobby is still grand, but in a slightly dilapidated way. The dining room in the restaurant hardly looks better, but sail on through into the "new" banquet wing, a fairly recent addition, where the ambience improves slightly.

When the Zhengzhou Guesthouse first opened in 1959, it was considered the premier hotel in the city. Since then, with the opening of the Plaza Regent next door, it has slipped a bit, but the kitchen still maintains a fine reputation. Chef Liu Chang Hai, who is considered by many as one of the foremost chefs in Henan province, keeps his staff under tight rein. The regular hotel food is simple but surprisingly good, and the banquet dishes can be excellent. (If you are staying next door and are unhappy with the food, you might just walk over to the Zhengzhou and order from the menu for a change of pace and scenery.)

Liu, whose father and uncle also were chefs, is a creative cook who has competed in national culinary competitions. One of his best dishes is deep-fried prawns coated in watermelon seeds. (The seeds have been peeled and have a crisp, nutty flavor.) *Teng zi ji* is not an original recipe, but this classic dish is prepared in impeccable style: a whole chicken is stuffed with spices and steamed for two hours until it is tender enough to dissect with chopsticks. The kitchen also delivers a fine red-cooked carp.

The regular menu consists of Sichuan, Hunan, and local dishes. Banquet dishes should be ordered twenty-four hours in advance, and the cost of a banquet meal with designated specialties is approximately 75 to 80 yuan per person with a party of six. For a simple dinner ordered from the menu, the price is 35 to 40 yuan per person.

FUZHOU

Having lived in Taiwan for three and a half years, I could hardly wait to visit Fuzhou, the capital city of Fujian province and the ancestral home of many of my Chinese friends from Taiwan. I was not even deterred when a Chinese Travel Service friend advised me to shorten my time in Fuzhou and add the extra days to my stay in Xiamen, a city to the south. "Fuzhou may be the capital, but it's an ancient city," he said. "Xiamen is by far the more captivating of the two."

As it turned out his advice would have been well-taken. Fuzhou is a small city with two distinctly different personalities. In the old sector streets are narrow and lined with tiny shops selling handmade bamboo pots and steamers, traditional Chinese musical instruments, and common household items. Because the Fujianese are a religious people, there are also an unusually large number of purveyors of brass incense burners, joss sticks, and bound packets of incense and (fake) paper money, which are used as offerings.

As you move away from the city center the atmosphere changes radically from that of a quaint Chinese village to a Las Vegas–like strip. High-rise hotels have been built here to accommodate the visitors who come to enjoy the famous hot springs. The landscape is cluttered with gaudy neon signs and shops selling schlocky handicraft items for tourists.

Fuzhou's historical roots date back to the sixth century, when it was founded by the Chen tribe. In the tenth century, it became the capital of an autonomous state known as Min Yue and by the Song dynasty (960–1279), it was a prosperous port, and remained so into the nineteenth century, when many European traders settled here. The city was bombed heavily during the Sino-Japanese War, and in 1948, it was taken over by the Communists. Since Fuzhou was designated as part of an Economic and Technical Development Zone in 1984, the city has seen an influx of foreign investment in the form of joint-venture enterprises.

Despite its schizophrenic personality, I managed to enjoy Fuzhou, leisurely riding by pedicab through the older sections and observing the comings and goings of daily life. I explored the superb downtown free market, astonished at the variety of fresh vegetables and seafood. In the early morning I strolled leisurely about the banks of West Lake, observing groups of elderly men and women gathering to chat or perform their morning exercise routines.

Since Fujian is a coastal province and Fuzhou has a reputation for fine seafood, I indulged in my passion and feasted on freshly caught fish steamed in its own juices with a sprinkling of finely shredded gingerroot and a dousing of black vinegar. I ate shrimp still in its shell and so fresh that the meat was almost quivering, and I partook of one of the most famous but extravagant of delicacies that Fuzhou offers, Buddha Jumping Over the Wall, a soup stew rich with the flavors of assorted seafood, meats, and wine, and prepared with over twenty ingredients. And then, as my friend had recommended, I shortened my trip and headed out to Xiamen.

BEIJING FANZHUANG (BEIJING RESTAURANT)

—

12 Dongda Lu
Tel.: 32334
Hours:
10:30 A.M.–2:00 P.M. (lunch),
4:30–9:00 P.M. (dinner)

The Beijing Fanzhuang has big plans. Over the next few years, so the manager claims, the second floor of the restaurant will be totally redecorated in the Qing style to resemble an ornate banquet hall of the Forbidden City. Waitresses will be costumed in splendid period clothing fashioned after that worn by ladies of the imperial court. Until the renovations take place, customers will have to be satisfied with the expansive, utilitarian-looking main dining room on the second floor and the simple tables arranged in the nondescript private dining area. There is one private banquet room at the extreme rear of the restaurant that is quite lovely and tastefully furnished with several exquisite Qing pieces. But the food is what makes a visit here is a pleasurable experience.

The Beijing opened in 1985 as a result of a joint-venture agreement between the Fuzhou Catering Company and a Beijing municipal catering firm. Initially, four cooks were dispatched to Fuzhou, along with countless ingredients. Even the ducks for the restaurant's famed Peking duck were imported from the north. Manager Seng Guide, who accompanied the chefs from Beijing and is a master chef in his own right, claims that the dish just couldn't be done properly with local ducks, which he says were inferior. Today, Seng has a local farmer raising the ducks to the restaurant's specifications, but there are still many ingredients imported from other parts of China. And although the number of Beijing chefs has decreased in the kitchen, the restaurant still prepares excellent and authentic-tasting Beijing and Shandong specialties.

The Peking duck does indeed rival some of the best served in Beijing. The meat is tender and juicy, with a crisp skin rendered of its fat. Dry-cooked fish *(gan shao guiyu)* is also delectable with a rich, dark sauce. Saucy chicken pieces *(jiang bao ji ding)* are exceptional in a glaze made with a sweet bean paste base, which is supposedly imported from Sichuan. Braised Two Winters *(shao er deng)* offers the complementary flavors of fresh bamboo shoot simmered in a rich braising liquid with black mushrooms. And huge prawns are succulent in the classic dish of oil-smothered prawns *(you men da xia)*. Other recommended specialties include rinsed lamb pot *(shuan yang you)*, stir-fried shrimp *(qing chao xia ren)*, and selected snacks, such as Three Treasure *shao mai (san xian shao mai)*, spring rolls *(chun juan)*, and Silver Thread loaves *(jin si juan)*.

The menu is translated into English. Initially, waitresses can be surly, but with a few words of encouragement their dispositions markedly improve. Since the Beijing is such a popular restaurant, reservations are recommended, with the menu to be settled beforehand. The food will probably be far better than if directly ordered from the menu. The average cost for a filling meal is approximately 50 yuan per person with a large party.

FUZHOU DA JIUJIA
(FUZHOU RESTAURANT)
—

36 Dong Da Lu
Tel.: 533057
Hours:
10:30 A.M.–2:00 P.M. (lunch),
5:00–8:00 P.M. (dinner)

The glossy brochure published by the Fuzhou Restaurant, leads a visitor to expect a lovely hotel surrounded by a charming garden with a gazebo at its center. Sadly, since the pictures were taken for the brochure, the restaurant has come under considerable disrepair. And the two noted master chefs Qiang Mugeng and Qiang Ququ, who have made this one of the most highly rated restaurants in Fuzhou, are often abroad performing demonstrations in other lands. Still, if you are looking for authentic Fujianese food, have the time to make advance bookings, and have the money for a lavish banquet, this is the restaurant you may want to choose.

The banquet rooms are simple but tastefully furnished, and waitresses are kind and accommodating. We made the mistake of ordering from the menu, and although some dishes showed promise (the steamed chicken with black mushrooms, *deng gu dun ji*, was actually superb), many were sloppy and overly salted. On another occasion, we did enjoy some excellent food, but reservations had been made and dishes ordered in advance.

The most famous delicacies served at the Fuzhou Da Jiujia are all local specialties. Supposedly no other version of Buddha Jumping Over the Wall (*fo tiao qiang*) compares with the one prepared here. Both Chef Qiangs were flown to Beijing expressly to prepare the dish for Ronald Reagan. Conch in chicken broth (*ji tang haibang*) and flattened shrimp with ham (*long sheng feng wei xia*) are also highly rated.

Reservations should be made twenty-four hours ahead, and plan on spending about 80 to 90 yuan per person for a lavish spread.

FUZHOU XIHU DA JIUDIAN (FUZHOU LAKESIDE HOTEL)

—

1 Hubin Lu
Tel.: 539888
Hours:
6:00 A.M.–11:00 P.M. (dim sum)

While the second-floor restaurant of the Fuzhou Lakeside Hotel restaurant offers what the management bills as authentic Cantonese fare at every meal, the best time to visit is for breakfast, when the room is filled with Hong Kong businessmen and tourists who are indulging their craving for hot Cantonese snacks. The air resonates with the sound of the Cantonese dialect, and with a little imagination, the somewhat glitzy decor and silk brocade outfits worn by the waitresses may even transport you mentally to Hong Kong.

Unlike many Cantonese dim sum parlors, the Lakeside Hotel does not parade its hot snacks around for the customer. Rather, you are given a mimeographed list on which you must check your preferences. All the standard dim sum are offered: barbecued pork buns *(cha sha bao)* are fluffy and light, although the filling may be slightly fatty. Fried turnip cake *(luobo gao)* is crisp and flavorful. Glutinous rice rolls with beef *(niu rou chang fen)* are excellent, as are custard tarts *(dan ta)*. Although there is no English menu, customers don't mind if you go to other tables and point. Waiters are friendly and will also try to help. Prices are moderate, and a selection of eight or nine dim sum costs about 10 yuan per person for a party of four.

HUAQIAO DASHA (OVERSEAS CHINESE MANSION) YAOCHI CANTING

—

Wusi Lu
Tel.: 557603 Ext. 681
Hours:
11:30 A.M.–1:30 P.M. (lunch),
6:00–8:00 P.M. (dinner)

Although countless sources had told me that the restaurant in the Huaqiao Dasha Hotel offered excellent Fujianese fare, I was once again reluctant. The first glimpse of the depressing lobby did little to allay my fears, and I felt even more hesitant after walking into the cafeteria-style dining room on the first floor. This couldn't possibly be the right place. And it wasn't.

The main restaurant is actually located on the second floor of an adjoining building, where another world awaits. The simple but attractive dining room is decorated with a hanging trellis complete with plastic grapes, and capable waitresses bustle about in ill-fitting polyester outfits. Never mind that the carpet is spotted and in desperate need of a thorough steam cleaning. By seven in the evening, all tables are completely filled, and the room is suffused with enticing smells emanating from the hot dishes on each table.

The food lives up to every enthusiastic endorsement. Dishes are simply served and often arrive on cracked china, but the flavors are undeniably good. The menu is fairly eclectic, but the kitchen shines when preparing local Fujianese specialties. Five-fragrance rolls (wu xiang juan) are crisp with a stuffing of ground meat and huge nuggets of fresh water chestnuts. The pork is a little fatty, but the aromatic filling is generously sprinkled with five-spice powder. Braised spareribs (yang shao pai) are meaty, tender, and glazed with a rich, reduced sauce. Sweet-and-sour Squirrel Fish is exemplary with a meaty fillet artfully scored, coated, deep-fried in a light batter, and coated in a tart sauce. And stir-fried rice noodles (chao xian mian) are a meal in themselves with a generous garnish of shreds of black mushrooms, carrots, garlic chives, chicken, and pork. For banquets with advance notice, the restaurant will also prepare the more ornate Fujianese preparations such as Buddha Jumping Over the Wall and conch soup.

Reservations are unnecessary if you are ordering from the menu, but tables fill quickly, so there may be a short wait unless you get there early. The cost of a satisfying meal will only be about 30 to 40 yuan per person. Banquet dinners are impressive and usually require about 70 to 80 yuan per person with a large group. Bookings should be made twenty-four hours in advance.

MA YING LI SHICHANG (FUZHOU CENTRAL MARKET)

Bayiqi Zhong Lu
Hours: 6:30 A.M.–7:00 P.M.

Any market offers a glimpse of the everyday life of the city, as well as providing an indicator of the standard of living of its inhabitants. While Fuzhou itself may occasionally appear to be run-down and slightly decrepit, its Central Market is a stark contrast—teeming with activity and packed with extraordinary ingredients.

The entrance to the market is alive with activity as two dumpling makers busily prepare *jiaozi*, one rolling out the skins and the other deftly filling them with ground meat. They can't seem to make them fast enough as customers impatiently buy them as quickly as they are made.

Inside the market, the stalls are heaped with all types of fresh vegetables, still glistening from the morning dew. The variety is impressive as leafy bundles of assorted greens vie for space with mountains of wild mushrooms, green beans, tomatoes, water chestnuts, cauliflower, taro, and carrots. A woman holds up plump cloves of garlic that have just been peeled, proudly displaying them to customers.

Nearby tables are laden with whole sides of pigs, neatly slaughtered and portioned into familiar cuts, and bamboo baskets brim with live shrimp, crabs, conch, and snails, while whole fish wriggle feistily on tables. In the center aisle, an elderly man uses scissors to cut pieces from a coil of taffylike candy that is stuffed with a mixture of walnuts, peanuts, and pine nuts.

A NOTE ABOUT FUJIANESE COOKING

—

If not as familiar to tourists as the food of some other provinces, Fujianese cooking has considerable significance in China itself. It is one of the eight noted schools of Chinese cooking as well as father to Taiwanese cuisine, a style with its own distinct flair but one that takes in both Fujianese and Japanese influences.

If pressed one could describe Fujianese cooking as a blending of Cantonese (southern) and eastern cuisines, with several unique characteristics. As in Cantonese dishes, the seasonings are often light, and sauces are mild to accentuate the natural flavor of fine ingredients. With some of the best soy sauce in China made in this area, Fujianese cooks have a penchant for red-cooking or braising foods to a tender, brownish-red doneness, a cooking method also popular throughout eastern China. And Fujianese chefs, as in the south and east, have elevated vegetarian cooking to a fine art.

In addition, the Fujianese are masters at making rich, clear soups and sauces that are delicate in appearance but burst with the full flavors of the ingredients within. It is not unusual to be served a large number of soups and soupy dishes at a Fujianese multicourse banquet.

Since Fujian is located in southern China and the province borders the sea, the climate is mild and temperate. Its fertile soil and gentle rolling landscape offer ideal growing conditions for all types of produce, both wild and cultivated. Rice, corn, peanuts, wild mushrooms, and all types of vegetables thrive. Yet it is the sea that dominates the cuisine, offering a fine selection of fish, crab, shrimp, whelk, snails, oysters, mussels, and squid. In fact, although some might disagree, many consider Fujianese seafood dishes to be the best in the country.

Wild and cultivated mushrooms are another specialty of Fujianese cooking. Most free markets offer mountains of different varieties. The most famous are the golden needle or enokitake mushroom, which are stir-fried with other ingredients, served in soups, or relished cooked, cooled to room temperature, and sprinkled with a little sesame oil.

Further south, crab, steamed and served with a vinegar dipping sauce, or stir-fried quickly with ginger and scallions, is always fresh and superb. Oysters are lightly dusted with a breaded coating, thrown into omelettes, or mixed with garlic chives and wrapped in a crunchy spring roll skin. And squid, cut into bite-size pieces, is deep-fried until golden brown and crisp.

In every part of the province, one is able to sample rice noodles (mian xian), which vary in thickness. Although all types are popular, it is the thin, delicate variety that the Fujianese crave. Some are served in soups with a soothing, flavorful broth and a garnish of meat or seafood. Others are stir-fried lightly in a mellow sauce and combined with pork, shrimp, fish shreds, chicken, black mushrooms, garlic chives, and other assorted ingredients. These noodles exemplify the best aspects of the Fujianese cuisine—simplicity, freshness, and delicacy.

RONGCHENG JIUJIA (RONGCHENG RESTAURANT)
■

Zhonglou Dongjiekou
Tel.: 555816
Hours:
10:00 A.M.–2:30 P.M. (lunch),
5:00–9:00 P.M. (dinner)

While many guidebooks consider Fuzhou a culinary mecca where great restaurants abound, it is, in fact, a city where outstanding meals are few and far between. There are however, a few eateries located in the center of the city that offer consistently good food at reasonable prices. And the Rongcheng Jiujia is one.

Known as the Shi Yan Canting until 1986, the restaurant also housed one of Fuzhou's top culinary training centers. The school has since moved, but some of the finest graduates continue at the stoves, and the kitchen staff includes an impressive brigade of special-level and first-level cooks. Furthermore Rongcheng is run under the capable management of Zhuang Yi Si, who was for many years the manager of the famous Fuzhou eatery Zhu Cheng Yuan and is a former master chef in his own right.

Rongcheng Jiujia is slightly overdone. The main dining area for foreigners is on the second floor, where many of the tables are housed in pagoda-like open rooms. The restaurant does a booming banquet business, and the nine simply furnished private rooms are usually packed with parties of local residents or Taiwanese or Hong Kong tour groups. Nevertheless, waitresses are attentive and cheerful, and food generally arrives promptly.

The Rongcheng specializes in Fujianese cuisine and serves an excellent version of Buddha Jumping Over the Wall. Most restaurants require advance notice for this dish, but at the Rongcheng it may be ordered directly from the menu, and it is served in individual clay crocks topped with a clay Buddha. The Rongcheng may not offer the best version of this dish in Fuzhou but the flavor is quite delicious, and the price is extremely reasonable. (Elsewhere one small bowl can easily cost 120 yuan.)

Other famous local dishes that are recommended are the sweet-and-sour Squirrel Fish, whelk soup (ji tang haibang), pepper-coated spareribs (jiaoyan paigu), Ten-Treasure fried rice noodles (shi jin chao yi mian), and an extraordinarily delicate fish dumpling soup *(gao tang yu jiao).* The restaurant also prepares a selection of dim sum, including spring rolls, rice noodle rolls *(fen bao),* and a sweet soup *(tian tang).*

Reservations are strongly recommended since the Rongcheng is a popular booking place for the tourist agencies. A multicourse banquet may cost as much as 60 or 70 yuan per person for a full table of ten. A filling meal may be ordered from the menu for about 50 yuan per person with just a small party of two.

WENQUAN DASHA (HOT SPRING HOTEL)

Wusi Lu
Tel.: 551818
Hours:
7:00–9:30 A.M. (breakfast),
12:00–2:20 P.M. (lunch),
6:00–8:30 P.M. (dinner)

Depending on your tastes in restaurants, you might be put off by the display at the entrance of the second-floor restaurant of the Wenquan Dasha, particularly if you are looking for authentic Fujianese cooking. Meticulously arranged in an ornate wrought-iron portable bar is a still-life sculpture containing selected French wines, several brands of cognac, and an impressive number of top-shelf liquors. Could this, you may be wondering, be the Chinese restaurant, or have you somehow stumbled upon a European eatery? And the tuxedoed maître d' who will probably greet you may add to your uncertainty.

A quick glance at the menu, which is masterfully translated into English, should dispel any doubts. The kitchen's repertoire is varied and full of Fujianese and eastern regional Chinese classics.

Since the Wenquan Dasha is a joint-venture hotel, there is a strong Hong Kong flavor throughout, and the small restaurant, which holds only about twelve tables, is designed with a decidedly sophisticated flair. The linen is pristine white and crisply starched. Waitresses glide about the room in floor-length, close-fitting Chinese dresses slit to the thigh. Yet customers in jeans will feel as comfortable as those who are more formally attired. Judging from our experience, the staff is courteous and helpful to everyone, foreigners and local Chinese alike.

Seafood is very fresh and often lightly sauced to accentuate its sweet flavor. Grilled prawns in the shell are excellent, their sweet meat brimming with the exquisite flavor of the water. Steamed crab and fish are equally memorable. Sautéed whelk in a white wine sauce is superbly seasoned in a light coating of a reduced wine glaze that tastes like a meeting of French and Chinese influences. Other delicious items include the braised grass carp with scallions, stewed spareribs with soy bean paste, stewed duckling with garlic, braised bean curd with black mushrooms, fried noodles with assorted meat, and deep-fried chicken Fuzhou-style.

Steamed pork dumplings are juicy, packed with a ground meat filling, and served with a good, spicy dipping sauce.

Reservations are unnecessary and prices, although a trifle high, are justified by the food and the service. All major credit cards are accepted, and a filling meal ordered from the menu will cost about 50 yuan per person for a party of four to six.

XIAMEN

My first sight of Xiamen was at night, and after ten, a time when most Chinese cities have shut down for the evening. Even then, its harbor area was buzzing with activity and restaurants were still ablaze with light as the last of the evening's customers slowly straggled out onto the sidewalk and leisurely strolled home.

At five-thirty the next morning, free markets already were overflowing with customers and breakfast snack houses were doing a brisk business. Xiamen is, like Guangzhou, a city on the move, thriving with activity and growth. There's no time to sleep: everyone's too busy trying to make money, stretching every minute of the day to its ultimate.

Xiamen is actually an island located in the southeastern coast of Fujian province and is connected to the mainland by a one-and-a-half-mile causeway. It lies in a deep bay that forms a peaceful basin protecting it from the South China Sea. Since it was declared one of China's four economic zones for intensive development in 1981, the city has not been the same. Investments from Hong Kong and Macao began pouring in immediately, bringing its share of entrepreneurs. The recent relaxation of relations between Taiwan and China has also had a profound impact on the city, and Taiwanese businessmen are investing in all types of ventures at an astounding rate.

Accordingly, Xiamen is a blending of old China with the new, a study in contrasts. The broad main streets are filled with shops and department stores selling the latest goods for export, while just a block away small alleyways are lined with old wooden structures built during the last century and tiny teahouses that serve simple snacks. Looming prominently on the horizon and casting an eerie glow at night when it is fully lit is a huge neon sign in English advertising Kent cigarettes, a glaring reminder of the growing presence of foreign investment.

Hong Kong executives and Taiwanese relatives are everywhere in Xiamen, which has become one of the most popular stops on the China itinerary. One especially feels their impact in the food. While Xiamen is famous for the local dishes at its own seafood and fish restaurants, the newest and best eateries are joint-venture businesses offering the specialties of its newest residents. At a number of Cantonese restaurants where the flashy decor is an exact duplicate of that in many a Hong Kong–style eatery, you can sample excellent dim sum until noon, then feast on more substantial classic Cantonese entrees. And at tiny but charming private one-room restaurants owned by Taiwanese, local Fujianese dishes are prepared in the Taiwanese manner, a subtle variation of the native style.

For a change of pace from the frenzied mood of the city proper, Gulangyu Island is a mere five-minute ferry ride away. It is a charming sanctuary where no motor vehicles are allowed and the architecture and red-tiled roofs are a reminder of Europe at the turn of the century. The island is also famous for the many who are accomplished musicians, particularly violinists, among its residents. In the late afternoon or early evening, as you stroll along the quiet streets that meander through the town, you can catch lilting strains of music floating out from open windows, offering a pleasurable and unexpected serenade to the passing pedestrians.

DONGHAI DA JIUDIAN (EAST OCEAN HOTEL)

1 Zhongshan Lu
Tel.: 26840
Hours:
7:30–10:30 A.M. (dim sum),
11:00 A.M.–2:30 P.M. (lunch),
5:00–9:30 P.M. (dinner)

There is some controversy, as one would expect, as to the best hotel restaurant in Xiamen. Many contend it is a tie between the Overseas Chinese Mansion, Lujiang Hotel, and the East Ocean Hotel. Others maintain that the last has recently moved to the forefront, and after sampling the cuisine at all three, I must agree.

The Donghai Da Jiudian still leaves a lot to be desired, especially at dinnertime, but the morning dim sum are quite good, and visitors who are feeling a little homesick may feel reassured by the presence of foreigners, especially Hong Kong residents enjoying the fare. The dining room has a decidedly Hong Kong flavor, with its elaborate chandeliers and prominent glassed enclosure where a chef clad in whites slices and chops up pieces of the roast pork, duck, chicken, and roast suckling pig that hangs on skewers before him.

The main menu, which is translated into English, is quite extensive with a combination of traditional Fujianese and Cantonese-style specialties. Foremost among them are steak Chinese-style, sweet corn and crabmeat soup, and pork ribs capital-style. There is also a small menu of seasonal specialties in Chinese on all tables, and this may be where the best eating lies. Boiled shrimp are succulent and fresh, and stir-fried crab with scallions and gingerroot is a Cantonese classic prepared with impeccable style here. And a number of excellent hot pot specialties *(shaguo doufu, shaguo yu)* feature different toppings of meat, seafood, and chicken with bean curd and other assorted vegetables.

Service could be a little more attentive, especially at peak dining hours. Reservations are unnecessary, and prices are moderate. Expect to pay about 40 to 60 yuan per person for a party of four. MasterCard credit cards are accepted.

HAOQINGXIANG JIULOU (HAOQINGXIANG SNACK HOUSE)

▬

30 Dayuan Lu
Tel.: 22973
Hours: 7:00 A.M.–11:00 P.M.

Although not quite so popular as the Wuzaitian, the Haoqingxiang is another small eating place offering local snacks. Freshly made fish balls *(yu wan)*, tossed noodles *(ban mian)*, and glutinous rice dumplings wrapped in bamboo leaves *(zhengzi)* are some of the specialties. Outside are small stalls with other snacks, including freshly made deep-fried spring rolls with a garlic, chive, and oyster filling and crisp pitalike flatbreads stuffed with thin slices of Daikon radish and a block of powdery peanut candy and sprinkled with fresh cilantro, black vinegar, and Fujianese bean sauce.

HUANGZEHE HUASHENG TANG DIAN (HUANGZEHE PEANUT SOUP HOUSE)

▬

22 Zhengshan Lu
Tel.: 24670
Hours: 6:00 A.M.–8:00 P.M.

For a bit of local color and a taste of one of Xiamen's traditional simple snacks, visit the Huangzehe Huasheng Tang Dian. For just 35 cents, you can sit at one of the cozy wooden booths that line the side of this tiny shop and sample the soothing, delicious soup made of cooked peanuts in a sweetened broth. The shop has been preparing this famous specialty since its opening in 1945. Steamed buns and assorted pastries are also offered at the bakery on one side of the shop.

Mornings are particularly busy, and it may be a bit of a chore to stand in line at the front counter to pay and receive a plastic coin redeemable at the counter in the back. And there the situation falls just short of bedlam. It's best to wait until the rush passes and visit in early evening or late afternoon.

NANPUTUO SUCAI JIA (NANPUTUO VEGETARIAN RESTAURANT)
—

Nanputuo Temple
Tel.: 22908
Hours:
12:30–2:00 P.M. (lunch),
6:30–8:30 P.M. (dinner)

The Nanputuo Temple, which is a fifteen-minute ride from the city center, is one of Xiamen's major tourist spots. This lovely Buddhist temple was built over one thousand years ago during the Tang dynasty (618–907), destroyed during the Ming dynasty and later rebuilt during the Qing. Most recently, it has been restored to a colorful, and in some cases, gaudy magnificence.

Two attractions draw hundreds of tourists to the temple site: the Buddha sculptures, which are magnificent, and the legendary vegetarian cuisine, prepared at a restaurant at the temple. Getting to Nanputuo Temple is easy enough—just follow the crowds—but eating there is a more complicated matter, for, as we discovered, it now houses *two* restaurants. (Both, it turned out, use the same kitchen.) One is located on the temple premises on the site of the old restaurant; the other is next door in a brand new, modern complex completed in 1986.

The new restaurant caters more to private parties and large groups. There are some tastefully furnished private rooms for customers who wish to pay princely sums for their meals, but the main dining room, although clean and recently built, is totally devoid of personality. The broad expanse of a room is filled by large round banquet tables, and customers are all seated together with little regard to their comfort and privacy. (Occasionally, wooden screens are arranged to separate the groups.) Food is served in a similarly careless fashion. Waitresses wheel out carts laden with identical steaming platters, and everyone is served the same dish. Little thought seems to be given to presentation, and most of the dishes are bland at best.

In the original restaurant, which is directly connected to the temple, a cozier and more intimate atmosphere reigns. There are two small rooms filled with small wooden tables, and at mealtimes the air is alive with the appealing din of customers enjoying one another's company and the food. Unfortunately, the fare is not much better than that next door, and many of the dishes are the same. At both restaurants, diners are given a choice of set menus with varying prices. At the older restaurant, smaller parties can eat a filling lunch for 15, 20, or 30 yuan per person. Next door, only banquet meals with about twelve courses are served for larger parties (the group must have a minimum of twelve people) and prices range from 150 yuan to 400 yuan per table.

Reservations are essential at both eateries. With a large group, allow twenty-four hours' advance notice. For smaller parties, several hours before will suffice.

TAIWAN LIAOLI
(TAIWAN RESTAURANT)
—

Gugong Lu Kou
Tel.: 31994
Hours:
11:00 A.M.–3:00 P.M. (lunch),
5:00–11:00 P.M. (dinner)

Lan Tian Si, a Taiwanese former chef, saw the future before a number of other people in Xiamen. In 1985, he returned to Fujian, a place many of his relatives had fled over forty years before, to relocate and start a private restaurant offering Taiwanese food. Lan anticipated the tremendous influx of tourists from Taiwan, and he correctly assessed their demand for their native fare. Even from the beginning, this hole-in-the-wall eatery thrived, and today, it is one of the most popular in Xiamen, even among the locals. All six chefs, whom Lan trained, are still in attendance, and business is so good that an expansion is being planned.

Like most private restaurants in China, it is a minuscule place. The main dining room has only six tables with folding chairs and decorations are basic. Chinese calligraphy hangings line one side of the restaurant, and the most prominent decorative feature in the room is the front wall which is plastered with banners announcing winners of the Philippine Chinese Cultural Track and Field Team. Nearby, another sign prominently reads "Taibei."

The kitchen is located several doors down in a street stall where live fish, shrimp, and lobster lazily swim in tanks until they are grabbed to be thrown into a pot. Lan insists on freshness and he is equally adamant about prompt service. You are barely seated before a very young waiter or waitress arrives, brandishing menus and offering advice on the restaurant's specialties. No sooner are the foods ordered than the cooked dishes are rushed back to the table, directly from the fire, still bubbling and spitting from the heat.

Some of the best items are seafood, all impeccably fresh. Boiled shrimp are so sweet in their own juices that they do not need any sauce. Baked squid *(kao youyu)* is succulently tender and lightly seasoned. Seafood stew *(hai xian geng)* is filled with fish, tiny oysters, shrimp, bamboo shoots, and hairy seaweed, all bathed in a fragrant hot-and-sour soup and sprinkled generously with fresh coriander. Many nonseafood dishes shine as well. Spring rolls *(chun juan)* are wafer thin and filled with a delectable filling of ground meat seasoned with five-spice powder. Braised "three-cup" chicken *(san bei ji)* is rich and hearty with tender chicken pieces coated in a reduced braising sauce. And home-style bean curd *(jia chang doufu)* is an unusual departure from the traditional version with a sweet-and-sour sauce.

Prices are quite reasonable, but seafood can be expensive. For a smaller party of four, a filling meal with a varied selection of dishes will cost about 80 yuan per person. With more people, the price is progressively cheaper. Since the restaurant is so popular, reservations should be made a day before.

TAIXIA JIUJIA
(TAIXIA RESTAURANT)
—

40 Gongyuandong Lu
Tel.: 24588
Hours:
10:30 A.M.–2:30 P.M. (lunch),
5:30 P.M.–12:30 A.M. (dinner)

You have to look very carefully for the Taixia Jiujia. The entrance is almost completely obscured by a huge sign advertising the decoration department of a local store, and the restaurant itself barely seats twenty-five people. The atmosphere in the yellow stucco dining room is intimate, and space is at such a premium that stacked cases of Tsingtao beer provide the decor for one side of the room. But after sampling some of Taixia's fresh and superbly prepared seafood dishes, you can easily understand how the restaurant has become so popular.

The Taixia reflects the trend of the future. Owing to Xiamen's liberal economic policies a Taiwanese businessman invested in the venture in 1988, hiring local residents to manage, and trained the cooks himself. The cuisine is a blending of traditional Fuzhou cooking with a heavy Taiwanese accent.

The menu is limited but appealing. A daily seafood list offers the freshest catch of the day with market prices. Whole fresh shrimp *(bai zhuo xia)*, with heads intact, are sold by the ounce and boiled until just cooked, then served with a vinegar dipping sauce. Deep-fried squid with a Sichuan peppercorn dipping salt *(jiao yan you yu)* is superb with a light batter that is fried until golden brown and crisp. Lobster *(long xia)* and snails *(xian lo)* are offered when available, and the method of preparation varies depending on the daily whim of the chef. Other recommended dishes include the cold-tossed Golden Needle mushrooms, deep-fried squab, and the stir-fried rice noodles or rice noodles in broth *(chao mian xian* or *mian xian tang)*.

The waitresses seem barely old enough to be serving tables, but all are charming, and service is exceptionally civilized. Hot towels steamed in a nearby rice cooker are presented immediately upon arrival.

Prices can be expensive, particularly if you order delicacies like lobster or snake. (For most meals allow a budget of 80 yuan per person.) The restaurant caters to a monied Japanese and Taiwanese business clientele, and the menu features many delicacies, apart from the fresh seafood. Reservations for dinner are an absolute necessity, but at lunch the crowd tends to be sparse, and seats are always available.

WUZAITIAN XIAO CHIDIAN (WUZAITIAN SNACK HOUSE)
—

49 Datong Lu
Tel.: 34820
Hours: 7:30 A.M.–11:30 P.M.

Many local residents contend that the true specialties of Xiamen are found only in the snack houses, and the most famous of these is the Wuzaitian in the middle of the city. Wuzaitian is a Xiamen institution; its doors first opened in the 1950s with a menu that offered fifteen or twenty simple dishes, and it has been a favorite eating place for locals ever since.

Foreigners may be a little put off its general griminess, but the Wuzaitian is just the type of simple eatery that appeals to Xiamen natives. The food is quick and cheap, and the ingredients are fresh. For tourists, it might provide an interesting view of everyday life with a special introduction to Xiamen's simpler snacks.

The shop has about three different stalls where the snacks are prepared. In one spot, a woman stands in front of a huge wok filled with boiling water and cooked noodles. She scoops out the noodles with a handled strainer and deftly transfers them to a bowl, adding fish balls and broth. The shop offers two soupy variations of the fish balls, one with the noodles *(yu wan mian)* and the other plain in a soup *(yu wan tang)* In another area, two cooks are at work filling wontons *(pian shi tang)* and placing them in a glassed-in case, in preparation for the expected crowds. Nearby a cook lifts bunches of glutinous rice dumplings *(zhengzi)* wrapped in bamboo leaves out of a steamer, allowing them to cool. Customers take seats at tables with stools in a small side room. A filling meal can easily be had here for under 10 yuan.

XIAMEN MANA JIUJIA (XIAMEN AGATE GARDEN RESTAURANT)

■

Xia Da Men Qian, Yi Tiao Jie,
Di Si Jia
Tel.: 27622
Hours: 11:00 A.M.–10:00 P.M.

No guidebooks list the Xiamen Mana Jiujia: it's still a secret treasure, and news of its existence is passed along by word of mouth among the local residents. But it is so unusual that it probably won't be long before it's discovered.

The restaurant, like its address (which translates into "the fourth house from the Xiamen University Gate"), is a bit improbable. Former professor Deng Chi Leng was a biology teacher at Xiamen University when he went for a walk on Gulangyu Island and chanced upon some snails. An accomplished cook, he decided to bring them home and experiment. The results were quite successful, and he returned again and again to the island for more, each time improvising with new dishes and offering them to his friends. The response was so enthusiastic that Deng decided to start a small restaurant, and so, in 1986, the Xiamen Mana Jiujia opened its doors. Deng has been so successful that he has given up his teaching, and he is at the restaurant full time. He also owns a snail farm, which provides the mollusks for his and other restaurants in the city.

The eatery is tiny with five small tables and a forlorn-looking sofa with dated newspapers scattered about its cushions. Overhead a simulated trellis adorned with dusty plastic grape clusters lends a slightly homey touch. The food, however, is outstanding. Although the menu offers several other dishes, the specialty remains the snails. Snails cooked Napoleon-style (Napolun wo nui) are prepared in the French manner, stuffed in their shells and dripping with garlic butter. A superb Chinese rendition called sha cha snails (sha cha wo nui) named after the spicy sauce with the same name features paper-thin slices of room-temperature snails served with a pungent dressing seasoned with ginger, garlic, and a sesame-paste base. Other highlights include snails stir-fried with mushrooms (suan gumu nui) and a delicate soup of asparagus with snails (lu sun wo nui tang). Nonsnail selections that are equally memorable are the steamed eel with black bean sauce *(man yu zheng dou si)* and the stir-fried rice noodles with shreds of black mushrooms, carrots, and scallions *(chao mian xian)*.

At lunch, the restaurant usually is not very crowded, but dinner is another matter; reservations are a must and may be made several hours in advance. Prices for a meal vary, but expect to pay at least 70 yuan per person for a small party of four, and less as the number of the group increases.

ZHONGSHAN LU CAI SHICHANG (ZHONGSHAN ROAD FOOD MARKET)

Zhongshan Lu
Hours: 6:30 A.M.–7:30 P.M.

Xiamen is one of the most colorful cities in eastern China, and its grand market, located on the main street of the downtown section, is an appropriate match. Seafood of all kinds, including five different varieties of shrimp, live fish, lobster, razor clams, crabs, squid, and cuttlefish are available and arranged haphazardly in immense piles. Chicken and pigeons cackle in cages, vegetables are everywhere, and the air is suffused with a faint odor of five-spice powder, mingling with the almost overwhelming scent of ripe fruit. Vendors sit at tables offering tastes of pineapple, mango, and papaya. There seems to be no end to the products available in this land of plenty.

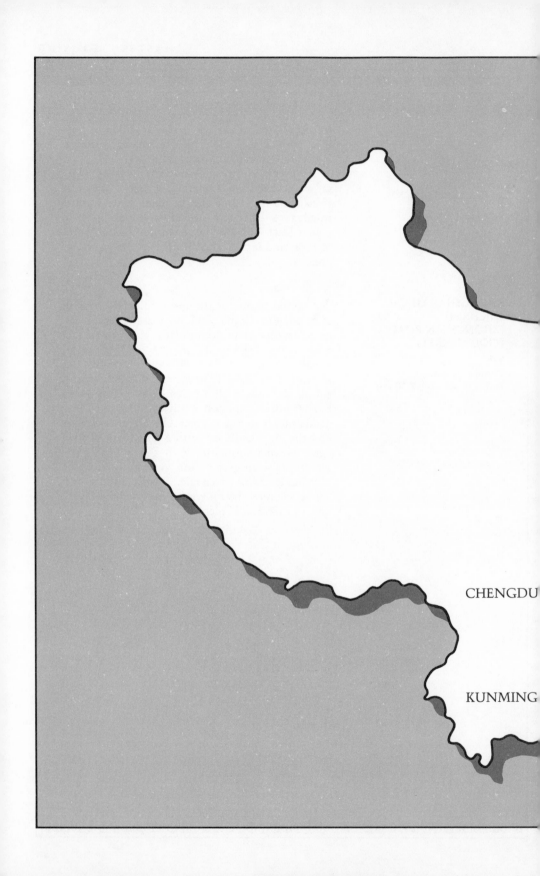

CHENGDU

KUNMING

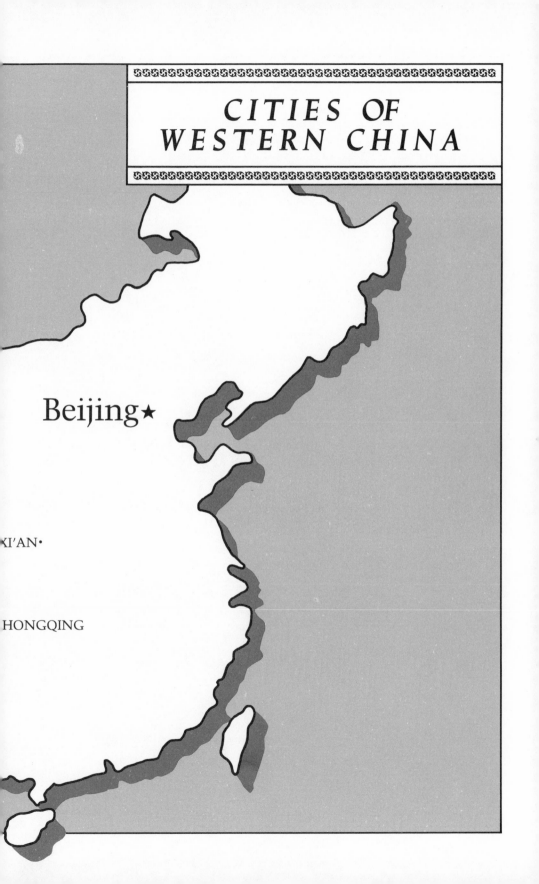

CITIES OF
WESTERN CHINA

Beijing★

XI'AN·

HONGQING

SICHUANESE COOKING
(WESTERN)

§

It is harder to enter Sichuan than it is to go to heaven.

—LI BAI, A TANG DYNASTY POET (699–762)

Tucked away in the southwestern corner of China, Sichuan is a province that developed—and thrived—in virtual isolation from the rest of the country. Possessing a fertile basin surrounded by mountains; endowed with miles of rivers, streams, and lakes, and blessed with a mild, semitropical climate, Sichuan is rich in all food products. Vegetables of every kind (some say over three hundred varieties) grow plentifully, as do subtropical fruits like oranges, tangerines, and kumquats. The ample land provides grazing for raising cattle, pigs, ducks, and other types of fowl as well as for cultivating rice and wheat. The forests nurture all types of wild game and a virtual garden of mushrooms and edible fungi. And nearby acres of bamboo groves thrive, offering a home to the province's unofficial mascot, the panda, and an unending supply of fresh bamboo shoots. Sichuan has justly earned its nickname of the Land of Abundance.

Sichuanese cooking is representative of the western regional style, a school that also includes the provinces of Hunan, Yunan, and parts of Guizhou.

Perhaps as a result of their remoteness, however, the Sichuanese have always been strongly independent, and their cuisine is equally flamboyant and bold. Pungent seasonings like gingerroot, garlic, and numbing Sichuan peppercorns are matched by the fiery presence of chili peppers, fresh and dried or in pastes and oils. The sauces are an extravagant blending of contrasting flavors, offering simultaneous accents of sweet, sour, hot, bitter, and salty in one mouthful.

There is some debate as to the introduction of chili peppers to Sichuan. All agree that they are not indigenous to China, and some culinary historians maintain that they were brought during the seventeenth century with other New World products. Others argue that they arrived much earlier, during prehistoric times, by way of India. When the Chinese first settled in the area some two thousand years ago, they adopted the native products, and the hot pepper was prominent among them.

Also widely debated is the explanation for the chilis' strong presence in the cuisine. Popular arguments hold that they were originally used to camouflage the flavor of foods that had spoiled in the warm climate, or to spice up the meager supply of ingredients, but neither is convincing. The ancient Sichuanese were masters at preserving methods like pickling, salting, and smoking, and the province is a treasure trove of food products.

A more likely theory is that peppers were originally used to provide a natural air-conditioning system in the body, as in India and Burma, Sichuan's warm-climated neighbors. The peppers cause perspiration, which as it evaporates leaves the body cooler. Also, many Sichuanese cooks contend that the spicy seasonings sensitize the palate, extending its ability to enjoy the broad spectrum of flavors in the sauces.

Textural contrast also plays a basic role in the Sichuanese style with the prominent use of water chestnuts, bamboo shoots, and black fungus or wood ears emphasizing crunchy and resilient qualities. And chefs tend to use a heavy hand when adding oil to a sauce, reasoning that it adds a rich, lustrous sheen to the dish. Both trademarks underline the sensual nature of the cuisine.

While spicy home-style specialties like Ma Po bean curd, fish-flavored pork, and dry-cooked beef are most often recognized as signature dishes, many refined banquet-style recipes such as camphor-smoked duck and sizzling rice with pork slices are also common in the Sichuanese repertoire. In fact most banquet dishes are mildly seasoned and are attributed to imperial cooks who fled to Sichuan from other parts of China seeking political asylum. These same cooks brought divergent influences from other regional styles that they incorporated into the native cuisine.

Adding still another dimension to the Sichuanese cooking style is the extensive selection of snack dishes, or dim sum. Simple yet irresistible, such classic favorites as *dan dan* noodles and chili oil dumplings add to the treasury of classic dishes that make this cooking style one of the most popular in China and abroad.

CHENGDU

For years, I had waited to visit Chengdu. From what I read about Sichuan's isolated location, I envisioned an exotic city unlike any other I had previously visited. I imagined it to be rustic, yet metropolitan, dynamic and colorful with narrow streets lined with ancient wooden dwellings and headstrong people who spoke in a strange, unintelligible dialect, steam emanating from their noses as they savored dishes laced liberally with hot peppers.

Of course the Chengdu that greeted me on my first visit some eight years ago had little in common with my preconceived notions. For one, it was much larger and more modern than I had envisioned. With its broad, busy avenues and high-rise hotels, Chengdu reminded me of many other cities in contemporary China. It was teeming with vitality and humanity, messy with new construction, and frequently fouled by pollution. Still, there were glimmerings here and there of the magical place I had long imagined.

Chengdu first emerged about two thousand years ago when it became the capital of the kingdom of Shu during the Zhou dynasty. It narrowly escaped destruction by the Mongols during the reign of Kublai Khan. Chengdu has really only come into its own as a center for trade, culture, industry and education since the founding of the People's Republic of China in 1949.

Chengdu is situated in the heart of Sichuan province, an area regarded to be one of the most fertile in China. The temperatures are subtropical, and bamboo forests thrive in the lush climate. Accordingly, so do rice, wheat, citrus fruits, tea, and an extraordinary range of vegetables, which is apparent when you visit the largest street free market, which is one of the most colorful and well endowed in China. The market is actually one of the few places in the city where the Chengdu of the past blends with its modern persona.

It was here, on one busy morning, that I found traces of the place I had imagined as I strolled about the stalls heaped with exquisite fresh produce and piles of fragrant spices, including dried and fresh chili peppers and Sichuan peppercorns. At every turn, vendors beckoned, holding up their products and proudly displaying their wares. The noise was piercing as customers and sellers fiercely bickered over prices, each one obviously enjoying the battle and not eager to give up before both were satisfied. Intermingled with the food stalls were old iron stoves, their charcoal stoked to a red-hot temperature, filled with crisp flat breads baking inside. Along the sidewalks in back of the market stalls were small noodle stands and old teahouses where customers, satisfied after the rigors of purchasing their required provisions, sat and relaxed, gossiping with friends and savoring the frenetic street scene just as their forefathers had before them.

CHEN MA PO DOUFU (GRANDMOTHER CHEN'S BEAN CURD RESTAURANT)

41 Jiefang Zhong Lu, Er Duan
Tel.: 331636
Hours: 10:30 A.M.–8:00 P.M.

Any connoisseur of Sichuanese cooking is familiar with Ma Po bean curd, one of the most classic dishes of the Sichuanese repertoire. And the story of its origin is almost as well known as the dish itself.

According to legend, Ma Po bean curd was first created at a restaurant in the northern section of Chengdu, near the Wanfu Bridge, during the reign of Emperor Tongzhi (1864–1874) in the Qing dynasty. Chen Xingsheng and his wife, who was the cook, ran a small eatery under his name that offered tea and simple dishes. Chen's wife was reputed to have a pockmarked face, and customers came far and wide to taste her special bean curd recipe, eventually renaming the dish Grandma Chen's pockmarked bean curd. The restaurant soon came to be called Grandma Chen's Pockmarked Bean Curd Restaurant and the name still stands today, even though the location has changed several times. (The Ma Po Bean Curd restaurant is expected to move yet again in the near future.) Despite the moves, the original sign, though slightly tarnished by age, still hangs proudly in the restaurant.

According to the present manager, Fang Changyuan, Ma Po bean curd is prepared today using the same method perfected by Grandma Chen over one hundred years ago. Fang speaks quite knowledgeably about the subject, since he has overseen the restaurant for some years and is a first-level chef. To make the dish, bean curd is cut into cubes and braised with ground pork in a spicy sauce enlivened by hot chili paste. Just before it is served, the dish is dusted with a generous sprinkling of Sichuan peppercorn powder, adding additional spice.

Although Ma Po bean curd is probably the most requested dish on the menu, the kitchen prepares as many as thirty different varieties of bean curd. Manager Fang says that in order to maintain the consistent quality of the product, the restaurant has its own bean curd maker, who daily produces over one thousand pounds for the restaurant's customers, who are said to be in the thousands.

Fang maintains that while Ma Po bean curd may be ordered in restaurants all over China, no version compares to Grandma Chen's, owing to her exacting standards. To begin with, the soybeans are specially selected for the bean curd. Only those of the highest quality are acceptable. The pork, which is added to the dish, must be very lean, and only from the shin. And fresh garlic, which is added for its pungent but not overbearing flavor, is brought in from Wenjiang county outside Chengdu, where the most fragrant in the area is thought to be grown.

Selected banquet dishes were added to the menu several years ago, but the bean curd and home-style dishes are more appealing. Besides the Ma Po bean curd (which is so spicy, it may blow your socks off), there is a less spicy home-style bean curd *(jia chang doufu)*, with a mellow, reduced sauce; and earthenware pot bean curd *(shaguo doufu)*, which is also milder and delicious with the bean curd cooked and served in its own pot. Shrimp bean curd *(xia ren doufu)* and Three-Treasure bean curd *(san xian doufu)* also are recommended. The restaurant also prepares several versions of *dou hua*, which is a more tender, delicate form of bean curd. The sweet bean curd soup *(tian douhua)* and hot-and-sour soft bean curd *(suan la douhua)* are well worth sampling.

For those who would like to try something other than bean curd, the kitchen also turns out very respectable renditions of fish-flavored pork shreds *(yu xiang rou si)*, sizzling rice with meat slices *(guo ba rou pian)*, and an unusual spring roll *(chun bing)*, stuffed with finely shredded vegetables, wrapped in a fresh spring roll skin, and drizzled with sesame sauce.

Reservations should be made at least twenty-four hours in advance; and the cost for a filling meal is about 40 to 50 yuan per person.

CHENGDU CAI SHI CHANG
(CHENGDU FREE MARKET)

There are two main markets in Chengdu: the more formal government-owned Renmin Shang Chang Shichang Bu, housed in a rather somber looking building off of Renmin Road, and the Chengdu Free Market, the livelier, more colorful of the two.

At the Renmin market, in a series of interconnecting buildings all types of processed food products including cookies, cakes, dried beef, canned provisions, coffee, teas, spirits as well as almost every conceivable commodity (sports products, electronic goods, toys, clothing, and shoes) are sold. It is certainly a place to pass through for a glimpse, but it's dark, and like many government-owned concessions, everything tends to blur into a slightly depressing haze of food and goods.

The Chengdu Free Market is exactly the opposite. The atmosphere is electric as vendors scream out the names and prices of their provisions. Customers brazenly haggle for the best price. The variety of poultry, seafood, meat, and vegetables plus the superior quality of the products underlines the bounty of the area. Towering piles of leafy greens, plump eggplants, ivory bean sprouts, and glistening cucumbers and peppers are framed in exquisite still-life pictures.

As soon as a huge truck arrives, its entire bed filled with freshly picked soybeans, and customers appear with empty burlap bags into which the beans are quickly shoveled. The load of beans is gone within twenty minutes.

Nearby, in endless glass cases lacquered camphor duck and barbecued meats are hanging. To the rear preserved ducks, chickens, and strips of meats are piled high, ready as reinforcement provisions. Further up the street, the sidewalk is covered with bulging burlap bags, each one unfurled to reveal a treasury of dried chili peppers, Sichuan peppercorns, walnuts, and dried beans. Just behind the bags, a young man is making fresh spring-roll skins, his hand deftly manipulating the loose dough as he rubs it in a circle across the surface of a hot grill and then quickly removes the cooked skin. Meanwhile, his wife is busy stuffing wontons and dumplings.

On another side street (Guo Kui Lu) the market continues for a distance with vendors selling all kinds of eggs. There are fresh duck and chicken eggs, quail eggs, thousand-year-old eggs, and preserved duck eggs. You can stand and watch women pressing dark clay around duck eggs to create the salty, preserved dish.

If you walk away from the center of town toward the Minshan Hotel, the market continues with a street as well provisioned with gardening items as a nursery. Small shrubs and plants, seeds, and gardening implements are stacked on tables left and right. Beautiful bouquets of vivid flowers draw a host of bees. Gradually, the greenery is replaced with endless rows of fish tanks filled with shimmering tropical fish swimming languidly about.

There are many fine markets in China, but none compare to this. It is truly a festive celebration of food, especially in the early morning when business is at its peak.

CHENGDU CANTING
(CHENGDU RESTAURANT)
—

143 Shangxi Dong Dajie
Tel.: 25338
Hours: 11:00 A.M.–8:00 P.M.

One of the oldest and most respected dining halls in the city of Chengdu is the Chengdu Restaurant. Disregard the worn carpet and peeling paint at the entrance and proceed upstairs to the main dining hall where large tables fill the second-floor dining room and pleasant private rooms with sliding glass doors are positioned off to the side. These are the temporary quarters of the restaurant while the new enlarged facilities are being built, and judging from the average construction period in China, the eatery might be here for some time.

The Chengdu first opened in 1958 and, since it is one of the city's technical training centers for cooks, immediately attracted a talented brigade of chefs. Today, the kitchen has no fewer than six special-level cooks, most of whom have served abroad. In fact, several were involved in the noted Sichuan Pavilion restaurants in New York and Washington when they were at the height of their success.

On a good day, the kitchen can turn out some excellent versions of the dishes that Sichuan cuisine is best known for. Camphor duck *(zhang cha ya pian)* is memorable, with its smoky, tender skin and meat. Sizzling rice with fish slices *(guo ba yu pian)* is a perfect example of the contrasting sweet and sour nuances of classic Sichuanese cooking. The restaurant makes several variations of the sizzling rice theme, including pork, shrimp, chicken, and black mushrooms. Fried beef cakes *(niurou jian bing)* are addictive with their flaky skins, anise beef filling, and penetrating flavor of Sichuan peppercorns. Other specialties of the house include chicken with peanuts *(gong bao ji ding)*, fish-flavored pork *(wu xiang zhu rou)*, and dry-cooked green beans *(gan shao si ji dou)*, as well as snacks like *dan dan* noodles *(dan dan mian)* and hot chili oil dumplings *(zhong shuijiao)*.

It is possible to just walk into the restaurant and order from the menu, which unfortunately is not translated into English. But for the best results, book a table and order some of the special dishes in advance. Reservations may be made as late as several hours in advance. For a filling meal (be certain to specify that you want to sample the local dishes and avoid shark's fin and bird's nest), expect to pay about 50 to 60 yuan per person for a party of four to six.

JINJIANG CANGUAN (JINJIANG GUESTHOUSE) JINJIANG HOTEL GARDEN CAKE BAKERY

—

36 Renmin Nan Lu
Tel.: 24481
Hours: 7:30 A.M.–8:00 P.M.

For those who have had their fill of Chinese pastries and crave some western sweets, the small bakery on the first floor of the Jinjiang Hotel should satisfy even the most demanding sweet tooth. At a small counter up the stairs beyond the reception desk, wooden boxes and shelves are usually brimming with all kinds of confections. The earlier the hour, the better the selection. Since the bakery accepts local currency, natives and foreigners alike usually line up for the sweets, and most items run out by noon.

There are at least six types of baked rolls each day, stuffed with cinnamon-apple seasoned coconut, Chinese sausage, or red bean paste. The rolls sell for under 2 yuan apiece. Crusty French baguettes, although somewhat yeasty and heavy, are available for 2½ yuan apiece. The bakery also makes a selection of cakes, including airy sponge cake, cream cake, and several types of mostly insipid chocolate cakes. Probably the best items are the filled rolls and sponge cake, and although the offerings don't quite measure up to a three-star French bakery, they aren't too bad for a bakery located in deepest China.

LONGCHAOSHOU CANTING (LONGCHAOSHOU RESTAURANT)

■

618 Chun Xi Nan Duan
Tel.: 26947
Hours: 11:00 A.M.–8:00 P.M.

While main dishes like fish-flavored pork and sizzling rice have gained just renown as some of the most popular culinary treasures in the Sichuanese repertoire, in Chengdu, it is the dim sum that are relished by the native Chinese. Like Canton, Chengdu is known for its small eating places where you can nibble on dumplings or slurp up a messy bowl of noddles. At the Longchaoshou Canting, all the bite-size foods of Chengdu are available, and you can feast to your heart's content.

The restaurant is spread out over two floors. The first floor is definitely the more informal of the two, with its cafeteria-style dining where masses enjoy the freshly made snacks. The atmosphere is positively frenetic with tables packed with hungry customers gobbling up the different foods off of their plastic trays. Near the entrance, people impatiently try to push their way to the head of a line where a counter is filled with cakes and pastries. In the back of the dining area, you can actually watch some of the snacks being made. In one open kitchen workers sit in circles deftly stuffing dumplings and shaping wontons. Others carry steamers stacked with multiple tiers over to a huge stove to be cooked.

For under 10 yuan, a whole meal of various small eats can be purchased with a ticket and then presented at the proper counter where trays are already stacked and waiting. The food is a trifle sloppy and recommended for those with less discriminating palates who are looking for a cheap but filling meal.

Upstairs the atmosphere is from another world as foreigners and locals mingle in a room with a decor that is flashy, yet inherently Chinese. Traditional wooden lanterns hang from the ceiling, illuminating large round tables and mirrored booths along the sides of the room. A huge bar stocked with almost every conceivable beverage—hard and soft—is an imposing presence along the opposite wall with dangling Christmas lights blinking on and off. Waiters and waitresses are lined up along the bar, at attention and ready to fulfill their customers' every need. Meanwhile, cheesy Chinese popular music plays in the background.

Many of the same snacks seen on the first floor are served here, though in a more refined form. There are the classic creations like dumplings in hot chili oil, *dan dan* noodles, cold vermicelli noodles in hot chili oil, and Three-Treasure *shao mai*. Among the more unusual items are steamed rice-powder cake *(bai feng gao)* and *san he ni*, which are mudlike pieces of soybean powder with crushed peanuts and sugar. The selection changes every month.

There are three set menus for diners to choose from. The standard meal, which offers a selection of ten to twelve snacks, costs 20 yuan. For 30 and 40 yuan, various cold appetizers and hot entrees are added, depending on the price and the number of people. (The larger the table, the more expensive and exotic the dishes.)

MINSHAN FANDIAN (MINSHAN HOTEL)

BAI CAO YUAN (GOOD HEALTH RESTAURANT)

—

17 Renmin Lu Er Duan
Tel.: 52611
Hours:
11:30 A.M.–2:00 P.M. (lunch),
6:00–10:00 P.M. (dinner)

Food as medicine has always been a recurring theme in Chinese cooking, and it is particularly strong in Sichuan province, where many Chinese herbs are grown. Until recently, it has been restricted to home kitchens and small eateries, but some Chinese chefs are now taking advantage of the worldwide interest in health and nutrition to bring this concept into the restaurant kitchen. The result is the creation of gourmet restaurants that offer traditional and innovative Chinese dishes that combine high-quality ingredients with traditional herbs and spices. One such establishment is the Bai Cao Yuan, on the twenty-first floor of the newly built Minshan Hotel.

As the menu explains, the Bai Cao Yuan is named after the legendary Emperor Shen Nong, who "tasted all kinds of plants" and followed a regimen combining food with various medicinal herbs and seasonings: "We combine the traditional way of keeping people in good health with the skill of culinary art under the guidance of the old thought 'the uniformity of man and nature.' " In keeping with this practice, the restaurant employs three dietitians as well as a chef as consultants.

The Bai Cao Yuan's decor and surroundings couldn't be more appealing. The restaurant is airy and light with windows on all sides providing a scenic view of the city of Chengdu. Handsome carved wooden tables and chairs are arranged throughout the large room, with a traditional garden taking center stage. Waitresses, costumed in long *qipao*, or high-collared Chinese dresses, slink around the room trying to attend to the customers' demands. For the most part, they succeed, but service can be slow, particularly if a large group has just arrived.

Diners are offered a choice of four menus or set meals with an accompanying 20-, 30-, 40-, or 50-yuan price tag. Some of the dishes are the same for each meal with more refined foods added as the price increases. A 40-yuan meal includes four appetizers, four entrees, two soups, four dim sum, and two desserts. The courses are small tastes, and most are attractively served in individual porcelain or bamboo containers.

Some of the dishes offered are camphor-smoked duck, red-cooked beef slices, sweet-and-sour fish, stir-fried pig's livers, steamed chicken with wolfberry soup, delicious steamed dumplings, an unusual milk drink, and steamed apple pear soup. The food is quite good with nonoily spicy sauces, but one wonders exactly how many of the dishes are true to the maxims of Chinese pharmacology. It's still worth a trip. Seats are usually available, so reservations are unnecessary.

SICHUAN BINGUAN CANTING (SICHUAN GUESTHOUSE RESTAURANT)

▬

31 Zongfu Jie
Tel.: 61115
Hours:
11:45 A.M.–2:00 P.M. (lunch),
5:30–8:00 P.M. (dinner)

Recent guests at the Sichuan Guesthouse may not recognize what used to be the old Dengfeng Hotel, long an institution in the city of Chengdu. The buildings have been greatly expanded and redesigned to resemble a modern hotel, although a bit of the small-time flavor still exists.

While a recent meal ordered off the menu in the dining room was sloppy and the service slow, the food was still a cut above the fare cooked at most hotels, and if you are interested in planning a banquet, this is probably where you should do it. Through the years, the chefs here have established an impeccable reputation, and with a little advance time and attention, the kitchen does rise to the occasion and prepare excellent food. In fact, one of the finest banquets I have ever had in China was held at the former Dengfeng, and most of the same chefs are still in attendance.

Prices are not cheap, and guests can spend anywhere from 100 to 120 yuan per person, depending on the menu and the size of the group. Although the kitchen will plan the meal, you can make several suggestions. Some of the best dishes are the sizzling rice meat slices (guo ba rou pian), dry-cooked beef shreds (gan bian niu rou si), stir-fried chicken with hot peppers (gong bao ji ding), and Sichuan dumplings (Sichuan shui jiao). Reservations should be made twenty-four hours in advance.

SICHUAN PEN REN JUAN KEXUEHUI
(SICHUAN CULINARY INSTITUTE)

—

A number of years ago, the Chinese government decided to restore Chinese cuisine to its former stature. As a result culinary institutes across the country that had closed during the Cultural Revolution reopened their doors, and even new schools were established. One of the best and most sophisticated is the Sichuan Culinary Institute in Chengdu.

Although it opened only in 1985, the school has already attained an excellent reputation, with an enrollment of about 280 full-time students and a professional staff that consists largely of special-level chefs. The institute building is equally impressive with six classrooms (one a newly built amphitheater that can accommodate one hundred students at a time), a testing kitchen, and a full library with video facilities. The school is also in the process of expanding with the construction of a five-story building that will house two restaurants that will be open to the public and student dormitories.

The Sichuan Institute attracts students from all parts of China who want to train as chefs or to teach cooking, or who are already cooks but would like to upgrade their level. Those from the first category are accepted after high school and train for three years. The others study for two years and one year, consecutively. The curriculum includes courses in culinary chemistry, nutrition, sanitation, culinary history, food theory, cooking technique, and foreign languages in a format that combines lectures and practical hands-on classes.

The school also offers classes to foreigners on a weekly basis, but arrangements must be made well in advance. Visits to the institute also may be arranged through the director, Wang Yi Ming. The institute's telephone number is 686923.

WEN SHU YUAN (GOD OF WISDOM MONASTERY) VEGETARIAN RESTAURANT

—

Wenshuyuan Dajie, Beimen
Tel.: 662375
Hours: 12:30–2:00 P.M.
(other times by reservation)

On a small side street away from the bustle and clamor of Chengdu's city center lies the Wen Shu Monastery, a popular tourist site that is one of the most active Buddhist centers in the country. The temple was first erected during the Tang dynasty (A.D. 641–907), but was destroyed by fire during the Ming period (A.D. 1368–1644), only to be rebuilt during the Qing dynasty in 1691. Its main treasures are ancient paintings, a Burmese jade statue, and the vegetarian restaurant, which is almost more popular as a tourist draw than the temple itself. In fact, it is not unusual to see a line forming as early as eleven o'clock for the window where tickets are purchased for the food—even though the kitchen doesn't even start serving until twelve-thirty.

If you don't make advance reservations for a meal here, you will find yourself at the mercy of an archaic serving system. The menu, which is scrawled in Chinese and English on the wall next to the ordering booth, is fairly diverse and extraordinarily cheap. Among the featured items are mock meat shredded with green pepper, pepper chicken, Ma Po bean curd, sweet-and-sour fish, Eight-Treasure rice, and fried bamboo shoots. Of course, everything is completely vegetarian, and no item costs more than 3 yuan.

Once the tickets are in hand, you must then proceed over to the next line near the temple kitchens, where tickets are exchanged for the food. Since tables are at a premium, it's advisable to stake one out before you purchase tickets. And don't be distressed by the mobs: just be firm and hold your ground. Despite the pandemonium that reigns and the seemingly endless ordeal of getting your food, the dishes are well worth it. Just relax and think of it as an adventure.

You can easily eliminate the trauma by booking a table in advance and ordering a set-price menu. Prices vary from a fifteen-course meal for 6 yuan per person (with a table of twelve people) to 100 yuan per person for an extravagant banquet of thirty different courses. The banquet food is much more refined than that on the regular menu (some of the dishes are beautiful masterpieces), and the small banquet rooms are quite charming. You can even peek into the open kitchen while you are waiting for your meal and watch the monks preparing the food. Reservations should be made at least one day before, and once the price is established, the temple will choose the dishes. You can offer suggestions, but the manager seems to have unerring judgment where the food is concerned. In past meals, the selected menu has always been above reproach.

WENJUN JIUJIA (WENJUN JIUJIA)

1 Qintai Lukou
Tel.: 24397
Hours:
12:00–2:00 P.M. (lunch),
5:30–7:00 P.M. (dinner)

The setting and decor of the Wenjun Jiujia are as poetic as the story behind the restaurant. Many years ago, during the Xi Han period (202 B.C.–A.D. 8) a famous calligrapher named Si Mi Xiang Ru fell in love with a wealthy landlord's daughter, Zhou Wen Jun. Her father forbade the relationship, and so they fled to another village and opened a small eatery, the Wenjun Jiujia. The restaurant thrived, with Zhou as the hostess serving the wine and Si writing his calligraphy, which decorated the walls of the restaurant. Alas, the father soon discovered them and recalled his daughter home with her husband.

The present Wenjun Jiujia opened in 1986, but it is built in the ancient Chinese style of the original with ornate carved wooden ceilings, majestic hanging lanterns, and a maze of interconnecting private and public dining rooms, many with adjoining balconies and porches. As in the restaurant of old, Si Mi Xiang Ru's bold calligraphy and paintings hang on almost every wall.

Despite its newness, the Wenjun Jiujia has a fine reputation thanks in part to its talented head chef, Liu Shang Yu, who has already traveled to the Culinary Olympics in Germany and to Malaysia to demonstrate his cooking abilities. The menu is varied and full, offering the traditional dishes that one finds at every restaurant in Chengdu, such as *dan dan* noodles, camphor-smoked duck, and delicious steamed dumplings along with several of the chef's signature creations: duck braised with tea *(wenjun cha ya)*, garlic-braised fish *(da suan lianyu)*, stuffed bean curd *(wenjun doufu)*, drunken fish *(xiang ru zui yu)*, and deep-fried rice balls stuffed with crushed peanuts *(san da pao)*.

The restaurant is very popular with locals, who book tables for family gatherings and weddings, so reservations are in order, but you only have to book a few hours before unless you are ordering special dishes. A full day's notice for a banquet, particularly on a weekend day, is recommended; 60 to 70 yuan per person will buy a filling and delectable meal.

SICHUANESE SNACKS
(DIM SUM)
■

*A*n old Chinese friend who grew up in Sichuan province, when asked to recommend the best eating places in the city, answered "Oh, in Chengdu, there are many good restaurants, but when you go there, you simply must eat the snacks."

Like Cantonese dim sum, Sichuanese snacks are extraordinarily diverse. Many are bite-size, pick-up affairs like dumplings, steamed buns, and dried beef jerky. Others demand chopsticks and spoons, such as Ma Po bean curd and dan dan noodles. They are deep-fried, steamed, pan-fried, smoked, salted, boiled, and pickled. They range from sweet to savory, and many constitute a meal in themselves.

The consumption of dim sum is not quite as ritualized in Sichuan as it is in Guangdong and Hong Kong. Certainly, as with any pastime involving food, there is always much conversation and merriment, but most eateries have no set order regarding the serving of these foods. Most fine restaurants serve a refined and stylized version of dim sum at the conclusion of banquets, and there are snack houses in Chengdu that offer exclusively an extensive variety of dim sum. The customer pays a set price and can enjoy a selection for the meal, but these places are hardly considered the sacred meeting places that teahouses are in Guangdong. In Sichuan, most snack houses are sloppy little places where eating is a quick, casual affair usually done on the run. Sichuanese dim sum are, in a sense, the Chinese version of fast food.

Sichuanese Dim Sum Glossary

*L*ike *Cantonese dim sum, Sichuanese snacks, which number in the hundreds, vary with the chef and the season. Many old recipes have been slightly improved and updated and some new innovations have been added to the repertoire, but most remain unchanged out of respect to the customers who long to reexperience the tastes they have come to adore.*

The following glossary offers a brief explanation of the most popular and traditional dim sum.

BAO XIAO MIAN (Long Folded Noodles) *there are countless variations of the noodle dish to be found in snack houses all over Sichuan province. The recipe and shape of the noodles may vary, but the toppings are pretty consistent. Generally, the dough is rolled out, folded over several times, sliced, and cooked and then served folded with pieces of spicy braised meat and a blanched vegetable, all surrounded by a mellow broth.*

DAN DAN MIAN (Dan Dan Noodles) *thin noodles swimming in a hot-and-sour serving sauce with a sprinkling of crisp fried shallots and chopped deep-fried soy beans.*

DAN HONG GAO (Fried Stuffed Egg Cakes) *this snack most closely resembles a round pancake made with a thick egg batter and stuffed with both sweet and savory fillings.*

FA GAO (Steamed Rice-Powder Cakes) *these light, muffinlike cakes are relatively bland and made with a raised ground rice-powder batter.*

HONG SHAO ZHU (Red-Cooked Pig's Lung) *while this dish may not appeal to many foreigners, it is famous in Chengdu. The pig's lung is braised until tender in a soy sauce–based liquid, then sliced thinly and served at room temperature with a splash of spicy hot-and-sour sauce.*

JIU CAI HEZI (Fried Chive Pies) *like people in northern China, Sichuanese are fond of garlic chives, using them liberally in dumplings, stir-fried dishes, and in this case, as a filling in a fried pie with a flaky skin.*

LA YU FEN SI (Cold Pea Starch Noodles with Hot Oil) *to produce these thin noodles, mung beans are ground to a paste, from which the starch is removed; the pasta is rolled from what remains, and then boiled and served in a spicy dipping sauce.*

MA PO DOUFU (Ma Po Bean Curd) *while some might consider this dish to be an entrée, the Sichuanese often eat this specialty of cubes of bean curd lightly braised in a pungent tart and spicy sauce as a snack.*

NIUROU GAN (Dried Beef Jerky) *in Sichuan, unlike other parts of China, beef is a popular meat, both in cooked dishes and dried as a snack. There are numerous types of dried beef jerky with varying textures and flavors. Some, made with fruit juice, are slightly sweet and soft; others are dry and crisp with a spicy, hot taste.*

NIUROU JIAOBING (Fried Beef Cakes) *flaky cakes stuffed with a ground meat filling and redolent of the numbing flavor of ground Sichuan peppercorns.*

NIUROU MIAN (Red-Cooked Beef Noodles) *one of the most famous Sichuanese snacks is bowls of noodles topped with pieces of beef braised in a spicy soy sauce–based cooking liquid and surrounded by a rich broth.*

NUO MI QIU (Sweet Rice Balls) *as in many parts of China, rice balls (yuan xiao) are favorites in Sichuan too. The fillings vary, but one of the most popular forms is stuffed with red bean paste, then sprinkled with a fine powder of chopped peanuts and sugar.*

SAN XIAN ZHENG JIAO (Three-Treasure Steamed Dumplings) *the Sichuanese love all types of dumplings. Three Treasure dumplings are plump with ground pork, shrimp, and fresh bamboo shoots.*

ZHONG SHUI JIAO (Cook Zhong's Dumplings, or Dumplings in Red Chili Oil) *one of the most popular forms of dumplings in Sichuan, these have a clear, near-translucent skin, a ground meat filling, and once boiled, are served in a pungent chili dipping sauce. The original recipe was said to have been created by a cook named Zhong; hence the name.*

CHONGQING

I was hardly prepared for my reaction to Chongqing. Largely un-derrated, this city has been described as smoky, drab, and indus-trial. And because of its soaring temperatures, it is frequently referred to as the "furnace of China." But from the minute the cab started its precipitous descent along the winding mountainous road that leads into the city from the airport, I was transfixed.

Chongqing has a dramatic skyline that is uniquely its own. At first glimpse I immediately thought of San Francisco, but the buildings are distinctly Chinese. The city sprawls out over steep hills, its tiny wooden houses, covered with tarpaper and perched on stilts, stacked one next to the other vertically and horizontally, stubbornly and mysteriously clinging to the craggy cliffs without any visible means of support. Winding in a meandering fashion among the shacks are countless stone steps, their beveled edges worn down with age.

In the midst of the hills and meager hovels of the old city stands the magnificent Renmin Hotel, a replica of the Temple of Heaven in Beijing. Newly restored, its cavernous cone-shaped roof and massive yet ornate structure reflects the grandeur of China's past with their almost overwhelming presence. In the heart of the old city are the colorful and crowded markets, their stalls brimming with fresh produce, fruits, spices, and dried meats. And rows of small shops offer all types of deep-fried snacks and noodles, and contain tables equipped with bubbling caldrons for the Chong-qing version of Mongolian firepot.

Directly across the Yangtze River stands the new financial dis-trict of Chongqing, its gleaming high-rise structures in striking contrast to the drab dinginess of the old city and a harbinger of industrial modernization. This new section is also a testament to Chongqing's prominent position in contemporary China: it is the largest city in Sichuan province, an industrial center, a transportation hub for air and rail travel, and a starting point for the Yangtze River cruises.

Chongqing became the capital of the area (which was then known as the State of Ba) more than three thousand years ago. The city wall was believed to have been built during the Warring States period (475–221 B.C.) and later expanded during the Ming and Qing dynasties. Until 1938, Chongqing was still surrounded by its old walls but it was devastated during the war, when it was bombed repeatedly by the Japanese from 1938 to 1941. Reconstruction and recovery began in 1949 with its liberation by the Communists one month after the founding of the People's Republic of China.

As in Chengdu, its sister city in Sichuan province, the climate in Chongqing is muggy and subtropical. The fertile countryside provides the city with a wealth of ingredients, and while Chengdu has long been considered the culinary mecca of Sichuan province, I found the food of Chongqing to be consistently superior. Both places offer a similar repertoire of Sichuanese classics, and in Chongqing, you'll also find local favorites like tea-smoked duck succulently tender and delicately smoky; oxtail soup, meaty yet delicate; and a selection of delectable beef dishes, each one better than the last. In Chongqing a foreigner may be initiated into the intense ritual of eating Chongqing firepot, a dish some may not initially appreciate gastronomically but one that will certainly provide an unforgettable dining experience.

CHONGQING BINGUAN (CHONGQING HOTEL)

—

41-43 Xinhua Lu
Tel.: 49301
Hours:
7:00 A.M.–12:00 P.M. (dim sum),
10:00 A.M.–2:00 P.M. (lunch)
4:30–8:30 P.M. (dinner)

Since its opening in 1959, the Chongqing Hotel has always had a fine restaurant. Two years ago, the hotel established a joint venture with a Hong Kong firm and brought in first-class chefs from Hong Kong to polish the chefs' cooking skills. Today the food is better than ever, with a kitchen boasting as many as seven special-level chefs, an unusual number for any eatery.

The location of the restaurant may confuse most customers. The dining rooms are situated several doors down from the entrance of the hotel proper. Proceed up the scruffy hallways to the third floor where the restaurant has been redecorated in a dark, rather somber manner to resemble a respectable Chinese eatery with a Hong Kong flavor. The tables and chairs are carved in sleek, dark wood, ceiling lights are garish chandeliers, and waitresses wear traditional tight-fitting, high-collared dresses. Assistant food and beverage manager Ren Bang Qun rules her dining room with an iron hand, and service is efficient and attentive.

The menu, which is translated into English, features Sichuanese classics with a few personal specialties of the chefs. Deep-fried spareribs *(fang xiang paigu)* are succulently tender, coated with a rich, dark sauce flavored with star anise. Strange-flavored chicken *(guai ban ban ji si)* is shredded chicken in a sesame-based sauce and a generous dousing of Sichuan peppercorn powder. Camphor duck *(zhang cha ya)* is smoky and so tender that even its bones are almost edible. Other recommended dishes include sizzling rice with pork slices *(guo ba rou pian)*, spicy bean curd *(ma la doufu)*, and spicy chicken with peppers *(gong bao ji ding)*. Excellent dim sum is served every morning in the second-floor dining room.

Reservations are unnecessary, but if you are planning a special meal, it is advisable to call and make the proper arrangements in advance. Prices are fairly expensive. A filling meal for four to six with six to eight courses will cost about 70 to 80 yuan per person. The restaurant also adds a 10 percent surcharge if you pay in local currency.

DA YAN GOU FU SHIPING SHANGCHANG (CHONGQING CENTRAL MARKET)

—

Zourong Lu, Jiefangbei
Hours: 5:30 A.M.–7 P.M.

Sichuan is called the Land of Abundance, and nowhere is this more evident than in the province's markets. Since it was in this area that agricultural reforms originated in China, free markets have prospered. In Chongqing, the central market, just down the street from the People's Liberation Monument, is a striking testimonial to both the bounty of the land and its liberal growing policies.

One can't help but be impressed by the quality and quantity of goods. Although the Central Market cannot quite compare to the central free market in Chengdu, it is still quite remarkable. Upon entering through the Zouronglu door one is greeted by the sight of huge piles of dried beef. Sichuanese love to snack on pieces of dried beef jerky, and the market offers several varieties, with flavorings that are subtle as well as spicy. There's also pressed duck and roast goose, some still warm from the oven and dripping with fat.

Further on there's the vegetable section, which in summer is a veritable field of products. Piles of ripe tomatoes share tables with snow peas, green peppers, cucumbers, eggplant, lettuce hearts, and tender bamboo shoots. At another booth, burlap bags are unfurled to reveal brightly colored dried red peppers, fragrant Sichuan peppercorns, walnuts, peanuts, and dried wood ears. Nearby a merchant lazily swats flies away from a whole pig's head. In the poultry section, live chickens cackle in cages, their heads hanging out between the bars. Freshly killed ducks and plump chickens are lined up in military precision, awaiting the customer's inspection. Bean curd of all types, seafood—even rabbit—it's all here.

LAO SICHUAN CANTING (OLD SICHUAN RESTAURANT)

—

15 Ba Yi Lu
Tel.: 41957
Hours:
10:30 A.M.–1:30 P.M. (lunch),
5:00–7:30 P.M. (dinner)

The first hint of the specialty of Lao Sichuan is at the entrance: a statuesque wooden cow is seated to the left of the doorway, its friendly eyes gazing down at those who enter. The theme is carried through to the menu, where names of dishes are carefully printed on bright red paper—silhouettes of cows. Some of the most famous dishes are oxtail soup *(niu bian tang)*, five fragrance beef *(wu xiang niurou)*, and red-cooked beef *(hong shao niurou)*.

In many parts of China, beef is not a popular meat. This is not the case in Sichuan, where ample land provides grazing fields for cattle. Since its opening in the 1940s, Lao Sichuan has excelled at the preparation of beef dishes. The restaurant does serve other types of foods, but everyone agrees that it is in the beef category where the kitchen excels. In fact, so diverse and popular are the beef specialties that the restaurant easily goes through one thousand to fifteen hundred pounds of meat daily.

Although Lao Sichuan is one of the most famous restaurants in Chongqing, the premises are quite humble. There are two tiny private rooms, the more appealing of which is entered at the rear of the restaurant, up an unsteady wooden stairway. The room is designed to resemble a traditional Japanese house. A smoked glass screen stands at one side, while directly across, empty panes made of carved wood offer a view of the main dining room. Downstairs, booths line one wall while the rest of the dining room contains large round tables. At peak hours the atmosphere is hectic. Inevitably there is a bowl of the restaurant's famous oxtail soup at every table, while bones, slung informally on the floor, are scattered in piles underneath the tables. Obviously, it is a very casual place.

One can easily order a complete meal of different beef dishes and still experience an extraordinary range of flavors, textures, and styles of cooking. Some of the restaurant's most noted specialties are their room-temperature beef appetizers. *Deng ying niurou* are transparent shreds of beef with a spicy, hot flavor. (Lao Sichuan is especially famous for this dish, and sells it in quantity to other restaurants and shops.) *Fengwei niurou* is beef with a texture comparable to dried flakes with a slightly sweet flavor. *Wu xiang niurou* are thin slices of braised beef with the rich flavor of star anise. In winter the restaurant also offers a type of smoked beef appetizer *(yan xuan niurou tiao)*. For hot entrees, Lao Sichuan offers red-cooked beef *(hong shao niurou)*, dry-cooked beef shreds *(gan bian niurou si)*, spicy beef chunks *(pao tong niurou)*, and the ever-famous beef soup *(niurou tang)*, which is slightly fatty but nonetheless delicate, its soothing broth richly seasoned with rice wine and Chinese wolfberries.

If you would just like to order from the menu, reservations are unnecessary, but you should plan to arrive before the prime eating hours if you don't want to wait for a table. For a banquet or a meal in the private room, book twenty-four hours in advance. A generous selection of beef specialties is available for 50 yuan per person.

MINGSHI HUOGUO DIAN (MINGSHI HOT POT RESTAURANT)

▬

57 Renmin Lu Shizhong Qu
Tel.: 350042
Hours:
11:00 A.M.–3:00 P.M. (lunch),
5:00–9:30 P.M. (dinner)

When economic reforms were established in China in the early eighties, resourceful entrepreneurs began to open private eateries, but they were mainly confined to tiny hole-in-the-wall noodle and dumpling shops. Today, owing to the success of these ventures, a few fine restaurants are now opening with more ambitious menus, and in some cases, fairly sophisticated decor.

Such is the case with the Mingshi Huoguo Dian, where sleek wooden tables and chairs and brightly painted walls hung with stylish photographs provide a charming setting for the serving of Chongqing-style Mongolian hot pot. The streets of Chongqing are filled with tiny stalls serving hot pot, but almost all are rather squalid. At the Mingshi, the kerosene odor can become rather overwhelming, and toward the latter part of the meal, the conversational din may be deafening, but there is certainly not a more appealing place in the city to enjoy this local specialty.

The restaurant opened several years ago and is owned by six partners. The premises were once a nursery, and according to one of the owners, a number of the nursery workers were rehired as waiters and waitresses. The intent of the eatery, so it was explained, was to introduce hot pot to a higher level of clientele. Since the restaurant is booked every night with stylishly dressed Chinese customers, it seems as if this goal has been achieved.

Hot pot is a fondue-type dish in which different raw ingredients, including meat, seafood, vegetables, and noodles, are dipped into boiling broth in a do-it-yourself-type manner. At the Mingshi, each table is equipped with an adjustable gas burner. The customer is given a card listing all the different possible dipping ingredients and a pencil, so that you can order what you please. Diners can also choose the type of broth: *hong tang huoguo* is a pungent broth spiced with chili paste, Sichuan peppercorns, gingerroot, and black pepper. *Qing tang huoguo* is a more traditional soup made with chicken broth and seasoned with gingerroot and a hint of pepper. *Yuan tang huoguo* is for those who would like to try both types of broth. The dipping ingredients include eels, squid, fish fillets, bean curd, oyster mushrooms, baby cabbage hearts, sweet potato noodles, and every conceivable type of pig's innard, including tripe, brains, kidneys, and even arteries. Chongqing cooks do not believe in wasting anything.

Many foreigners may not find Chongqing hot pot to their liking. The broth is oily, and a few of the dipping ingredients are for adventurous eaters, but you can just stick to the less exotic items. And natives maintain sampling hot pot is an integral part of the Chongqing experience.

Since the Mingshi is so popular and seating is limited, reservations are a must; bookings should be made twenty-four hours in advance. The price is approximately 35 yuan per person, depending on the selection of dipping ingredients.

RENMIN BINGUAN (RENMIN HOTEL)

—

Sichuan Restaurant
175 Renmin Lu
Tel.: 351421
Hours:
11:30 A.M.–2:00 P.M. (lunch),
5:30–8:30 P.M. (dinner)

It is almost impossible to prepare the visitor for the breathtaking beauty of the Renmin Hotel. Built to resemble the Temple of Heaven and the Tiananmen gate with a central dome tower connecting two massive wings, this magnificent structure has become a popular tourist site since its opening in 1953. And while the food in the small dining rooms just to the left and right of the entrance of the grand auditorium may not be quite as spectacular as the structure, it is certainly worth the visit.

The dining rooms, which hold only eight tables apiece, offer similar Chinese-English menus specializing in classic Sichuanese fare. The decor is appealing, with an attractive full-length wall mural depicting a lively village scene from ancient China. Statuesque waitresses in traditional Chinese costumes are helpful and efficient, offering advice on the specialties and in some cases, dissuading customers from ordering mediocre dishes. Linen is starched and spotless, another plus for the restaurant.

The hors d'oeuvres selection is quite impressive, with such unusual items as spicy rabbit in orange peel, shredded pig's ear in pepper oil, and pig's stomach with pepper sauce. For those with more timid palates, there are traditional dishes such as strange taste chicken, cold-tossed spinach with sesame oil, or bean sprouts with garlic paste. In the entrée department, our waitress steered us clear of the seafood dishes, apart from the stir-fried eels (which were delicious), explaining that since Chongqing was so far inland, seafood was not always fresh.

Highly recommended dishes at the Renmin include the crisp spring chicken, smoked goose with tea flavor (though on occasion, the goose can be fatty), fried spring chicken diced with pepper, stir-fried pork shreds Chongqing style, Ma Po bean curd, and the stir-fried pork shreds with bean sprouts. All are generously flavored with a healthy dose of chili peppers, garlic, and gingerroot. Natives might argue that the seasoning here is too tame, but most foreigners will find the level of spiciness to their liking. Also, chefs seem to show a light touch with cooking oil, so most dishes are lighter than usual. Even the steamed buns are surprisingly good with their delicate skin and lean, fragrant meat filling.

Prices are reasonable. For a filling meal with four or five courses, the price is about 30 yuan per person. Reservations are unnecessary.

WEIYUAN
(WEIYUAN RESTAURANT)
—

37 Zourong Lu Jiefangbei
Tel.: 43592
Hours:
11:00 A.M.–2:00 P.M. (lunch),
5:30–8:00 P.M. (dinner)

In Chongqing, a city of particularly discriminating gastronomes, there is practically no dissension on the topic of the best eatery. Some have their old favorites, but nearly everyone agrees that Weiyuan is number one.

Weiyuan is actually just a small, humble place (a former Japanese-style residence, the manager confessed) laid out over three floors, which are staggered at different half-levels. The first floor, which contains the largest number of tables, has pseudo-brick wall paneling with recessed lighting and cracked linoleum. On the second floor, which is a glassed-in balcony overlooking the lower level, four tables are arranged, allowing an unrestricted view of the customers below. The location also offers the opportunity to see what everyone else is eating before ordering.

During the 1930s, Weiyuan was originally part of Yizhishi, but in 1949, a group of chefs and workers left to open a new restaurant. The rest, as they say, is history.

One explanation for Weiyuan's consistent quality may be that it is a technical training center for young chefs, who start in classrooms and then graduate to the kitchen. At present, there are ten special-level cooks working in Weiyuan's kitchen, and the superb food is a testament to their skills.

It is hard to recommend specific dishes when each one sampled tastes better than the one before. Red-cooked fish with whole garlic cloves is extraordinary. The fish meat is fresh and flaky and the garlic cloves are tender and sweet, and all are coated in a rich, reduced sauce. Braised chicken wings with bamboo shoots (gui fei ji) is another favorite, with the tender chicken, crisp bamboo shoots, and pungent wine sauce. Tea-smoked duck (zhang cha yazi) is meaty and memorable with a delicate, smoky flavor. The braised spareribs (yan xun paigu) also are excellent, with tender meat that falls away from the bone. Corn soup (yu mi geng), which is generously studded with bits of smoky Chinese ham, has a potent corn flavor. And steamed dumplings are exemplary with their juicy meat filling generously seasoned with ginger and scallions. Other recommended dishes are the steamed whole fish *(qing zheng jiang tuan)*, red-cooked oxtail *(hong shao niu bian)*, crispy duck *(xiang su quan ya)*, and sizzling rice with pork slices *(guo ba rou pian)*.

Portions are generous, service is efficient, and the price is most reasonable. A very filling meal can be had for at most about 60 yuan per person. Reservations are definitely suggested, and bookings should be made twenty-four hours in advance.

YIZHISHI CANTING (YIZHISHI RESTAURANT)
—

114 Zouronglou Jiefangbei
Tel.: 42680, 47089
Hours:
11:30 A.M.–1:30 P.M. (lunch),
5:30–7:30 P.M. (dinner)

If you are walking through the downtown section of Chongqing, you can hardly miss the Yizhishi Canting. The outside of this eatery is quite eye catching, with its carved wooden paneling and traditional Chinese flavor, while inside, the atmosphere is more informal, as cozy booths line one side of the restaurant, with the remaining space filled with small wooden tables. Yizhishi is a favorite meeting and eating place for locals, especially young people, and at mealtimes, the restaurant is packed with couples and groups of friends. If you don't care to eat but would like to people-watch, you can go downstairs where a bar and ice cream salon provide a casual rendezvous long after the restaurant closes.

Yizhishi originally opened in Chengdu at the beginning of the century. As it prospered, plans were made for a branch in Chongqing, which opened during the 1940s and fared even better than the original. In 1955, the Chengdu branch closed, and many on the staff immigrated to Chongqing. Today, the kitchen employs three special-level cooks. The premier master chef, Liu Dao Ren, has been cooking at the restaurant for thirteen years. He assumed the management from his father, Chiu Chang Ming, who reigned in the kitchen for forty-five years and who was responsible for establishing the eatery's fine reputation.

While some may balk at the degree of spiciness in the food (Sichuan peppercorn powder is used liberally here, and the virgin palate may have a hard time dealing with its intensely numbing flavor), local residents contend that the food is authentically Sichuanese in its seasoning. Many dishes are very good, but some are really overspiced, oily, and a bit sloppy. And waitresses, who are usually overwhelmed with the rush of customers, can be surly. Pay them no mind and enjoy the food and the carnival-like atmosphere.

For appetizers, you can try the four-flavor chicken *(si wei ji)*, though the peppercorn powder in this dish in particular can be lethal, or the tangerine peel rabbit *(chen pi tu).* The main entrées include some Sichuanese classics. There's Ma Po bean curd *(Ma Po doufu),* spicy chicken with peanuts *(gong bao ji ding),* pickled vegetable and meat slice soup *(suan cai rou si tang),* and double-cooked pork *(hui guo rou).* Dry-cooked fish *(gan shao jiang tuan)* is excellent with a fillet of fresh fish simmered until flaky in a sea of whole garlic cloves, and Sichuan dried meat *(Sichuan la rou)* has a unique flavor with its pungent dried meat slices and bed of stir-fried seasonal vegetables. Yizhishi also prepares a medley of dim sum, the most popular of which are the steamed dumplings *(bai ji zheng jiao),* Three-Treasure open-face dumplings *(san ding shao mai),* and *dan dan* noodles *(dan dan mian).* All dim sum must be ordered twenty-four hours in advance.

For banquets, reservations are recommended, but for more informal meals Yizhishi is a casual place where you can drop in and order from the menu. For a multicourse meal, 40 yuan per person is sufficient.

HOT POT CHONGQING-STYLE

There are three nicknames for Chongqing:
Hazy City, Mountain City, and Hot Pot City.

—Chinese saying

Hot pot is popular in many parts of China, but in Chongqing, this fondue-style soup dish takes on another dimension. Its status may start to become apparent as you watch locals intently dipping their various sliced meats, seafoods, and vegetables into a bubbling broth, and then voraciously devouring them once they have cooked. While the hundreds of hot pot stalls dotted throughout the city began to suggest the devotion of the populace to this dish, the zeal with which Chongqing-style hot pot is consumed cannot truly be understood by a foreigner, unless you share the dish with a native who is a hot pot connoisseur.

Xu Ning is the chief economic writer for the Chongqing Daily *newspaper. By day, he researches Chongqing's latest joint-venture agreements and the prices of locally produced commodities. At night, he often indulges in one of his favorite passions: Chongqing-style hot pot.*

"People say that Chongqing hot pot has the following taste characteristics," says Xu Ning as he stares intently at the pot of broth in the center of the table, almost willing it to begin boiling. "The flavors are spicy, fresh, hot, and salty—making it desirable to many people. A banquet meal may have many different courses, each with its own flavor, but with hot pot, there are many different tastes involved in one dish. And you can adjust the flavor to suit your own tastes. Furthermore, a hot pot allows you to pick and choose whatever you want to eat. The atmosphere is very relaxed, and everyone enjoys it."

The most famous style of hot pot in China is Mongolian fire-pot, a dish introduced by the northern tribes of Mongolia, who cooked foods simply over an open fire. In the northern rendition, the diner dips thin slices of lamb and beef plus a selection of vegetables, bean curd, and noodles into a boiling chicken broth and cabbage soup. In the refined eastern and southern version, seafood, chicken, and snake replace the meat. Chrysanthemum blossoms are also added, providing a touch of elegance.

In contrast, Chongqing-style hot pot, like much of the local cuisine of Sichuan province, is homier, heartier, and quite oily. Some seafood and green vegetables are used, but dipping ingredients here tend to consist of tripe and pig's innards such as kidney, liver, brain, and arteries.

According to Xu Ning, the original version of Chongqing hot pot was made with ingredients that were considered undesirable for other dishes. "The story is rather vague," explained Xu as he neatly portioned green vegetables at various positions in the pot of boiling broth so that they would cook evenly. "But during the 1920s an enterprising boatman was cruising down the Yangtze River when he came upon a factory where old work oxen were being slaughtered. All their various parts were sold except the tripe, which was discarded. Since it was winter and he was familiar with the concept of Mongolian firepot, he decided to set up a stand and revise the dish slightly, using tripe, adding chili paste, and adjusting the seasonings and the broth to suit the tastes of the locals. The dish was an instant success, and other shops imitated the idea. Today, hot pot is avidly consumed year round."

Since then the dish has been adapted slightly, and one now has a choice of two dipping broths: one is chicken based with the pungent seasonings of gingerroot and black pepper; the other is made from pork bones and has the additional seasoning of chili paste, Sichuan peppercorns, sugar, wine, and black pepper. Both are exceedingly oily and heavy. For foreigners, hot pot may prove to be an acquired taste.

"Families all over Chongqing eat hot pot," enthuses Xu Ning, as he smacks his lips after fishing a piece of cooked eel out of the pot and pops it into his mouth. "There are easily over one thousand eateries in the city specializing in this dish, on every street and lane. In Chengdu, there are teahouses galore where everyone gathers to eat snacks; in Guangzhou the Cantonese are infatuated with their looks, so there are beauty parlors on every corner; but in Chongqing, what you have are hot pot shops."

XI'AN

It has been said that of all China's cities, next to Beijing Xi'an has a heritage that is richest in history and culture. And so it was with great anticipation that I set out for my first trip to this city— which more than lived up to its reputation. Xi'an did not disappoint me. A battalion of terra cotta soldiers, uncovered at the site of the tomb of the emperor Qin Shi, was certainly the most extraordinary sight. Undeterred by the crowds of tourists milling about me, I stood transfixed by a space the size of a football field filled with lifelike clay warriors lined up in military precision. Their faces, carved meticulously out of stone, were haunting, and they left everyone around me momentarily spellbound. Later, at the excavation site of the Banpo Neolithic village, I was equally fascinated by the sophisticated tools and ornate pottery left by inhabitants who are believed to have lived around 6000 B.C.

Although Xi'an may not strike the contemporary traveler as a huge metropolis, it was, at the height of its imperial splendor during the Tang dynasty, the largest city in the world, with a population close to two million. Xi'an also served as China's capital for eleven dynasties and was the center of commerce during the days of the Silk Route, from the eleventh century B.C. to the tenth century A.D. Its decline began toward the end of the Tang dynasty, when order in the governing of the city gave way to excess and corruption. And during the Qing dynasty, Xi'an was further devastated by Muslim uprisings.

Xi'an's revival began after Liberation, when the city embarked on a campaign that slowly reinstated it as a center of commerce and education. Its fortune was further ensured in 1974 with the discovery of the terra cotta warriors, which made it an obligatory stop on almost every tourist itinerary.

In Xi'an I found other unexpected pleasures. At the majestic Big Wild Goose Pagoda, my fellow travelers and I raced up the steps of the cavernous multitiered building like young children, gazing down with pleasure at the lovely view of the city that rewarded us at the top. On a small side street near the Drum Tower, we wandered into the tranquil grounds of the great Mosque, the largest Muslim monastery in China. It was midmorning, and the mosque was eerily peaceful, its yard and inner rooms awash in hazy sunlight with the low murmur of chanting in the background. The temple was in the process of massive renovation, but there were still many indications of its beauty. Brightly colored banners were hung in the doorways in honor of a recent holiday, creating a festive mood.

Xi'an is not considered one of China's culinary capitals, but good meals are there for the tasting. At the Tang Student Institute in elegant dining rooms ornately decorated to resemble parlors from the Tang period, lovely waitresses in period costume serve traditional Tang dishes. For humbler fare, one can partake of a Muslim ritual and taste the traditional hearty dish of *pao mo*, a stewlike soup made with lamb and vegetables.

Perhaps the best time of all can be had at the De Fa Chang Restaurant, located directly across from the Bell Tower. In a bright, airy dining room with a carnival-like atmosphere, you can feast your way through seventeen courses of dumplings, each one folded into a different shape and stuffed with a different sweet or savory filling. The meal ends with the dramatic serving of a fiery Mongolian hot pot. The lights are dimmed as the dish is presented, and customers hold their breath as the brass pot filled with bubbling broth is placed on the table, its shape outlined by the merry flames emanating from the Sterno below.

DE FA CHANG JIUJIA (DE FA CHANG DUMPLING RESTAURANT)
—

Xi'an Zhong Lu
Tel.: 26021
Hours: 6:00–9:00 P.M.

If you wish to indulge a craving for Chinese dumplings, or investigate the diversity of forms this food can take, the De Fa Chang should satisfy both desires. Prominently positioned in the center of Xi'an, directly across from the Bell Tower, it is a reliable, bright, and clean eatery that specializes in all types of dumplings.

The first floor contains small tables where customers devour the standard pork filling and three-flavor variety (pork, shrimp, and water chestnuts). Here, the boiled dumplings are deliciously hearty and filling, and are made by machine. Upstairs, a slightly less chaotic, festive atmosphere reigns as diners gather around large banquet tables for the "dumpling banquet," which consists of multiple courses of ornate, hand-folded dumplings, stuffed with myriad fillings. There are from seventeen to thirty-five varieties with fillings such as mushroom, walnut, beef with green pepper, cassia with water chestnut, ham, shark's fin, egg and pea, bamboo shoot and tomato sauce, and chicken with mushrooms. Most are steamed, but there are a few that are fried and boiled.

Since its opening in 1935, this eatery has enjoyed a consistently fine reputation. Its popularity was ensured from the beginning, since it was the first restaurant in Xi'an to serve dumplings with pork filling, in addition to the local favorite of lamb. The dumplings—so it was reported—were endowed with a true Beijing flavor, perhaps because of the original manager, who was from the capital city. The name of this eatery, interestingly enough, has little to do with dumplings. Roughly translated, *de fa chang* means "by keeping the business honest, you can get rich for a long time." Apparently, the restaurant has abided by this creed—business is brisk, and reservations for a banquet should be made forty-eight hours in advance during the prime tourist season (September–November and April–June) and twenty-four hours ahead the rest of the year.

Downstairs the dumplings are extremely inexpensive and shouldn't be more than 10 yuan per person. Upstairs, the cost per person for a banquet depends on the number of dumplings served. The price for reserving one table for a standard dumpling banquet is 400 yuan, excluding drinks. (A table will seat ten people.) With smaller parties, the cost is approximately 70 to 80 yuan per person.

DONG YA FANDIAN (EAST ASIA RESTAURANT)

—

46 Luo Ma Shi
Tel.: 717396
Hours: 8:00 A.M.–8:00 P.M.

One would not expect to find good Shanghai food in Xi'an, but with the proper encouragement, this restaurant will prepare surprisingly tasty renditions of some classic eastern regional dishes. Tucked away on a side street just off the main thoroughfare in downtown Xi'an, the East Asia is part of a small tourist hotel. The banquet rooms for foreigners are located on the upper two floors, beyond the somewhat gloomy entrance. Upstairs the linen tablecloths are generally clean, and the walls are decorated with the bold slashes of Chinese calligraphy hangings.

The East Asia was formerly located in Shanghai proper, but in 1956, for some inexplicable reason, the entire main staff relocated in this restaurant in Xi'an. Today, the same master chef, Song Guo Qing, manages the kitchen, and a number of the same chefs—as well as their sons—still perform in the kitchen.

The East Asia's waitresses were charming and helpful, but by all means call Chef Song and ask him to personally order some dishes for your party. He may recommend simmered fish tails, sweet-and-sour pork chops, chicken with special hot sauce, sauteed shredded eels with bamboo shreds, and mushrooms with bamboo shoots. The kitchen also creates excellent dim sum, but they should be ordered in advance.

The normal cost of a good meal is 35 to 50 yuan per person, and with several days' notice, the restaurant also prepares traditional Tang dynasty banquets. The price, however—800 to 1,000 yuan per table of ten—is not cheap. For most meals, reservations should be made a day in advance, but seats usually are also available on a walk-in basis.

JIEFANG LU JIAOZI GUAN (LIBERATION STREET DUMPLING HOUSE)

■

229 Jiefang Lu
Tel.: 21385
Hours: 8:00 A.M.–7:00 P.M.

If you choose to visit the Liberation Street Dumpling House you can be certain of being led to it by the crowds gathered in front of it. On a recent morning, as soon as the doors were opened, every table was filled, and a huge line had formed in the kitchen to buy the famous filling. (Apparently, it is sold by weight, and customers like to buy it and make dumplings at home.)

The only problem on the day of my visit was that the dumpling machine was refusing to spew out dumplings. Two huge caldrons of boiling water were waiting, dough had been put correctly in one hole and pork filling in the other, but still the dumplings would not come. (According to a friend these machines have been available in China for several years and are now used in dumpling houses all over the country. But she also confided that they have two distinct disadvantages: they do not pleat the dumplings, nor do they add very much filling.)

Finally, after several minutes of tinkering, the machine responded, and soon the boiling water was swimming with perfect half-moon shapes. It was not long before a bowl piled high with dumplings was seen on every table.

The Liberation Street Dumpling House has always been a popular place with local residents. The menu downstairs is quite basic—a few cold dishes and pork-filled dumplings. Upstairs, in the small dining room that contains four tables, you can make reservations in advance, pay 15 to 100 yuan per person, depending on the varieties, and enjoy a multicourse dumpling banquet.

To my mind, this is more of a place to sample the plain dumplings downstairs, communing with the locals. It's reasonably clean (particularly if you get there early), and where else can you get a filling meal for under 5 yuan?

JINHUA FANDIAN (GOLDEN FLOWER HOTEL)

---

8 Changle Xi Lu
Tel.: 32981
Hours:
6:00–9:30 A.M. (breakfast buffet),
6:00–9:30 P.M. (dinner buffet)

For the most part, seeking out western food in China is hardly worth the time, and in a foreign country my policy has always been to stick with the native cuisine. Still, there are some travelers who need to comfort themselves with some familiar fare every now and then, and even I, after a long trip, admit craving salads and the simpler dishes of home.

Fortunately one hotel in Xi'an, the Golden Flower, offers some surprisingly good western dishes. Since Xi'an is not particularly known as a gourmet mecca, this may be the perfect city in which to give in to those primal homesick urgings. And if you stick to the breakfast and dinner buffets, the overall price—considering the variety—is quite reasonable.

Opened in the spring of 1985, the Golden Flower has acquired an excellent reputation, and seems intent on maintaining it. (A somewhat rare phenomenon in China.) In addition to a considerable number of Chinese cooks, the restaurant employs a Swiss, a Dutch, and a Filipino chef to plan and oversee the western menu.

For 33 yuan, the breakfast buffet is a cornucopia of all the standard offerings one might expect in any first-class buffet: sumptuous fruit platters, a choice of juices, egg dishes, cereals, grains, bacon, sausage, and ham; but in addition, there's a wonderful pastry table with assorted Danish, delicious banana bread, and pecan rolls studded generously with caramelized nuts. Sticky buns this good are a rarity in this country, let alone China, and after suffering through the western-style breakfast served at most Chinese hotels, the Golden Flower will seem like heaven.

At the dinner hour, the same space becomes slightly more formal, with the addition of a string quartet that serenades the guests. Across a miniature moat that divides the room is the Chinese restaurant; if you must you can sample the Chinese dishes, which tend to be mediocre and overpriced. Stay instead with the western buffet, ignoring the à la carte menu, and enjoy the appe-

(continued)

tizer table, which usually offers about eight different varieties of composed salads plus the makings for tossed salad, onion quiche, chicken wings, and a soup. (The various dishes change seasonally.) The starters are truly good, and you could easily make a meal from them.

The entrées tend to be heavy, but there is a wide selection of meat, seafood, and vegetable dishes. (The meat is imported and can be excellent.) For dessert, the cakes were slightly disappointing, but the fruit salad was delicious, and that might be all that you can eat at this point. For 60 yuan plus beverages you can hardly go wrong.

TANG XIENG XIANG (TANG XIENG XIANG RESTAURANT)

—

33 Zheng Lou Xi Da Jie
Tel.: 22170
Hours: 9:00 A.M.–9:00 P.M.

For adventurous souls who are in the mood for both a bit of local color and a taste of an unusual, inexpensive, regional dish there is the Tang Xieng Xiang, which specializes in *pao mo*, a hearty lamb soup.

Pao mo is as much of a ritual as a food. It is said to have originated some 1,400 years ago during the Tang dynasty. According to a local food expert in Xi'an, Zhao Kuang Yin, the first emperor of the Song dynasty, who reigned A.D. 961–963, discovered this humble peasant dish one day when he was passing along the street. He smelled the rich lamb broth, tried some, and later added the soup to the imperial menus.

To partake of *pao mo*, customers are seated and given large empty bowls with dried, round baked breads that slightly resemble English muffins. As cold dishes and finger foods are served, the diners methodically break up the breads into tiny pieces directly into the bowls. They usually use about one and a half muffins, making a nice little mound of dried bread bits. As soon as everyone has finished, the waitress returns to retrieve the bowls, carrying them out to the kitchen, and she is careful to remember whose bowl belongs to whom.

As if on cue, once the bowls have disappeared, everyone attacks the cold platters, which may include smashed cucumbers with hot sauce, pickled garlic, red-cooked beef slices, barbecued lamb tripe, lamb tendons, and vermicelli sheets in a vinaigrette. All in all, these dishes can be quite good, but they are served merely to appease your appetite while the main dish cooks.

Once the cold dishes have been consumed, a hot soupy lamb dish made with tomatoes, bean threads, and scallions is served. The lamb is cooked until tender and is fragrant with spices.

Although you may feel a little full at this point, the next dish is the focal point of the meal. The original bowls are returned, now containing a fragrant lamb mixture. The lamb is succulently tender and redolent with star anise, cinnamon, scallions, ginger, and soy sauce. The broth is rich,

(continued)

and the bread bits are now swollen with its flavor. The dish is the consistency of gruel. Extra broth is served and added if desired, and the local practice is to add lots of chili paste to spice up the food. The dish is filling and unusual, and about as homey and hearty as you can get. It is particularly enjoyed by the local residents in the cooler weather. And the cost per person for the entire meal is under 10 yuan per person.

TANSHIJIE FUSHIPIN SHANGCHANG (TANSHI STREET FREE MARKET)

Dong Da Jie—Xi'an Center
Hours: 6:00 A.M.–7:30 P.M.

In Xi'an, there are priorities for sightseeing. Outside the city are the terra cotta soldiers and the Banpo Neolithic village, and in the city center, the Big Wild Goose Pagoda and the Great Mosque are a must. But if you are roaming around the downtown area, are tired of department stores, and would like to get an inkling of the daily life of the residents, you can visit the Tanshijie Fushipin Shangchang.

Not too long ago, Xi'an was considered to be a fairly provincial place, but the city has matured almost overnight as money from the tourist industry has bolstered its economy. This has also created a consumer audience with income to spend on clothing, as evidenced by the "sleek" Chinese fashions available at this market and the abundant supply of fresh ingredients. Mountains of squash, mushrooms, wood ears, and greens sit next to boxes piled high with ripe fruits. Wriggling fish share the stands with shrimps and eels. There are also all kinds of dried foods and spices. And for those who have never seen a Chinese market and wouldn't otherwise have the opportunity, this market offers a brief respite from the ancient relics and a lively glimpse of contemporary life.

WU YI CANTING
(MAY FIRST RESTAURANT)
—

351 Dong Dajie
Tel.: 71866
Hours: 8:30 A.M.–9:00 P.M.

Thanks to the influx of tourist dollars elevating the standard of living and to the demand for improvement, Xi'an's reputedly mediocre dining is changing for the better. But in order to get a truly great meal here, customers—particularly if they are foreign—often have to implore, cajole, even challenge the staff and cook to deliver their best—and sometimes magically, as our meals at this restaurant confirmed, the cooks will comply.

The May First Restaurant, as we were told by local authorities and travel agents, is considered one of Xi'an's premier eateries, but we were forewarned that the food can be inconsistent. Rather than take any chances, we called ahead to discuss the menu in depth and to get suggestions.

As a result, the meal was superb. Mock monkey brain mushrooms, cooked in a delicious white sauce, were served with a mousseline of chicken shaped into goldfish. Duck, cooked until tender and boned, was dipped in an egg-white batter and deep-fried. Mock shark's fin was fashioned from tiger lily buds and served on a bed of bamboo shoots. And the snacks, which consisted of deep-fried eggplant skins stuffed with sweet potato filling, black rice congee, and walnut cakes, were superb.

Of course, the cost for our meal was considerable. Expect to pay at least 100 yuan per person for a banquet. If you spend some time and effort in organizing the meal, the results will be well worth it.

XI'AN PENGREN YANJUSUO (TANG STUDENT INSTITUTE)
—

192 Jiefang Lu
Tel.: 26833, 29407
Hours: 10:30 A.M.–9:00 P.M.

Located on the main street of Xi'an, the Tang Student Institute is undistinguished, and its entrance is tiny and dirty. But you should continue up the stairs, where murals depict lovely ladies from the Tang dynasty. As you enter, you will be greeted by waitresses wearing similar outfits and filmy pants, in imitation of the Tang style. The design of the restaurant (with some modern adaptations) is also authentic to the Tang era, some twelve hundred years ago.

The restaurant is part of the training center dedicated to the study of Tang cooking established by the Ministry of Commerce in 1985. Twenty students, under the guidance of a staff of sixteen, practice and prepare traditional Tang dishes for the public. The director of the training center, Wang Zi Hui, is a nationally recognized authority on Tang cooking.

The menu changes with what is seasonally available, which restricts the preparation of a number of Tang dishes. Accordingly, you may be surprised at the foods that appear at your table. For instance, crisp-skin chicken, a popular contemporary dish, will precede sweet black rice syrup with fruit, a Tang specialty. While the food here is not really outstanding, the kitchen will inevitably produce one or two dishes that shine, and the experience of sampling Tang dishes is an interesting one. On our last visit the most flavorful dishes of the meal were the cold appetizers (among them the hot-and-sour chicken, the spicy hot beef, and the green beans were all especially good), the stir-fried eels with bean sprouts, the "camel's feet" hot-and-sour soup, and the vegetarian sizzling rice.

Reservations should be made at least twenty-four hours in advance, and the cost of a full Tang banquet is 100 yuan per person. The restaurant will plan the menu, and it is advisable, when making the reservation, to instruct the staff not to spend money on items like sea cucumber and shark's fin.

A NOTE ABOUT TANG COOKING
—

The Tang dynasty (618–907) was an expansive period for all areas of Chinese culture—including food. Chinese civilization has begun its southern descent, enriching the food supply with subtropical fruit and vegetables. Outside trade with Middle Eastern countries brought into play a host of new products including spinach, kohlrabi, and coriander. Exotic spices like cardamom, cloves, and nutmeg also became popular, and potent peppers made their way from India.

Meat was not common in the everyday diet, except for game, when available. Instead, fish of all kinds were harvested from rivers, ponds, lakes, and the ocean. Crabs, oysters, shrimp, and squid were also widely available.

Legumes—particularly millet—formed the bulk of the diet staples, but during this period steamed bread, noodles, and buns were first discovered by the wealthy classes. They quickly won favor, and dumplings, won tons, and sweet and savory cakes (also imported from the Middle East) were relished.

As far as cooking techniques and methods were concerned, braising and red-cooking continued to be popular in the north, whereas stir-frying was already a familiar process with chefs in the north and south, who brought the technique to the masses all over China. Another important culinary landmark of the time was the development of tea-making into a ritual and its spread as a universally popular beverage. (Previously, it had been enjoyed only in Sichuan province.)

One of the most influential factors defining the Tang style was the credited pharmacological effects of different foodstuffs. Tang texts were quite explicit about which seasonings were appropriate for each ingredient. All foods, especially seasonings, were believed to exert a hot or cold influence on the body, but the desired effect was neutral.* Thus, ingredients and spices were paired to cancel each other out. Ginger, a "hot" seasoning, became a natural flavoring for seafood, which was believed to be in the cold category, for example. In fact, many of these established pairings became the basic framework upon which modern sauces are based, and they are still as vital today as in ancient times.

* Edward H. Schafer, *Food in Chinese Culture* (New Haven: Yale University Press, 1977).

KUNMING

Kunming is not yet numbered among China's key tourist cities. Since it is situated in the extreme southwestern portion of the country at the center of Yunnan province, it is not the most accessible destination. Yet its dramatic scenery, agreeable climate, and unusual ethnic population make it a place that will fascinate all visitors.

Even from the air, as you approach the city, the sights are memorable. There are the towering snow-capped peaks that fill the horizon to the north, east, and west; the flat, fertile plain where the city is located, on the shores of the shapely Lake Dianchi; and off to the southeast, rising up from the ground in clusters, are the bizarre-shaped, primeval-looking limestone configurations that make up the Stone Forest.

One of the first things you will notice upon your arrival is the clear, dry air. After suffering from smothering pollution in most of China's major cities and enduring the damp humidity of the southern regions, you'll have the opportunity to breathe deeply, savoring Kunming's fresh air and enjoying the scenic mountain vistas, as yet unobscured by smog.

The weather is considered by many to be the most ideal in China. Although Kunming's location is subtropical, its high altitude tempers the heat, providing a moderate climate, with an average annual temperature of sixty degrees Fahrenheit. Flowers bloom year-round: camellias, azaleas, primroses, magnolias, orchids, and lilies are planted throughout the city in profusion. Accordingly, Kunming has earned the two nicknames as the city of "eternal spring" and the "kingdom of flowers."

Twenty-two ethnic groups make their home in Yunnan Province, but only a fraction live in the city of Kunming. Still, you will feel their presence: here and there in the city you'll catch glimpses of ethnic dress. Many set up blankets along the sidewalks in front of the modern hotels, accosting foreigners with appeals for changing money, while others sell bright woven shawls and handsome batik bags.

The city is an odd blend of new and old. In Kunming's northern sector ancient wooden dwellings and shops line many of the streets, and mazes of alleys contain colorful flea markets, food stalls, and snack shops selling dumplings and bowls of noodles. Further south, the streets broaden to spacious avenues, and high-rise buildings prevail. In the past few years, Kunming has seen an explosion of growth, particularly in the tourist trade. English signs are posted in many restaurants and eateries, advertising "coffee bars" and announcing western specialties.

Despite the introduction of some western dishes, there is still ample opportunity to enjoy native Yunnan cuisine. For those with a taste for adventure and the finances to support such a meal, chefs will prepare elephant nose braised in soy sauce, stewed bear's paw, and in the proper season, a multicourse banquet made with the famous local wild mushrooms. There are simpler specialties like pan-fried cheese, Yunnan ham, and steamed chicken in a Yunnan pot. And for those looking to enjoy a simple, hearty dish and to savor one of Yunnan's oldest signature foods, there is the famous Cross-the-Bridge rice noodles, a one-hundred-year-old specialty that is a delectable meal in itself.

CAIHU FANDIAN
(GREEN LAKE HOTEL)

—

6 Cuihu Lu
Tel.: 22192
Hours:
12:00–2:00 P.M. (lunch),
6:00–9:00 P.M. (dinner)

There is not a large selection of fine restaurants in Kunming, but one of the best is located on the first floor of the Green Lake Hotel, opposite the Green Lake Park. Built in 1956 and recently renovated, the hotel has an entrance that seems a trifle disheveled, and young travelers with backpacks are often scattered about. But just through the glass doors toward the rear of the hotel, the dining room beckons with its handmade sign proclaiming the daily specials.

The restaurant is large but not as overwhelming as many hotel eateries can be. About thirty round banquet tables are evenly spaced about the floor. The floral yellow wallpaper is bright and tasteful, and large traditional Chinese paintings line the walls. Service can be slow, but waitresses clad in turquoise pinafores and white shirts offer customers hot towels plucked from sterling silver baskets as soon as they are seated.

The menu is in Chinese and English, and although somewhat limited offers a selection of some well-prepared local dishes. Fried cheese is golden brown on the outside with a tender, ricottalike center. Barbecued sliced pork is deliciously tender and pungently seasoned with cumin and chili peppers. Yunnan spring rolls have crisp skins with a plump vegetable and meat filling. Fried green onion and ham is smoky and rich with the unique flavor of the Yunnan ham. The restaurant also offers steamed soup in Yunnan clay pots and the classic Cross-the-Bridge rice noodles. And if you are lucky enough to be there between the end of July and mid-August, the restaurant offers more than thirty different types of wild mushrooms, prepared in myriad dishes.

Since the kitchen employs five special-level chefs, the restaurant is well-suited to banquet-style cooking. If you reserve before four o'clock of the same day and are willing to spend about 140 yuan per person, you will be treated to a magnificent feast. Otherwise, reservations are unnecessary, and for about 40 yuan per person, you can order from the menu and enjoy a satisfying meal.

CROSS-THE-BRIDGE RICE NOODLES
—

Like most Chinese, the Yunnanese are extraordinarily fond of all types of noodles. One of their favorite dishes is called Cross-the-Bridge noodles, a filling and unique specialty that constitutes a meal in itself.

For this famous dish, plates of paper-thin slices of raw fish, pork fillet, and chicken are served along with portions of yellow garlic chive strips, blanched leafy vegetable, pieces of bean milk skin, chopped coriander, and some thin, spaghetti-type noodles. The diner also is given a large, deep bowl of hot chicken soup.

First the uncooked meats and seafood are added to the soup, along with the vegetables. Then the noodles are portioned in with as much coriander and garlic chives as desired for seasoning. The meat and seafood cook instantly, since the broth is so hot. (Most Yunnanese caution foreigners about burning their mouths on the scalding liquid. The thin layer of oil lying on top of the soup prevents steam from rising and camouflages the high temperature of the broth.) Variations of the dish abound, since the vegetables change seasonally and renditions may be simple or more complex depending on whether meat or a combination of meat with seafood is served.

There is some dispute as to how this dish came by its unusual name. According to the version printed at the famous Cross-the-Bridge Restaurant in Kunming, the dish originated about 150 years ago in southern Yunnan at a simple restaurant that served this specialty exclusively. Since the eatery was on an island, customers had to cross a bridge to eat the noodles. Word spread, and soon the crowds were so enormous that customers had to make an appointment to cross the bridge.

Cross-the-Bridge noodles are available at many restaurants throughout the city of Kunming, but there is a branch of the original Cross-the-Bridge Restaurant at 80 Nanting Jie near the center of town. The branch opened in the late 1930s and later expanded in 1949. Conditions are basic, but a bowl of the noodles can be sampled for less than 4 yuan. The restaurant also cautions its customers to wait until the broth has cooled slightly "Dear customers," a large sign beseeches, "don't be in such a hurry to eat. You may not see the steam but the soup is very hot. Even if you don't believe it, don't try it too quickly."

KUNMING FANDIAN DUI WAI CANTING (OUTSIDE DINING ROOM, KUNMING HOTEL)

—

14 Baita Lu
Tel.: 22063 Ext. 2116
Hours:
12:00–2:00 P.M. (lunch),
6:00–7:30 P.M. (dinner)

The Kunming Hotel offers mediocre food in a clean, comfortable setting. It's more for the diner who requires sustenance rather than surprises. But for the budget-minded, more courageous traveler, there is the Kunming Hotel's Dui Wai Canting just around the corner on busy Baita Lu.

Don't be confused by the first entrance, which leads you into a coffee shop–ice cream parlor. Continue walking down the street to the second entrance, which will take you into the dining room. It's a simple, no-frills type of place: about twelve folding tables with worn chairs are randomly scattered about, some of which may still contain evidence of the previous customer's meal.

Service is rather lethargic, and it may take a while for the waitress to bring a copy of the tattered menu, but you can use the time to look around and see what your neighbors are eating. Once the food is ordered, it arrives minutes later, still steaming. If you arrive at a peak dining hour, the tables will inevitably be packed with diners attacking their food with gusto.

The food is a trifle sloppy but nicely seasoned, and portions are generous. You can sample the standard Yunnan specialties such as steamed chicken in a Yunnan pot *(qi guo ji)*, fried cheese *(jian ru bing)*, and Yunnan spring rolls *(Yunnan chun juan)*. There also are some excellent Sichuanese favorites such as diced chicken with hot peppers *(gong bao ji ding)*, fish-flavored meat shreds *(yu xiang rou si)*, home-style bean curd *(jia chang doufu)*, and cabbage and bean curd soup *(baicai doufu tang)*.

The china dishes may be chipped, and chopsticks are disposable, but you can bring your own beer, and you can't beat the prices. For five to six courses and rice, the price will be about 8 yuan per person for a party of four to six.

NANYUAN FANDIAN (NANYUAN NATIONAL DANCE AND MUSIC RESTAURANT)

260 Luoshiwan
Shuanglongqiao
Tel.: 37225, 35742
Hours:
12:00–2:30 P.M. (lunch),
6:00-9:30 P.M. (dinner)

For some reason, even though everyone in town had suggested that the Nanyuan was the best restaurant in the city, I resisted going there. Maybe it was the description of the Yunnanese minorities' dance program that takes place every night after dinner, making me fear that the eatery was more like a dinner night club and most likely a tourist trap. Even after local food authorities encouraged me, I was reluctant, but after a visit to the restaurant to look around, I relented, and the meals there proved to be some of the best sampled in Kunming.

The Nanyuan, which opened in 1988, is the place where many foreign tourist groups are taken. The main dining area is on the second floor in a sprawling room with an apparently endless supply of banquet tables. A makeshift stage stands at one corner near a garden with an impressive rock sculpture decorated with a prominent neon sign proclaiming "Guest Is Emperor." For smaller parties, there are square tables randomly arranged near the stage, and more are added throughout the evening as customers straggle in. In the back, four private rooms provide dining for groups who desire privacy.

Generally, the crowd is a mixture of local residents accompanied by relatives and overseas friends, or Taiwan and Hong Kong tourists. The entertainment begins even before the official show as you watch everyone merrily toasting and feasting away. Things usually don't get out of hand.

Surprisingly, the food tends to be excellent, and the menu offers an eclectic selection of Yunnan, Guangdong, Sichuan, Suzhou, and minority specialties. The wisest approach however, is to stick to the local dishes. Simmered Yunnan ham with cheese *(huo jia ru bing)* is delectable, with the smokiness of the ham contrasting nicely with the creamy blandess of the cheese. Yunnan baked duck *(Yunnan kao ya)* is crisp and tender. Chicken in a Yunnan pot *(qiguo ji)* is superb with its clear, fragrant chicken broth and tender meat. Peppercorn spareribs *(jiao yan paigu)* are unusually spicy, and the snacks are outstanding, particularly the flaky turnip cakes *(luobo si)*, Nanyuan steamed dumplings *(Nanyuan tang bao)*, and steamed shrimp dumplings *(xia rong zheng jiao)*.

The food is also a prelude to the show, which begins promptly at eight o'clock and features native minority folk dancing and singing. Some of the numbers are a little sentimental, but most are quite charming with young girls dressed in the colorful costumes of the Dai and Yi minorities of Yunnan. Their dancing teachers stand on the side, intently watching and coaching their every move. A four-piece ensemble with traditional Chinese instruments accompanies the dancers.

This is probably one of the most popular restaurants in the city, so reservations are highly recommended. Bookings should be made the day before. Prices vary depending on the dishes ordered. A very satisfying meal ordered from the menu can be had for 45 yuan per person (or you can specify a set meal). Banquets range anywhere from 40 to 130 yuan per person for a full table of twelve people.

TANG MING KAFEI CANTING (TANG'S CAFÉ)

Wangchengpo Haigenglu
Tel.: 41529
Hours:
11:00 A.M.–2:00 P.M. (lunch),
5:30–9:00 P.M. (dinner)

Tang's Café is not easily described. On a rather desolate stretch of road just outside the city, you will come upon a small group of buildings with a gaily painted archway. If you continue just a bit further, you will see a building with a neon sign annouuncing "Coffee Shop Welcome," which signals the location.

Upon entering however, there is little evidence of any coffee shop. In a masterful feat of design, the owners have built a huge stage on the ground floor apparently carved out of a mammoth tree. The first floor is merely a club (or maybe this is where you are supposed to drink coffee) and the scene for local entertainment, which takes place nightly. The restaurant is located on a huge open balcony overlooking the stage on the second floor. The entire interior is designed to resemble a dark jungle, and stuffed birds are positioned throughout, hanging from tree branches. Garish tables of inlaid marble with wooden trim are arranged about in nooks in the elaborate landscaping.

You may be approached by a wizened old man with a long scraggly beard offering small boxes of Yunnan tea and plates of layer cake with bright pink frosting. This is Tang Pin Zi, the managing director of the restuarant, who speaks passable English (Tang once served as cook and manager for the mess hall of the U.S. forces stationed in Kunming.) Tang will translate the menu, which is written and Xeroxed, and he will probably recommend some of the most expensive dishes, punctuating each sentence with the phrase "my friend."

Opened in 1987, Tang's Café is the product of a joint-venture partnership between local Chinese and overseas Chinese from Burma. For the first two years, Tang's became known as one of the best restaurants in the city, but lately the kitchen seems to be slipping, and the food tends to be inconsistent. A visit to Tang's is more for the experience than for the food, so you might go after dinner and just order coffee.

The menu is varied but the strengths of the kitchen lie in the preparation of local specialties. As in other restaurants in Kunming, during July and August you can enjoy a mushroom feast with the different types of local wild mushrooms. Yunnan spring rolls *(Yunnan chun juan)* have a delicious filling but can be greasy. Steamed chicken in Yunnan pot *(qi guo ji)* is nicely flavored with a mellow broth and plump pieces of chicken. Baked chicken *(kao ji)* has a nicely seasoned crisp coating with juicy meat. Deep-fried frog's legs *(gong bao niuwa)* are incredibly meaty (each one weighs half a pound) but very expensive. Three-way cooked chicken *(da ji san wei)* and three-way cooked fish *(xian yu san chi)* are costly but offer the diner three different dishes made with the same chicken or whole fish.

Prices are very high if you are ordering the costly delicacies, but for a meal of the local dishes, the price should be about 60 yuan per person. Reservations are recommended but not always necessary.

YUNXIULOU CANTING (YUNXIULOU RESTAURANT)

—

168 Wujing Lu
Tel.: 35766
Hours:
12:00–3:00 P.M. (lunch),
6:00–9:00 P.M. (dinner)

Since its recent opening in 1987, the Yunxiulou restaurant has slowly acquired a fine reputation among a small band of knowing individuals. Even many locals are still unaware of its presence, since it is quite a distance from the city center, and since the eatery specializes in Yangzhou and Huiyang, or eastern-style cuisine. But it is an undiscovered jewel for foreigners.

The entrance and first floor are a little run down, but proceed up the stairs to the second floor, where bright bouquets of fresh flowers gaily preside at the center of every table, and a striking floor-to-ceiling tile mural with bold colors frames the rear wall of the restaurant. To the right, a row of large windows gives the room a bright, airy feeling, and waitresses nattily costumed in white silk blouses, red bow ties, and scarlet-colored skirts scurry about. The service is excellent, and dapper-looking Xu Wei Min, the manager, rules with an iron hand.

It is surprising to find a restaurant specializing in the classic dishes of eastern regional cuisine in Yunnan, a province located in the extreme west of China. According to Xu, during the Sui and Tang dynasties, some thirteen hundred years ago, large groups of Chinese emigrated from Nanjing, bringing with them the local dishes. Today, although the Yunnanese prefer the heartier and robust specialties of the western school, many crave the refined and subtle seasonings of eastern China. Yunxiulou offers both.

The kitchen excels at age-old eastern classics such as stir-fried eels (qing chao shanyu), red-cooked chicken (hong shao ji gu jiang), steamed dumplings (xiao long bao), dry-cooked pomfret (gan shao changyu), and Yangzhou fried rice (Yangzhou chao fan). But there is also an impressive list of local dishes such as Cross-the-Bridge noodles (Guo Qiao mi xian) and deep-fried spareribs with hot and sour sauce (you cuan da pai).

Dishes arrive promptly, still sizzling from the fire. Service, if anything, is overly solicitous. There is a handwritten English menu, and in addition to the names of dishes, there is a page devoted to what the restaurant considers essential items, such as teapot, pepper shaker, ashtray, toothpick, and toilet paper. This is one restaurant that attempts to meet the customer's every demand.

Reservations for dinner should be made the day before, and a delicious multicourse meal ordered from the menu will cost about 30 yuan per person.

STEAMED CHICKEN IN A POT, OR STEAMPOT CHICKEN

*T*he classic Yunnan steamer has become justly famous for its unique design and attractive shape. Fashioned out of red clay, the pot has a central chimney that allows steam to enter, spraying the food within with a fine mist and creating a rich, clear broth.

Today, many soups are prepared in the Yunnan pot, but the classic recipe was originally made with chicken. In fact, according to some sources, the pot was created over one hundred years ago in Yanglin, near the famous Stone Forest, by a man who sold the pots with the steamed chicken. At that time, the dish was known as Yanglin chicken.

The first pots were crude, but gradually the design was refined, and flowers, birds, and lines of poetry were hand painted on the sides. Soon the dish came to be known by its present name—steampot chicken.

The most traditional recipe for steampot chicken is made simply with a whole chicken seasoned with rice wine, gingerroot, and scallions. Variations are made by adding black mushrooms and different types of Chinese herbs that lend flavor and transform the dish into a tonic that may be taken as a cure for various ills.

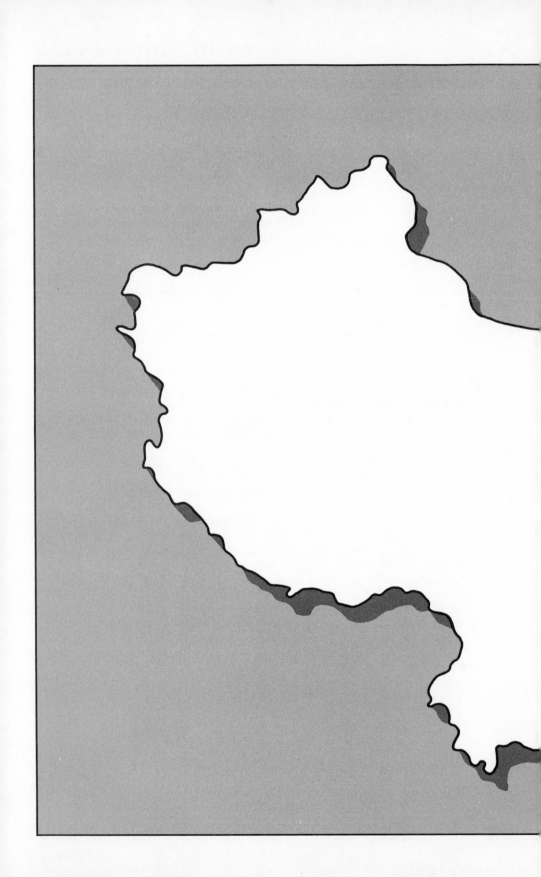

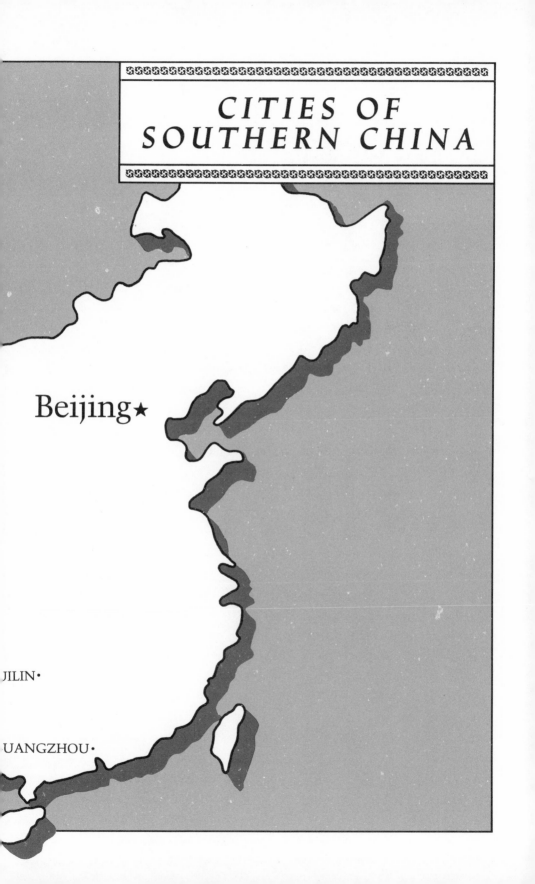

CITIES OF
SOUTHERN CHINA

Beijing★

JILIN·

UANGZHOU·

GUANGDONG COOKING
(SOUTHERN)

If you like good food, go to Canton.
If it moves on four legs, the Cantonese will eat it.

—TWO CHINESE SAYINGS

T he province of Guangdong, with its lush climate and rich supply of food products, has long been considered an eating mecca in China. There are not only delicious things to be tasted here but also an unabashed enthusiasm for and interest in food. The Cantonese—perhaps more than anyone else in China—simply *love* to eat. Just visit one of the host of fine restaurants, and you'll be certain to find it packed with customers at almost any hour of the day.

Eating is a particular pleasure in Guangzhou, the capital city, for resident and visitor alike. After consuming the rich, mellow flavors of Shanghai seasonings, and feasting on the fiery, oily specialties of Sichuan and Hunan, Guangzhou offers the simple, unadorned taste of the foods themselves. There are the whole steamed fish—so fresh that you know they have just been pulled from the water—and the delicious crunch of stir-fried vegetables, crisp at the stem, tender at the leaves, and imbued with the flavor of the hot fire heightened with wine and oil. It is these and other comparable dishes that have encouraged Chinese gastronomes to label Cantonese cooking the haute cuisine of China.

Guangdong has a long history as a culinary center. For centuries it has been a major rice bowl of China. From the period of the Han dynasty (206 B.C.–A.D. 220), rice has been a staple food in the south, and was planted in northern regions only during the Sung dynasty (960–1279), when strains were finally made adaptable to the cooler weather.

The climate of Guangdong, with its subtropical temperatures, fosters a cornucopia of ingredients for Cantonese chefs. All types of vegetables thrive year-round. Go to any market and compare the variety of products available there to those of the northern regions. Fruits—bananas, melons, pineapples, oranges, and litchis —are also plentiful, and occasionally used in whimsical combinations with meat and seafood. Since Guangdong borders the sea and lakes and ponds abound, fresh and saltwater varieties of all types of fish and seafood thrive. Crab, shrimp, lobster, grouper, pomfret, carp, and flounder are among the most popular species.

The Cantonese are equally fond of meat. Poultry, including chicken, duck, goose, and squab, is in great demand, as are pork and beef. Wild game such as civet, bear, snake, and raccoon is also favored, as are more unusual animals like monkey, dog, and rat, which have earned people here the reputation as diehard gourmands who will eat almost anything.

The primary cooking methods are stir-frying and steaming, two simple techniques that allow the natural flavors of the foods to come through. Barbecuing and roasting are also popular. Apart from the frequent use of scallions, gingerroot, and wine, Cantonese chefs are light-handed when it comes to seasonings, allowing the ingredients' intrinsic tastes to become accentuated in the cooking process.

Cantonese chefs have received just renown for their entrees, but they are also the acknowledged masters of the dim sum snack form. While dumplings are offered in eateries all over China, it is the Cantonese who consistently produce the most diverse and refined varieties. Most southern cooks also excel in the preparation of noodles, steamed breads, soups, and all types of sweet and

savory pastries. Some dim sum restaurant kitchens boast a repertory of over a thousand items.

For all these reasons and more, Guangdong has become a veritable gastronomic heaven. You may be impressed with the universal passion for food in China, but nowhere is this more apparent than in the stylish and sophisticated city of Guangzhou.

GUANGZHOU

Guangzhou did not excite me as much as other cities had on my first visit to China in 1979. It lacked the grandeur of Beijing, and had none of the frenetic chaos or special charm of Shanghai. Even the fact that it was clearly a step ahead of the rest of China, with its extravagant signboards advertising electrical goods and the colorful haute couture of its residents, did little to gain my affection.

After several years I returned to what seemed to be a different city entirely. An excitement and exuberance that clearly had been missing in earlier years now filled the streets. The drabness had been replaced by a colorful vitality that transcended outward appearances. There was some inner spark igniting a raw energy among the populace. Perhaps the mood reflected the sudden, joyful discovery of making money. The atmosphere reminded me of Hong Kong in earlier times—a less worldly, less sophisticated Hong Kong.

On that second trip, Guangzhou was ripped apart by construction but the city clearly had started to come into its own, assuming an identity that reflected its traditional Chinese roots while borrowing aspects of Hong Kong and the west. The streets had been broadened and were lined with high-rise office buildings, yet amid the new structures, lush parks with traditional Chinese pagodas and majestic monuments still preserved a sense of the past.

The Cantonese are avid gastronomes, and the city reflects this passion. Its markets are a living watercolor of the area's products. Tables are piled high with all types of vegetables; glass tanks contain pools of hefty, active fish swimming about, while baskets are piled high with shrimp, squid, scallops, and oysters; and live chickens and ducks squawk furiously from their cages. One can't walk three paces on any street without encountering purveyors of gorgeous tropical fruits, and bakeries at every corner churn out fresh breads, pastries, and cakes.

Thriving restaurants are packed with customers at every hour of the day. In the early morning they come to gossip or leisurely read the paper as they sip tea and enjoy freshly cooked dim sum. At lunchtime, there may be a grand repast or a simple dish of fried rice or noodles. Midafternoon finds many residents enjoying afternoon tea with more dim sum. Dinnertime calls for fresh seafood, stir-fried chicken, or pork, with plenty of bowls heaped with hot rice. And once the supper dishes have been cleared and after a brief respite, the snack houses once again are filled until late into the night. Each day is marathon of gastronomic appreciation—a celebration of food. In some parts of China, only festivals warrant a full day of feasting, but the Cantonese need no such excuse.

One can easily understand the passion of the Cantonese after tasting their food. There is a lightness and a purity in classic southern Chinese fare that is not found in any other regional style. An integral element is a profound appreciation of an ingredient's unadorned flavor. The chef usually relies on the product, the fire, and the natural juices that result to seduce the palate.

I can remember the excitement of returning to Guangzhou after visiting seventeen cities on a recent trip to China. My arrival marked the end of a two-month journey, and I had been sampling food from Beijing down through the middle of the country. I certainly wasn't hungry, but I could hardly wait to savor the fresh flavors of Cantonese dishes.

Despite two dinners the night before and a large breakfast the following morning, I was ready for my first meal in Guangzhou. We dined in the Northern Garden Restaurant where dark burnished wood, stained glass windows, and traditional calligraphy hangings make up the tasteful classic decor. Slowly we studied the menu, discussing our selections with our waiter. Soon the dishes arrived in swift succession, each one more delicious than the last. There were steamed grouper lightly seasoned with shreds of gingerroot and scallions, stir-fried crab, still in its shell, in black bean sauce, boiled shrimp with their heads intact, bursting with sweet juice, and quick-fried broccoli in pungent oyster sauce. We ate until we could barely move and then, after a brief stroll, we were ready for the ritual of afternoon tea and dim sum.

BEIYUAN JIUJIA (NORTHERN GARDEN RESTAURANT)

—

320 Dengfeng Bei Lu
Tel.: 333365
Hours: 6:30 A.M.–10:00 P.M.

There are those who would argue that this eatery, and not the Guangzhou Restaurant, is the best in the city, and you would be hard pressed to choose between them. Certainly, the Northern Garden, with its small rooms and ornate, leaded stained glass windows, its winding pavilions and central pool, is a bit more charming and more true to the old style of traditional Chinese architecture. With either place, however, you can't go wrong as far as the food is concerned.

Originally, the Beiyuan opened in the northern suburbs in 1958. At that time, the eatery was known as a "country" restaurant, since the kitchen specialized in simple, home-style dishes such as vegetables picked and cooked straight from the garden. But everything was made with only the freshest local ingredients. Years later, even after a move to a more central location within the city, this restaurant still maintains its high standards, and the kitchen's repertory of dishes has expanded and become refined. Even the tea is reputed to be brewed with spring water.

Dishes that are a must to try are the following: steamed fish (served whole and sprinkled with soy sauce, shredded gingerroot, and scallions); stir-fried crabs in ginger sauce; roast suckling pig (slightly fatty but still tasty); boneless duck with fruit juice; deep-fried crisp chicken; baked chicken in salt; and corn soup. And the stir-fried vegetable dishes are excellent, including those in oyster sauce.

For a larger group of people, such as a table, or a banquet, reservations should be made twenty-four hours in advance. For a smaller party (up to six), seats are usually available—even on a spontaneous visit. Be prepared to pay anywhere from 35 to 100 yuan per person depending on the menu. A Chinese-English menu is available.

CAI GEN XIANG
SUSHIGUAN
(VEGETARIAN
RESTAURANT)

—

167 Zhongshan Liu Lu
Tel.: 344363
Hours: 6:00 A.M. (downstairs
for dim sum)–9:30 P.M.

If you have never had the experience of tasting Chinese vegetarian food and you are in the mood to try something different, this is the place. Be forewarned, however, that the help can be a bit difficult, and the food may be a tad bland. Still, this eatery does make an honest attempt. The name of the restaurant is said to have been inspired by a Buddhist proverb: "As long as you preserve a tranquil mind, even vegetable roots will taste fragrant." Keep this saying in mind as you sample this restaurant's dishes.

As you enter, on the lower floor to your left is a glass case filled with all kinds of sweet and savory pastries. If you are in the mood for a snack, you can sit at one of the tables, drink tea, and sample the case's contents. Upstairs, in a simple room with wooden paneling, is the main restaurant. The tablecloth may be slightly soiled, but just ignore it and let the waitress order for you. We tried to consult with her as she chose the dishes, but she would have nothing to do with us. Finally, we gave up and just let her select on her own. All in all, she didn't do too badly.

One of the best dishes was a deep-fried spring roll affair stuffed with shredded black mushrooms, carrots, wood ears, and eggs (jia san si juan). There also were mock chicken rolls made with mashed potatoes wrapped in bean milk skins and deep fried. And a vegetarian rendition of the Cantonese classic of corn soup was surprisingly good.

The restaurant offers a number of ornate vegetarian dishes, but these must be ordered at least twenty-four hours in advance. Prices are relatively inexpensive. Expect to pay about 20 to 40 yuan per person—perhaps a little more when ordering banquet dishes. And reservations, except for a banquet, are not really necessary.

DATONG JIUJIA
(DATONG RESTAURANT)

63 Yanjiang Road
Tel.: 861038, 888988
Hours:
6:30–11:30 A.M. (dim sum),
12:00 P.M.–12:30 A.M.

The Datong, with its fifty-year history, is an institution in Guangzhou, but of late, it has undergone some changes. Two years ago the restaurant became involved in a Hong Kong–based joint venture. Since then, according to those polled, the dim sum has vastly improved, to the point where it may be the best in Guangzhou. Meanwhile, the regular menu has suffered slightly. You may opt for sampling a dim sum breakfast or brunch here, and selecting another restaurant for lunch or dinner.

The restaurant is spread out over five floors with foreigners restricted to the seventh-floor banquet room and sixth-floor dining room. The crowds are usually so intense that snagging a ride on the elevator can be a major feat. According to the restaurant's manager, this eatery serves eight to ten thousand customers a day. (An astonishing number, and somewhat questionable.) Needless to say, don't go expecting a quiet meal.

The decor of the sixth-floor dining room could best be described as glitzy Hong Kong. Flashy crystal chandeliers offset the somber burgundy velvet of the draperies and chairs. The carpet, also in dark velvet, is in need of a good cleaning. (It seems difficult to believe that the Hong Kong investors spent—so they claim—"millions" to redecorate in 1985.)

Despite the shortcomings, one or two dishes on the regular menu do shine. The roast Qingyuan chicken, named after the town 240 miles away where it's raised, has crisp, nutty skin and tender meat. The roast goose is also flavorful and not too fatty. And you can't miss with the fresh shrimp that's live when ordered, boiled quickly, and served in its shell with a dipping sauce.

Diner's Club, American Express, and Master-Card are all accepted. Expect to spend up to 20 yuan per person for a good selection of dim sum, 50 yuan per person for a good lunch or dinner, and at least 100 yuan for a full-blown banquet.

WINTER MELON

*W*inter melon, with its frostlike coating and delicate flesh, is now sold in different parts of China, but originally it was found only in the south, where it was said to be introduced from India. And no Cantonese banquet would be complete without the grand finale of a whole carved winter melon soup steamed in its own juices.

For the Cantonese, the appeal of winter melon is not just in its flavor. It is believed to have a cooling effect on the body, reducing thirst (making it a most popular dish in warmer weather), strengthening respiration, and relieving asthmatic breathing.

DONGFANG CANGUAN (DONGFANG HOTEL) FOOD STREET

—

120 Liu Hua Lu
Tel.: 669900
Hours: 10:30 A.M.–12:00 A.M.

It would be hard to miss the Dongfang Hotel. With its four massive wings that hold over eleven hundred hotel rooms, the structure sits in a prominent position directly across from the Guangzhou trade fair complex. There are numerous restaurants within the Dongfang, and the morning dim sum on the first floor, although not quite in the same league as the China Hotel next door, can be very good.

One of the Dongfang's unique offerings is the fast-food concession on the side opposite the China Hotel. It's really quite hard to miss, as there is a huge neon sign in English proclaiming "Food Street" right over the door. Also, at most times, there is a flurry of activity surrounding the restaurant, since it is popular with local residents and visiting businessmen looking for a quick bite to eat. Food Street is quite informal, with simple formica tables and plastic chairs. It's somewhat reminiscent of any fast-food eatery, but it's cleaner than one would expect, and the enthusiastic crowds give it a gay atmosphere.

The menu is inscribed in Chinese right on the paper place mat, but several capable waitresses do speak passable English. The best choices are the noodles and rice dishes, particularly the congee (there are seven varieties), wonton noodles, and special dishes like salt-baked chicken and barbecued pork. Prices are extremely resonable, and most meals do not cost more than 20 yuan.

GUANGZHOU JIUJIA (GUANGZHOU RESTAURANT)

2 Wanchang Nan Lu
Tel.: 887840, 884339, 887136
Hours:
6:30 A.M.–12:30 P.M.
(breakfast and lunch),
5:30–10:00 P.M. (dinner)

Seats are not easy to come by in the Guangzhou Restaurant. For weddings, reservations are made a year in advance; for banquets, where a table or two is concerned, at least three or four days' notice is necessary (unless your travel agent has connections). For smaller parties, you could try calling several hours ahead and hope that there is an opening. To be safe, book at least twenty-four hours in advance. Despite the bother, this restaurant is worth the trip.

The eatery is laid out on four floors with over two hundred tables. There are sedate private rooms with wooden fixtures and marble floors; and wide open balconies with elaborate chandeliers and mirrors. During peak hours waitresses rush around frantically serving platters heaped with steaming food, and throughout the place resounds the subdued roar of thousands of customers enjoying good food.

The Guangzhou first opened in 1936 under the name of Xinan Jiujia and since then the kitchen has been under the command of a long line of skilled and renowned master chefs. Under their tutelage, this eatery has established a number of delectable specialty dishes. Perhaps the most famous is the Wenchang chicken, named after the town on Hainan Island where this particular chicken came from. During the the 1940s—so the story goes—the owner of the Guangzhou heard that there was a superior variety of chicken in Wenchang County. He dispatched some workers to bring samples back, and from that point the chicken became an immediate staple on the menu. The bird is first blanched until tender in boiling water. Its bones are removed, and the meat is cut into bite-size pieces. The chicken is then sandwiched between slices of Chinese ham and steamed again so that the flavor of the ham blends with the chicken meat. The resulting dish is delicious.

Other dishes worth trying are the pan-fried duck with lemon sauce, blanched shrimp (a bag with the live shrimp is brought to your table for inspection before the shrimp is cooked), roast

(continued)

crispy-skin goose (should be ordered one day in advance), the exceptional stir-fried vegetables, and the fried noodles with garlic chives. During the morning hours, the restaurant offers a variety of dim sum, and among some of the best varieties are the crabmeat ravioli and pan-fried Chinese ravioli with yellow leeks.

Be prepared to spend about 30 to 100 yuan per person, depending on the menu. There is a limited but adequate Chinese-English menu available, and although most waitresses know little English, they are charming and very helpful.

NANYUAN JIUJIA (SOUTHERN GARDEN RESTAURANT)

▬

120 Qian Jin Lu
Tel.: 448380, 449211
Hours:
5:00–9:00 A.M. (dim sum),
11:00 A.M.–12:30 P.M. (lunch),
5:00–9:00 P.M. (dinner)

If ever there was a Chinese restaurant for the romantic, this is the one. Nestled in a bamboo garden overlooking tranquil pools of water are a series of interconnecting teahouses that make up this eatery. Many of the rooms are complete with elegant stained glass windows outlined in burnished wooden trim.

I first stumbled upon the Nanyuan on my initial trip to China in 1979. Since it is not centrally located (as is its cousin, the Beiyuan, or Northern Garden), it sees fewer foreign customers. (A blessing and a curse, since the atmosphere is slightly less hectic, but the waitresses understand only limited English.)

The food, as I've discovered, can be somewhat inconsistent. The first two meals I ate here were nothing short of superb. On one of my most recent visits, however, all the dishes were disappointing, perhaps because there were only two in our party and we ordered directly from the menu. Then again, the chefs may have had a bad night.

Some of the dishes that have been worth ordering are the fried boneless goose with ham, steamed chicken with ham and broccoli, fried shelled shrimp, stir-fried frog's legs, steamed winter melon soup with assorted meat, and whole steamed fish.

Prices are comparable with those at other major restaurants, running anywhere from 40 to 60 yuan per person for a filling meal. The Nanyuan is considered one of the top restaurants in the city. Perhaps the best advice is to book in advance, setting a price limit per person, and suggesting some dishes while allowing the restaurant to choose the rest. Then again, you could try some of the other restaurants in the city first, saving the Nanyuan for a moonlit night when you aren't too hungry.

PAN XI JIUJIA (FRIENDSHIP RESTAURANT)

—

151 Long Jin West Road
Tel.: 815718, 815755
Hours:
6:30 A.M.–3:00 P.M. (dim sum),
3:00–9:30 P.M.

The Pan Xi restaurant was once described by a prominent American journalist as a "small dumpling house." Never having eaten there, I believed it. So you can imagine my surprise when I finally paid a visit several years later and discovered one of the largest and loveliest restaurants in Guangzhou.

Overlooking the Li Wan Lake in the western suburbs, the building consists of a series of interconnecting rooms and pavilions, many of which overlook the water. And while the Pan Xi enjoys a fine reputation for its main dishes, it is the small "dot the heart" snacks that this eatery is considered to excel in.

One of the reasons for its renown in the dim sum area is its master chef, Luo Kun, who until his recent retirement ruled over its kitchen. Chef Kun is one of the true masters of the dim sum art and he is respected for his craft all over China. Under his command, the restaurant has built up a repertory of over one thousand different varieties of dim sum. Chef Kun's apprentices still carry on the tradition, and every morning, starting as early as six-thirty, the restaurant is mobbed with customers who go there to sip tea and partake of the sweet and savory pastries.

By all means pay a visit and savor the ritual of dim sum, a staple of Cantonese life. Grab a table, and once you have been served your choice of tea, look for the carts being wheeled about with the hot pastries. If the selection is limited, take your bill and go to the source, the individual dim sum stations where the food is being cooked, so that

(continued)

you can grab an order as it comes off the fire. (The cook will stamp your bill for you.) The dim sum is cheap, and you can easily enjoy a diverse selection for under 10 yuan per person. Some of the most famous dim sum are the shrimp dumplings, barbecued pork dumplings, water chestnut cake, and steamed open-face dumplings.

After the dim sum, the tempo of the restaurant relaxes slightly as customers savor such dishes as Eight-Treasure winter melon soup, stewed black mushroom soup, duck shreds with yellow leeks and silver bean sprouts, crab roe with hearts of vegetable (in season), fragrant steamed chicken, and stir-fried pork with fruit sauce. Customers should expect to pay about 35 to 50 yuan per person for a full meal.

QINGPING FANDIAN (QINGPING RESTAURANT)

111 Xiajiu Lu
Tel.: 889782, 888683
Hours:
7:30 A.M.–10:30 A.M.
(breakfast),
11:00 A.M.–1:00 P.M. (lunch),
5:00–9:00 P.M. (dinner)

When Wang Yuan, the manager and special first-level cook at the Qingping Restaurant, was thirteen, he had a vision. He wanted to study cooking and to develop the best-tasting chicken in all of Guangzhou.

Today, at the age of fifty-seven, Wang Yuan may have realized that dream. Every day hundreds of customers line up at the glass windows in front of the Qingping Restaurant, patiently waiting to buy some of his cold simmered chicken. (More than one thousand chickens are sold each day.) Inside the large two-story structure, tables are filled with diners enjoying his chicken as well as other selected delicacies.

Wang Yuan will not fully divulge the recipe for his award-winning chicken, but he will give some hints as to what makes it extraordinary. (You can hardly blame Wang for his caution: he has been trying to perfect this dish for over eighteen years.) First, he will use only chickens that weigh exactly two pounds, and his simmering mixture is a combination of rice wine, scallions, and gingerroot. The chicken is served at room temperature, cut into bite-size pieces (with the bone). A fragrant ginger-scallion dipping sauce is served on the side, but the chicken hardly needs it. The meat is wonderfully tender, and suffused with the flavorings of the marinade.

The restaurant is a no-frills place, its decor pleasant but undistinguished. Prices are quite moderate. Wang Yuan prides himself on his restaurant appealing to a broad, mainstream audience, and he seems to have astutely calculated a formula for success. The restaurant is mobbed nearly every night after seven. Lunch is almost as busy.

Reservations are recommended, and bookings should be made twenty-four hours in advance. Since the menu is in Chinese and dishes change frequently, the best method is establish a price per head when making the reservations. For a party of four to six, a very satisfying meal will cost 60 yuan per person. If the group is larger, the price drops accordingly.

QING PING SHICHANG (QING PING MARKET), ZHU GUANG SHICHANG (ZHU GUANG MARKET)

*A*t the Qing Ping Market, you will see some of the bizarre staples enjoyed by the venturesome Cantonese—snake, dog, cat, and monkey brain, as well as the superb fresh vegetables and seafood that have become the dominant trademark of the Cantonese style.

Judging by the vast quantities of its products, the Qing Ping deals more on a wholesale than a retail level. It is almost endless: You can easily wander for ten minutes among the piles of dried black mushrooms, all meticulously arranged according to their quality. There are also numerous varieties of Chinese medicines and herbs from dried cinnamon peel to preserved snake skins.

The liveliest times to view this market are early morning or the predinner hours, but even at midday or in the still of the afternoon heat, there's plenty to see, even if some shopkeepers will be taking their daily siesta. Most purveyors will immediately come alive at the sight of customers—especially foreigners —who carry with them the lure of foreign currency bills.

While the Qing Ping Market deals in quantities of items for wholesale, the Zhu Guang caters more to a retail audience. It may not have the diverse selection of goods, but it is a lively, well-stocked place. One of the best times to visit is at six *o'clock, when everyone stops on his or her way home, shopping for last-minute ingredients for dinner. At that time, the market is packed, and the air is electric as purveyors shriek out bargains for customers.*

If you start at one end and walk all the way through, crossing the street that splits the two entrances, you will see all kinds of ingredients—dried or preserved, fresh, and some even still breathing. Since Guangzhou is close to the sea and fresh water, there are all kinds of fish. The Cantonese are sticklers about eating only the freshest products. To attract attention a common ploy of the fishmongers is to let the fish flap about on the sidewalk, underlining their freshness. Of course, there are numerous stands with all kinds of vegetables, the varieties changing with the seasons. And there are the counters loaded with dry goods from multiple types of black mushrooms to pickled turnip and preserved black beans.

Further along there are portable deli cases with windows where barbecued pork hangs alongside roasted chicken and duck. Customers can buy an entire piece or a section. Once they've made their choice, the shopkeeper, wielding a sharp cleaver, cuts up the piece into bite-size pieces, adds a little sauce if desired, and wraps it up. The dish can then be served as a cold first course or a meat entrée.

The market is kept quite clean, and the turnover on the ingredients is frequent, so you might even consider a visit before dinner. As long as the sight of live fish doesn't deter you, a walk through the stalls may even stimulate your appetite.

THE AGE-OLD RITUAL OF DIM SUM

—

*D*im sum has always been as much a ritual in China as it is a food form. And from the earliest times to the present, in China, Hong Kong, and Taiwan (and even in New York and San Francisco), the formula has been much the same. It begins with the meeting of the participants, who may be relatives, friends, or business associates. The location is another constant, since habit plays an important role in the enjoyment of the dim sum process. A particular table in a particular dim sum parlor may have been in the family for generations. (For this reason, in some dim sum restaurants, getting a table at the busiest hours may be impossible.) Dim sum also usually involves food and talk, and the discussion may revolve around business transactions, gossip, or family affairs.

Once everyone is seated, the meal begins with the selection of the tea. Most dim sum houses have at least four or five choices, the most common being jasmine, black tea, Lapsang Souchong, and chrysanthemum. Traditionally, the tea was far more important than the dim sum itself, which was served to foil the potent effects of the drink. Today, however, the dim sum has taken main stage and the tea is but a prelude to the main event.

Dim sum—or dian xin, *as they are known in Mandarin—are most often, but not invariably, bite-size. They may be sweet or* savory, hot or cold, deep-fried, steamed, boiled, or stir-fried. The selection varies with the restaurant and the expertise of the chef. There are the dumplings—open-face and closed; the roll-ups, such as spring rolls, sweet rice sheet rolls, and rice packages in lotus leaves; and noodles and buns with sweet and savory fillings.

In most restaurants, dim sum are wheeled in on carts or carried on trays that periodically appear hot from the kitchen. At each table, the customer selects the variety and amount (usually three or four to a plate) merely by pointing. Their bill is then stamped indicating the amount to the waiter.

In some restaurants, such as in the Pan Xi in Guangzhou, a freer, slightly chaotic atmosphere reigns as diners roam the restaurant, going directly to the source to pick up their own snacks. At each small kitchen, where the dim sum is made in front of your eyes, anyone can personally grab a serving of whatever dim sum is desired. The cook then stamps the bill.

At the end of the meal, the waiter merely counts up the number of stamps to tally the total bill. Dim sum is usually quite cheap, and since the waiters do little more than refill the tea pot, a large tip is unnecessary.

The beauty of dim sum is in its variety and the informality. Any customer can choose whatever he or she wishes, sampling a taste here and there at leisure. Lingering is not discouraged. And just when you feel you've had enough, another cart of fresh, hot pastries will come by, and you can start all over again.

Dim Sum Glossary

In some dim sum parlors, particularly in Hong Kong, where ingredients are prime and innovation is encouraged, the dim sum are extraordinarily diverse. The chef might experiment with the traditional recipe, creating a new variation on an old theme, or even a completely new type. There are, however, a number of standard classics, and the following glossary covers the most traditional forms which will be found in all fine dim sum restaurants—in any country.

CHA SHAO BAO (Barbecued Pork Buns) *airy, globular buns with a yeast dough skin stuffed with slices of barbecued pork coated with oyster sauce.*

CHANG FEN (Stuffed Sweet Rice Rolls) *squat steamed rolls made with a slippery, white sweet rice-powder skin and stuffed with a beef, shrimp, or scallop filling.*

CHUN JUAN (Spring Rolls) *slender, deep-fried rolls stuffed with pork, bamboo shoots, and shrimp and wrapped in thin skins made of flour and water.*

DAN TA (Custard Tarts) *flaky tarts with a rich and eggy custard center.*

DOU SHI PAI GU (Steamed Spareribs in Black Bean Sauce) *bite-size spareribs coated with a fermented black bean sauce.*

JIAN DUI ZAI (Fried Sweet Rice Balls) *crisp balls of deep-fried rice-powder dough stuffed with sweet red bean paste.*

LO PO GAO (Fried Turnip Cake) *slices of a steamed puddinglike cake made with shredded daikon radish, chopped Chinese sausage, and rice powder that are pan-fried until golden brown and crisp.*

LUO MI JI (Stuffed Lotus Leaves)   *steamed packages of lotus leaves stuffed with glutinous rice, chicken, dried shrimp, and black mushrooms. (The lotus leaf merely provides flavor and is not eaten.)*

NIANG QING JIAO (Stuffed Peppers)   *steamed green pepper halves stuffed with fish or shrimp paste.*

NIANG XIEHAN (Stuffed Crab Claws)   *stone crab claws that are almost completely enclosed in a ball of shrimp paste, and then deep-fried to a golden brown.*

NIUROU WAN (Steamed Beef Meatballs)   *meatballs made with chopped beef seasoned with soy sauce, sesame oil, fresh coriander, and a few other flavorings.*

SHAO MAI (Steamed Shao Mai)   *opened-face dumplings with a thin flour-and-water skin, stuffed with ground pork and garnished with a variety of ingredients, including peas, chopped ham, and crab roe.*

XIA JIAO (Steamed Shrimp Dumplings)   *delicate dumplings with translucent wheat-starch skins stuffed with chopped shrimp and water chestnuts. Soy sauce and mustard are often mixed and used as a dipping sauce.*

XING REN DOUFU (Almond Bean Curd)   *a refreshing almond-flavored jelly usually cut into squares or diamond shapes and mixed with fresh or canned fruit salad.*

YIN ZHEN FEN (Silver-Tipped Noodles)   *a room-temperature dish made with homemade noodles that look like fat bean sprouts, and generally garnished with egg shreds, barbecued pork, and bean sprouts.*

YU JIAO (Stuffed Taro Balls)   *deep-fried balls or ovals made with a mashed, steamed taro skin and a pork, shrimp, and black mushroom filling.*

SHAHE FANDIAN
(SHAHE RESTAURANT)

—

318 Xianlie Lu
Tel.: 777239
Hours: 6:30 A.M.–9:00 P.M.

In this small town about twenty minutes outside Guangzhou, the streets are filled with festive crowds carrying colorful pinwheels that they have purchased at the local temple nearby. But the temple is often secondary in importance to a visit to the Shahe Restaurant, located on the main street, where the best noodles in all of Guangdong are prepared.

Shahe noodles are famous throughout China and abroad. The rice flour used is superior to most other brands, and the water for the dough is imported from the Beiyuan Mountains nearby to give the noodles their crisp texture and pleasing flavor. The recipe, it is believed, is still the same as the one developed in the thirteenth century.

The Shahe Restaurant is much newer. The noodles were first available through a noodle-maker, but in 1955, a small eatery was built. Still later, in 1973, a hotel was added, and in 1986 the restaurant was upgraded again to a huge three-story building complete with a department store. Today, seats are packed during most hours of the

day as local residents and Hong Kong tourists satisfy their cravings for these delicious noodles.

Traditionally the menu was varied but slightly limited. The standard selection has included the noodles served in a soup *(tang mian)* or dry-cooked *(gan chao mian)* with a choice of pork, chicken, or seafood and vegetable toppings. Sweet noodles *(tang mian)* are still lightly cooked and sprinkled with a brown sugar–sesame paste topping, and vinegary noodles *(su mian)* are prepared with bamboo shoots and shrimp in a sauce. The main variable was the size and shape of the noodle.

Recently, Leon Woon Song, who is the deputy manager and a special-level chef, went to Japan and was inspired to create different noodles using the natural juices of vegetables and seasonings. Today, the menu has expanded to include mustard, chili, carrot, and beet noodles. Depending on the season the Shahe may serve up to seven different kinds of flavored noodles. The noodles are prepared fresh daily (except Sunday) by four cooks who labor from four o'clock in the morning until five at night.

The main dining area is located on the third floor, and while the decor is pleasant, it is hardly exceptional. The main consideration here is the crowds, who flock to the restaurant and will do anything necessary to grab a table. Reservations may be useless. The wisest course of action is to arrive early, if possible, and be bold—grab a seat as soon as it is vacated. Service is quite efficient, so tables do change frequently. Prices are fairly moderate. A selection of four to five noodles dishes will cost about 30 yuan per person with a party of four.

SHE CAIGUAN
(SNAKE RESTAURANT)
—

41–43 Jianglan Lu
Tel.: 88217
Hours:
9:00–11:00 A.M. (dim sum),
11:30 A.M.–3:00 P.M. (lunch),
2:00–4:00 P.M. (dim sum),
5:00–9:15 P.M. (dinner)

The Cantonese have always been credited with the most adventurous palates in China, with their tastes running from monkey and dog to cat and snake. History records that the residents of Canton consumed snake meat as early as the Han dynasty (206 B.C.–A.D. 220) and drank snake soup in the Song (960–1279). But snake is not only a delicacy appreciated for its flavor, it is considered to possess many healthful properties and is often prescribed as a tonic for numerous ills.

The foremost snake restaurant in Guangzhou is the She Caiguan, which has been in business for over a century. Originally, Wu Man, the owner, who later became known as the Snake King, opened a shop selling snake meat, venom (as an aphrodisiac), and skins. In 1939, the shop expanded to a small eatery where customers could consume a limited number of snake dishes. Today, the four-story restaurant employs about sixteen cooks who are masters at the art of snake cookery, and the menu extends to over one hundred dishes.

The restaurant has undergone many changes, and the present decor is most appealing, with a sleek, sophisticated air. Linen is starched, the glasses gleam, and chopsticks rest on ornate stainless-steel holders. The waitresses may occasionally be brusque, but for the most part, service is efficient and cordial.

Snake cookery, according to Liang Jin, the manager of the restaurant, is an exacting art. To begin with, the snakes must be killed properly, so that their meat does not become tough. Similarly, in the cooking process, if the meat is not cut and cooked in the appropriate manner, it will be inedible. At the She Caiguan, the chefs are trained in the special skills and regularly tested.

The menu here is quite impressive. You can sample an entire multicourse banquet of snake specialties, or taste traditional Cantonese dishes. Among the most famous snake dishes that shouldn't be missed are the snake soup *(san she ji si tang),* a delectable concoction of flaky snake meat, bamboo shoots, black mushrooms, and ginger served in a mellow chicken broth. Deep-fried snake rolls *(xiang bo jin long juan)* are also excellent. And stir-fried snake meat with onions in a peppery sauce is delicious, but the snake meat on occasion can be a trifle tough.

Prices are not inexpensive, since snake is a delicacy and commands a high market price. For a multicourse meal with several snake dishes one can easily pay 80 yuan per person with a party of four to six. A snake feast with nine dishes can be arranged, and the meal will cost 400 to 600 yuan per table of ten. Reservations are a necessity, since the restaurant is so popular. Generally, twenty-four hours' notice is adequate, but during the cooler months, when snake meat is in demand (the Chinese believe that the meat contains warming properties), several days' notice is required.

TAO TAO JU
(HAPPY, HAPPY HOUSE)
—

20 Dishifu
Tel.: 885769
Hours:
6:30–11:00 A.M. (dim sum),
12:00–3:00 P.M. (lunch),
3:00–5:30 P.M. (dim sum),
6:00–9:00 P.M. (dinner)

Tao Tao Ju is a Guangzhou favorite, a restaurant whose name is synonymous with great dim sum, although it also prepares an extensive selection of Cantonese dishes. Since its opening over one hundred years ago during the reign of the Emperor Guang Xu (1875–1908), it has attracted an illustrious audience of customers, including scholars, authors, and well-known actors and actresses. The restaurant itself is huge, and in order to reach the dining area, you must first go through a small shopping arcade and up a flight of escalators. The main rooms for eating are on the second and third floors, with the higher level being preferable, with its traditional Qing dynasty decor. Exquisite stained glass panels are set into intricately carved wooden screens. The floor is subdivided into smaller rooms, each one with its own intimate appeal.

Seats are not easy to come by, even in the earliest hours of the morning. Many families send an emissary to scout out a place and reserve a table. Usually, if you are a small party, they will allow you to sit down and eat, as long as you are out before the family arrives.

Carts laden with hot, freshly cooked dim sum rotate regularly around the floor, but the food goes quickly and may be gone by the time it arrives at your table. The best approach is to grab your ticket and go over to the cart (even if it hasn't yet reached your table), selecting and claiming the dim sum that suit your fancy. You may take as many as you want.

The dim sum are excellent. Steamed *shao mai* are plump and juicy, redolent of gingerroot. Barbecued pork buns *(cha shao bao)* are fluffy and stuffed full of a barbecued pork and oyster sauce filling. Spring rolls *(chun zhuan)* are crisp and delicate. Shrimp dumplings *(xia jiao)* have translucent skins and a satisfying, tender filling. Custard tarts *(dan ta)* are superb, with a flaky crust and creamy egg center. The kitchen offers ten varieties of dim sum daily, and most of the classic Cantonese snacks are available. And seven different brands of tea are offered.

Reservations for dim sum are unnecessary, but you must be aggressive about finding seats and not mind sharing a table with other parties. For a filling selection of six or seven types of dim sum, the cost is about 5 yuan per person with a party of four.

ZHONGGUO DAJIUDIAN (CHINA HOTEL VILLAGE RESTAURANT)

—

Liu Hua Lu
Tel.: 666888
Hours:
6:30–10:30 A.M. (dim sum),
11:00 A.M.–2:00 P.M. (lunch),
5:00–9:30 P.M. (dinner)

The China Hotel, with its slick, expansive lobby and gleaming escalators, is hardly where you would expect to find some of the best dim sum in Guangzhou. But tucked away in the basement, across from the bowling alley and around the corner from the post office, is the Village Restaurant, an eatery that draws praise from tourist and local residents alike for its flavorful snacks. A number of the restaurants located at the China Hotel (both western and Chinese) have established solid reputations, but none draws the sizable crowds that are common at the Village Restaurant.

You will probably hear the restaurant before you see it. Unfortunately, there is always a wait, but lines seem to be longer on weekends, and you can always slip through into the restaurant and prevail upon one of the managers within to allow you to sit at one of the empty tables. (The restaurant keeps a certain number of tables free so that guests of the hotel can be seated immediately.) Then again, if you are a guest at the hotel, simply show a key and you will be seated.

The Village is hardly the place for those looking for a quiet and sedate meal. The huge dining room, with its green linen tablecloths and green-jacketed waiters and waitresses, is usually overrun with large families. Children run freely in the aisles, playing games with one another, and service can be slow—in some cases, almost nonexistent.

This is another place where you have to be forceful to get what you want. Carts are rolled about, filled with freshly cooked pastries, but too often, the most popular and desirable varieties sell out early or are gone before they reach your table. The best tactic is to take command, grab your card, and approach the carts as soon as they come out of the kitchen. For some dishes, you just have to plead with the waitress to take some directly from the kitchen stove.

Almost all the dim sum are excellent, but the best are the classic dishes like barbecued pork buns *(cha sha bao)*, spring rolls *(chun zhuan)*, turnip cake *(luobo gao)*, Eight-Treasure rice packages in lotus leaves *(ba zhen nuomi ji)*, *shao mai*, and custard tarts *(dan ta)*.

Prices are reasonable; a filling selection of six to eight varieties of dim sum costs about 15 yuan per person with a party of four. Since this is a joint-venture hotel, most major credit cards are accepted.

GUILIN

It is impossible to visit Guilin and be unaffected by its beauty. The horizon is mesmerizing, its lush, green rolling hills generously covered with graceful palm trees suddenly giving way to jagged upright stone peaks reaching toward the heavens. The light, which changes constantly, is diffused by low clouds and mist, which often enshroud the mountains, coloring the scene with subtle shadings. This hauntingly lovely picture is mirrored in the numerous lakes and rivers that flow about the countryside.

Guilin's dramatic landscape has been depicted in Chinese paintings for centuries, but no matter how astute or talented the artist, nothing compares to the reality of its natural splendor. The town itself is fairly undistinguished, a quaint little place dwarfed by the breathtaking panorama that surrounds it. It is situated on the Li River in the Guangxi Zhuang Autonomous Region in southeastern China. The eerie rock formations and numerous caves are remnants of a limestone seabed that covered the area some 370 to 325 millions years ago. Shaped by wind and water, they intoxicate and serve as a testament to the powerful primal forces of nature.

Guilin's climate is subtropical and its land is fertile, providing the area with plentiful fruits, vegetables, and fresh seafood. The cooking style is delicate and refined; chefs are strongly influenced by the Cantonese school, which favors mild seasonings and cooking techniques that underline the natural flavors of the ingredients. In one striking departure from the Cantonese way, Guilin residents do have a passion for chili peppers, sprinkling them liberally throughout their dishes.

Guilin has long had a reputation for having some of the worst food in China. This certainly was the case some eight years ago on my first visit to the area. We suffered through meal after mediocre meal, all of which were messy and unpalatable. Fortunately, with the recent influx of Cantonese businessmen to the area and a general upgrading of the living standard, the situation has changed, and selected restaurants now serve some well-executed Cantonese and Guilin classics, as well as passable dim sum.

On subsequent visits to Guilin, I have sampled a number of delicious dishes, but most vividly etched in my memory is one of the simplest meals. It was during my first trip to the city on a five-hour boat ride down the Li River. The day had dawned misty, but by midmorning the sun had melted through the fog, leaving the sky cloudless and piercing blue. I was seated on the upper deck of one of the boats that slowly make their way down the scenic Li River, floating past magnificent hills and shapely rock formations that are eerily reminiscent of a picture postcard. As my other friends on board dined in the cabin below on fresh stir-fried vegetables and seafood (the only good meal of the trip), I sat in the sun, astonished at the extraordinary scenery, and feasted away contentedly on roasted peanuts, sweet tangerines, and warm beer.

GINZA JAPANESE RESTAURANT
GUILIN GARDEN HOTEL

—

Yuanjiang Lu
Tel.: 442411, 443611
Hours: 12:00 P.M.–12:00 A.M.

Good Japanese food is a rare commodity in any city, particularly in China, but given the extraordinary number of Japanese travelers making pilgrimages to their neighboring country, it would make sense that a taste of soothing miso soup and crisp, perfectly cooked tempura be readily available.

The Ginza Japanese Restaurant, located in the Guilin Garden Hotel, is very attractive and designed in a modern Japanese style with clean wooden tables, bold-print patterned cloth hangings, and a glass and wood sushi bar in its front. Waitresses shuffle about in colorful, traditional Japanese kimonos complete with wooden thongs and white socks.

The place is fairly empty until after seven-thirty at night, when the *karaoke* begins, but the real business doesn't start until after nine o'clock, so you needn't worry about encountering crowds. The menu is in English, Chinese, and Japanese, making it possible for almost all customers to order for themselves, and since the hotel is under the auspices of the Ramada Inn chain, at least one waiter will speak intelligible English.

The head chef, who is from Hong Kong, trained for over a year in Japan before coming to China to work and to train the local crew. Apparently, he has done his job well, because even though he was not in the kitchen, the food we tasted was above reproach. Assorted sushi is freshly made and tightly rolled with a generous dot of *wasabi* (Japanese horseradish) in the center. Barbecued chicken wings happened to be slightly undercooked but were glazed with a pungent sauce flavored with chopped ginger and soy sauce. Deep-fried vegetable tempura is artistically presented with a varied selection of vegetables dipped in a light batter and fried until crisp. The dish is served with a delicate, gingery serving sauce. The menu also offers an extensive variety of filling noodle dishes, a bowl of which could easily serve as a meal in itself. Other suggested specialties include a prawn or scallop tappanyaki as well as a mixed meat and vegetable sukiyaki.

Prices, as with most Japanese eateries, are not cheap (except for the noodles, which are under 30 yuan per portion.) For a filling meal, expect to pay about 80 to 100 yuan per person. The restaurant accepts Visa, MasterCard, and American Express credit cards.

GUILIN FANDIAN (GUILIN OSMANTHUS HOTEL FAST-FOOD BAZAAR)

▬

451 Zhongshan Nan Lu
Tel.: 334300
Hours: 11:00 A.M.–11:45 P.M.

Guilin's largest hotel has long upheld a reputation as recruiting some of the best chefs in the city, but the food in the dining room hardly reflected this fact, save for an occasional expensive multicourse Chinese banquet. In 1988, the hotel made a bold move and built a fast-food bazaar next to the hotel and adjoining the night flea market. If standards remain as they are now, the food, atmosphere, and prices are all guaranteed to make it a popular eating spot for locals and tourists alike for years to come.

The bazaar is divided into two areas. The first, as you enter, is mostly for the quick and easy dishes. To the right are glass cases containing fried pastries and cooked meats. Directly behind, chefs stand at attention in front of their woks and stainless-steel stoves, ready to whip up the food at a minute's notice.

You needn't worry if you don't speak Chinese. The entire menu is pictured on the rear wall in living color, all labeled in Chinese and English. There are numerous rice dishes with meat and vegetable toppings, including barbecued pork, chicken, roast suckling pig, roast duck, and a host of noodles with as many toppings. Also offered are selected western dishes, such as steak, pork chops, and chicken shashlik. Tables and matching circular benches are grayish marble, and plates and napkins are paper.

On the other side of the room is the more formal dining area, which is still quite relaxed. The main difference is the expanded menu, and tables are covered with bright pink and red tablecloths. Here, the menu features a number of Guilin specialties, most prominently among them is the earthenware pot *(shaguo)* with assorted braised meat, seafood, and vegetables in broth. *Shaguo* pots are so filling that coupled with a simple dish of rice, they are a meal in themselves. Other recommended items are the stir-fried chicken with chestnuts, braised sliced fish, barbecued pork, braised bean curd, Guilin-style, and steamed spareribs with black bean sauce.

The food is simply prepared and well sea-soned, and the restaurant is bright and clean. Waitresses are friendly and allow you to bend the rules slightly, ordering from the menu on either side, no matter where you are sitting. This is a great place to go for a quick, honest meal. If you order the simpler dishes off the wall, a filling meal can be had for under 10 yuan. Dishes from the menu are slightly more expensive; expect to pay about 15 to 20 yuan with a party of four for four to five dishes.

GUILIN LEQUN SHICHANG (GUILIN LEQUN MARKET)

Lequn Lu
Hours: 6:00 A.M.–7:00 P.M.

For most travelers to Guilin, a prime activity of their stay is the half-day boatride down the Li River. In fact, many groups plan barely enough time to do much else. If you do find yourself with a bit of spare time in Guilin, it is a small, rather charming city to explore, and it is one of the few places in China where rented bicycles, are readily available, making personal sightseeing even easier.

Guilin does have a fine central food market. The main section of the market is housed in a huge three-story cement structure, and most of the action is on the first story, where the floor is overrun with vendors selling every conceivable food product. In packed stalls, dried goods like black mushrooms and black fungus sit next to jars of preserved pickles and salads.

Not long ago, Guilin had a serious food shortage. Nearly everything went to tourist hotels, and the markets often were bare. Today, thanks to the economic reforms allowing farmers to raise a portion of their crops for profit, produce is abundant and the markets are thriving. Beautiful leafy vegetables are framed by mountains of red and green chili peppers. Nearby, plump water chestnuts sit invitingly. Some are cut open, exposing their sweet, white flesh.

Outside the market building are countless rows of tables set up by farmers eager to sell their produce. Further on are tiny restaurants, barely large enough to hold a table with another Guilin specialty—*shaguo*, or hot pot. Customers gather around the table or simply crouch on stools feasting on this hearty local dish.

GUILIN TAI LIAN JIUJIA (TAI LIAN HOTEL)

102–8 Zhongshan Zhong Lu
Tel.: 223030, 223021
Hours:
6:30–10:00 A.M. (dim sum),
11:00 A.M.–2:30 P.M. (lunch),
5:30–10:00 P.M. (dinner)

If you were to poll most local residents and overseas Chinese vistors to Guilin, the Tai Lian restaurant would probably be voted as the most popular in the city. With its bustling, crowded atmosphere, grand crystal chandeliers, tuxedo-clad waiters, and hostesses in their close-fitting traditional Chinese-style dresses, the Tai Lian closely matches a sophisticated Hong Kong eatery. And the food, albeit a trifle sloppy, is almost as authentic.

The Tai Lian first opened in 1987 as a result of a partnership between a Hong Kong corporation and a Guilin overseas investment group. Most ingredients, according to assistant food and beverage manager Yang Wen Bing, are imported from Guangdong, making possible its presentation of many traditional Cantonese specialties.

One of the most popular offerings of the restaurant is the daily dim sum served in the early morning. Tables usually are packed, and customers, too impatient to wait for the carts laden with freshly prepared pastries to arrive at their tables, grab their cards and hover at the carts themselves, selecting the desired dumplings, buns, and other delicacies before they are eaten up.

In the kitchen, four master dim sum chefs toil to prepare the many foods. On most days there are at least twenty-five different kinds of dim sum but the kitchen is capable of producing at least seventy. The luncheon and dinner menu (in Chinese and English) is quite extensive, offering an impressive selection of Cantonese recipes, including shark's fin, abalone, pigeon, and duck. Seafood is also noteworthy. Recommended dishes include oil-fried squid *(you bao xian you)*, steamed fish *(qing zheng yu)*, baked crab with scallions and gingerroot *(kao pang xie)*, salt-baked chicken *(yan ju ji)*, fried duck with mashed taro *(li rong xiang su ya)*, and corn soup *(yumi geng)*.

For dim sum, arrive early, or you may have to wait for a table. The same is true for other meals; however, reservations for a banquet should be

(continued)

made twenty-four hours in advance. Dim sum is about 10 yuan per person for a varied selection, and for a filling lunch or dinner, the cost will be about 50 to 70 yuan, depending on the types of dishes. American Express, MasterCard, and Diner's Club are all accepted. Local currency, or *renminbi*, also is accepted without a surcharge.

GUILIN WEIXIANGGUAN (WEIXIANGGUAN RESTAURANT)

240 Zhongshan Zhong Lu
Tel.: 222559
Hours: 7:00 A.M.–8:30 P.M.

Local culinary sources insist that, if you come to Guilin, you *must* try the fried rice noodles, a famous local specialty. While most hotel and local restaurants offer variations of this dish, the oldest and most famous rice noodle house in town is located right on the main street of Guilin.

The Guilin Weixiangguan is for the diner who doesn't mind the squalor of a small, local eating place. Conditions are basic: there are about ten worn wooden tables with matching stools where customers can be seen, at any hour of the day, intently slurping away at huge bowls of rice noodles. Small canisters of hot chili paste are the centerpiece for each table, and if you watch any customer, you will see it used quite liberally. There are several varieties of rice noodles to choose from. The most popular is the *chao mifen* or stir-fried rice noodle made with thick strips of slippery noodles garnished with shredded bits of meat and vegetables. Rice noodles with fresh vegetables *(sheng cai mifen)* are soupier, with a topping of red-cooked meat and black mushrooms, sprinkled with fried soybeans, and surrounded by a hearty broth. Guilin fried noodles *(Guilin mifen)* are dry-fried with assorted meats and vegetables and a shiny glazing of sauce. All three varieties can be had for under 10 yuan and are a meal in themselves.

FAMOUS DIM SUM OF GUILIN

Guilin is situated in Guangxi province in the south of China. Because of its close proximity to Guangdong, the cuisines share many common characteristics. Generally speaking, the seasonings for most dishes are mild. Stir-frying and steaming are favored methods among Guilin's chefs. In fact, most Guilin residents adore Cantonese cooking, and one finds classic Cantonese specialties on the menus in most Guilin eateries.

Guilin residents also share a passion for dim sum. Foremost among these local treats are rice noodles, which may be fat or thin, long or short, and are stir-fried, dry-fried, and cooked in soup. Whatever their shape or cooking method, rice noodles tend to be slippery and smooth, since they are made from a dough of glutinous rice powder and water. Apart from their interesting texture, the noodles are quite bland and provide an ideal foil for meats, seafood, and vegetables.

Guilin cooks also prepare a number of special finger foods or pastries. One of the most famous is water chestnut cake (ma ti gao), which is a sticky, sweet puddinglike confection studded with water chestnuts. Deep-fried glutinous rice balls stuffed with a sweet filling of crushed sesame seeds and sugar are also held in high regard, as in other parts of China. In Guilin, taro, which is often steamed and used as a skin for dumplings, is molded into a beehive and deep-fried. The taste is pleasant, and the shape is quite unusual. In another snack, sweet, glutinous rice is stuffed with sweet sesame filling or a savory meat center, wrapped in bamboo leaves, and steamed.

Most of these finger foods are served with tea as snacks, or they may appear at a multicourse banquet, served in between courses as an "entremets," or palate cleanser.

GUISHAN FANDIAN
(GUISHAN HOTEL)
—

Chuanshan Lu
Tel.: 222811
Hours:
7:00–10:30 A.M. (breakfast),
11:30 A.M.–2:30 P.M. (lunch),
5:30–10:30 P.M. (dinner)

At first glance the Guishan Hotel dining room seems interchangeable with any other dining hall in China. With its nondescript wallpaper and piped-in Muzak, it would hardly win awards or hearts for creating a warm atmosphere. The mirrored bar at one end and imperial yellow tablecloths do provide a bit of color to an otherwise toneless scene, but then you aren't visiting for the decor or the atmosphere but for the food. And as far as reputations go, the hotel has one of the best in the city for providing consistently good Guilin and Cantonese fare.

Service is another drawing card. The waitresses, with their traditional Chinese green silk blouses and black skirts, are slightly disorganized but friendly, and dishes arrive promptly and hot.

As in any other major hotel, the menu is in Chinese and English, offering foreigners the convenience of just pointing to their designated choices. The stir-fried beef with water chestnuts is vastly improved with the addition of hot chili peppers, giving the dish some extra spice. (You can mention the peppers when you are ordering.) The beef slices are tender, water chestnuts are crunchy and sweet. Interspersed throughout are slices of pungent gingerroot. Guilin fried rice

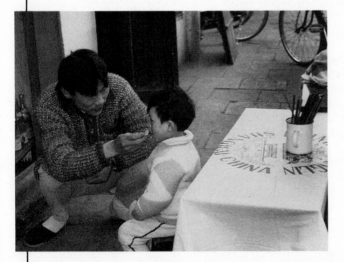

noodles are almost a meal in themselves with flat, smooth noodles amply garnished with garlic chives, pork shreds, and bean sprouts. The Guilin water chestnut and beef patty is subtle and delicately seasoned, but you can add a little more spice to suit your palate. (Like the Cantonese, Guilin natives place hot mustard and chili sauce on each table so that the customer may add additional seasoning to taste.) The Guilin soy bean sticks *(fu zu)* also are quite good (but can be salty) with their rich braising sauce studded with bits of chili peppers and yellow garlic chives. Another hearty, richly seasoned dish is the Eight-Treasure bean curd with chicken, squid, shrimp, and black mushrooms.

For Cantonese dishes, the corn soup, steamed whole grass carp, loquat or *pi pa* duck and stir-fried shrimp with cashews are the suggested favorites.

Reservations are unnecessary if ordering from the menu, but at peak dinner hours, there might be a short wait. Prices are moderate: for a filling meal with five to six courses, expect to pay about 50 to 60 yuan per person with a group of four to six. All major credit cards are accepted.

LIGUAN BINGUAN (BAMBOO GARDEN RESTAURANT) GUILIN RIVERSIDE RESORT HOTEL

Anjiazhou
Tel.: 222292
Hours:
6:30–9:30 A.M. (breakfast),
11:30 A.M.–2:30 P.M. (lunch),
6:30–10:00 P.M. dinner

In Guilin, contrary to the general rule, the best eating in the city happens to be in the hotel dining rooms.

One of the best-kept secrets is the Bamboo Garden Restaurant of the Guilin Riverside Resort Hotel. The decor is very appealing, with its whitewashed walls, wooden paneling, and large Chinese paintings. The clean design is a pleasing combination of Japanese and Chinese influences, reflecting the respective tastes of the joint owners.

Waitresses are helpful and speak some English phrases, and the menu is translated into English, a useful fact for most travelers. It does tend to get somewhat frenzied when the groups staying at the hotel are herded into the dining room, but they are fed quickly and herded back out again. You can avoid this situation at lunch, since the groups eat elsewhere and the dining room is empty, or by eating your dinner after seven-thirty.

Although they couldn't be rated as a four-star eating experience, the dishes we tasted were quite good. The barbecued meat platter is excellent, particularly the barbecued pork and duck, both of which are tender, lean, and may still be warm from the roasting process. Fried diced chicken with Guilin chili is masterfully seasoned with just the right mix of vinegar, soy sauce, ginger, and hot peppers. Fried chicken balls with water chestnuts are sweet and crunchy with the addition of the famous Guilin water chestnuts. Noodle soup with chicken and baby hearts of vegetable is also exceptionally tasty.

Even if you have the misfortune of arriving with the crowds, service is usually brisk and efficient. For a simple, but filling meal, expect to spend about 40 yuan per person.

GUILIN'S WATER CHESTNUTS

*H*uge, thin-skinned, crispy, and sweet, Guilin's water chest-nuts have become highly regarded throughout China. You can see them in the local markets piled high with their brownish-red skins intact. In restaurants they appear in countless dishes and are transformed to make some of the most famous delica-cies of the area. Chopped finely and mixed with sugar and glu-tinous rice powder, they are steamed into a puddinglike cake and served as a dim sum. Minced lightly and paired with ground beef, they are steamed to make a delicate meatloaf. Even simply sliced and stir-fried with meat, pork, or chicken, they transform an otherwise mundane dish into something special.

SICHUAN GARDEN RESTAURANT HOLIDAY INN GUILIN

▬

14 Ronghu Nan Lu
Tel.: 223950
Hours:
11:30 A.M.–2:00 P.M. (lunch),
6:00–10:00 P.M. (dinner)

Since it opened in 1987, rumor has been that the Holiday Inn in Guilin had a superior Sichuanese restaurant. And everyone agreed, including Guilin locals and foreign tourists. So after some hesitation, I decided to see for myself. My first visit, I was not all that favorably impressed. The food was sloppy and oily, and the service was arrogant and slow. But the next several meals forced me to change my opinion.

One of the first surprises you might have upon entering is the number of Chinese customers, both local residents and overseas visitors. The Sichuan Garden has become a popular place to take relatives and to entertain foreign guests.

The restaurant, which overlooks an outdoor courtyard, holds about twenty tables, each covered with a starched white tablecloth. Small touches like a colorful wall-to-ceiling mural with a flock of cranes (signifying longevity) and miniature ceramic eggplant chopstick holders placed at each table setting lend a certain charm.

The menu is in Chinese and English and offers all the expected Sichuanese classics: deep-fried crispy duck, Ma Po bean curd, spicy fish-flavored pork, hot-and-sour soup, and *dan dan* noodles. But there are also some unusual Chef's Special items that you don't ordinarily find on hotel menus, such as pig's ear in hot pepper oil, pan-fried eel dumplings, and stir-fried pork knuckle with pepper. These dishes change each month.

According to the manager, the eight main chefs are all from Sichuan province, imported for the exclusive purpose of working in the kitchens. Certain ingredients considered essential for duplicating the authentic flavors also are brought in. And for the most part, the chefs do an admirable job. Seasonings are finely tuned, and customers may specify how spicy they prefer their food by designating one or two miniature chili peppers on the menu. Most dishes also are available in half or full-size portions.

Reservations are necessary only from September through October during the peak tourist season, unless you would like to partake of a banquet. If so, it is recommended that you reserve two to three days in advance. For a banquet, the cost per person will be approximately 80 to 100 yuan per person. For an impromptu meal, ordered from the menu, the price will be about 50 to 60 yuan. All major credit cards, including Visa, MasterCard, American Express, and Diner's Club, are accepted.

GUILIN'S CHILI PASTE

While Guilin residents have a reputation of having a subtle palate attuned to the mild seasonings of Cantonese cooking, they also share a passion for fresh chili peppers and chili paste. A table in any Guilin restaurant would be naked without the mandatory pot of chili paste. After the chilis are picked in the fall, they are dried and pounded with garlic and soybeans. Salt and wine are added, and they are then sealed in urns to ferment for a season. Once opened, this condiment has a flavor that is not only fiery but mellow and slightly sweet.

Glossary of Chinese Terms

USEFUL WORDS

Baked bread—mianbao
Bitter—ku
Breakfast—zaocan, zaofan
Dinner—wancan, wanfan
Lunch—wucan, wufan
Noodles—miantiao
Rice—mi fan

Snacks/dessert—dianxin
Sour—suan
Spicy—la
Steamed bread—mantou
Sweet—tian
Vegetarian—su cai
Western food—xican

USEFUL PHRASES

Bottoms up—Gan bai.
I'm full—Wo chibao le.
I'm hungry—Wo e le.
I'm thirsty—Wo ke le.
I'm sorry—Dui buqi.

The bill, please—Qin jie zhang.
What is your specialty?—Ni zheli
  shenme tebie hao chi?
Where is the bathroom?—Cesuo zai
  nali?

BEVERAGES—YIN LIAO

Beer—pijiu
Coca-Cola—kekoukele
Coffee—kafei
Cold, boiled water—liangkaishui
Grape wine—putaojiu
Maotai—maotai

Milk—niunai
Mineral water—kuangquanshui
Rice wine—mijiu
Soda (Chinese 7-Up)—qishui
Tea—cha

USEFUL NAMES OF DISHES

APPETIZERS—Xiaocai

Cold platter—lengpan
Cold, tossed vegetables—liangbancai
Dumplings—jiaozi
Pickled vegetables—paocai
Spring rolls—chunjuan
Thousand-year-old eggs with bean curd—pidan doufu

SOUPS—Tang Lei

Corn soup—yumi geng
Egg-drop soup—danhua tang
Hot-and-sour soup—suan la tang
Rinsed lamb pot—shuan yang rou
Vegetable bean curd soup—baicai doufu tang
Wonton soup—huntun tang

CHICKEN DISHES—Jilei

Chicken feet—jizhua
Chicken gizzard—jizhun
Chicken legs—jitui
Chicken meat—jirou
Cold chicken with sesame dressing—zhima ji
Crispy chicken with five spices — cui pi ji
Salt-baked chicken—yan jiu ji
Smoked chicken—xun ji
Stir-fried chicken with hot peppers— gong bao ji ding
Tangerine-peel chicken—chen pi ji

DUCK DISHES—Ya Lei

Camphor-smoked duck—zhang cha ya
Crispy-skin duck—xiang su ya
Duck feet—yajiao
Duck liver—yagan
Duck meat—yarou
Peking duck—Beijing kao ya
Eight-Treasure duck—ba bao ya

PORK DISHES—Zhurou Lei

Barbecued pork loin—cha shao rou
Cold boiled pork with garlic sauce— suan ni bai rou
Dong Po pork—Dong Po rou
Double-cooked pork—hui guo rou
Fish-flavored pork shreds—yu xiang rousi
Lion's head—Shi Zi tou
Pig's trotter—zhu zhua
Pork liver—zhugan
Sausage—xiang chang
Spareribs—paigu
Suckling pig—ru zhu

BEEF DISHES—Niurou Lei

Beef in oyster sauce—hao you niu rou
Beef meat—niu rou
Oxtail—niuwei
Sliced beef in hot sauce—ma la niurou
Stir-fried beef with eggs—hua dan niu rou
Stir-fried beef with scallions—cong bao niu rou
Tangerine-peel beef—chen pi niu rou

LAMB DISHES—Yang Rou Lei

Baked leg of lamb—kao yang tui
Lamb shashlik—kao yang rou chuan
Mongolian lamb—shuan yang rou
Stir-fried lamb with scallions—cong bao yang rou

SEAFOOD DISHES—Hai Wei

Abalone—bao yu
Conger eel—hai man
Crab—pang xie
Crab in sweet and sour sauce—cu liu xie rou
Dried scallop—gan bei
Fish-flavored shrimp—yu xiang xia ren
Fish meat—yu rou
Fish roe—yu zi
Fish slices in sweet and sour sauce—cu liu yu pian
Furong shrimp—Fu rong xia ren
Grouper—shi ban yu
Hundred corner shrimp balls—bai jiao xia qiu
Jellyfish skin—hai zhi pi
Live shrimp—huo xia
Lobster—long xia
Lobster Cantonese—yue shi chao long xia
Mackerel—qing yu
Oyster—hao
Pomfret—yin chang yu
Prawns—ming xia
River carp—cao yu
Salmon—gui yu
Saltwater shrimp—yan shui xia
Scallop—xian bei
Sea cucumber—hai shen
Shad—fei yu
Shark—sha yu
Shark's fin—yu chi
Shelled shrimp—xia ren

Smelts—hugua yu
Snapper—jia ji yu zhendiao
Squid—you yu
Squirrel fish—song shu yu
Spicy prawns in tomato sauce—gan shao ming xia
Steamed whole fish—qing zheng yu
Stir-fried crab with ginger and scallions—jiang cong chao pang xie
Stir-fried squid with hot peppers—gong bao you yu juan
Westlake fish—Xi Hu cu yu
Yellow fish—huang yu

VEGETABLES—Shu Cai Lei

Bamboo shoots—zhu sun
Beansprouts—dou ya
Bitter melon—ku gua
Broccoli in oyster sauce—hao zhi jie lan cai
Carrot—hu luo bo
Cabbage—bai cai
Cauliflower—cai hua
Chili pepper—la jiao
Chinese broccoli—yie lan cai
Chinese chives—xiyang cong
Cucumber—huang gua
Dried black mushrooms—dong gu
Dry-cooked string beans—gan bian si ji dou
Eggplant—qie zi
Fish-flavored eggplant—wu xiang qie zi
Five-Treasure vegetable platter—wu zhen su cai
Garlic—suan
Ginger—jiang
Green pepper—qing jiao
Hot-and-sour cabbage—suan la bai cai
Kohlrabi—cai guo
Lotus root—lian ou

Mustard cabbage—jie cai
Mushroom—mogu
Pea pods—wan dou jia
Pickled cucumber slices—ma la
   huang gua (pian)
Radish—bai luo bo
Rape—you cai
Scallion—cong
Spinach—bo cai
Summer bamboo shoot—zhu sun
Tomato—fan qie
Water chestnuts—ma ti
Winter melon—dong gua

BEAN CURD—Dou Fu

Bean curd skin—fu pi
Bean milk skin—fu yi
Braised bean curd—hong shao dou fu
Dried bean curd skin—fu zhu
Fermented bean curd—fu ru
Ma po bean curd—ma po dou fu
Northern style bean curd—guo ta
   dou fu

NOODLES—Mian Tiao Lei

Bean threads—fen si
Buckwheat noodles—qiao mai mian
Rice-flour vermicelli—mi fen
Stir-fried noodles—chao mian
Tossed noodles—ban mian
Wheat noodles—mian

FRUIT—Shui Guo Lei

Apple—ping guo
Banana—xiang jiao
Cherry—ying tao
Honeydew melon—ha mi gua
Kumquat—jin ju
Orange—ju zi
Peach—tao zi
Pear—li
Plum—mei
Strawberry—cao mei

VEGETARIAN—Su Cai Lei

Assorted vegetables over sizzling
   rice—shi jin guo ba
Mock goose—su er
Two winters—shao er dong
Vegetarian eight-treasure chicken—
   su ba bao ji
Vegetarian spring rolls—su chun
   juan

EGGS—Dan

Egg white—dan ging
Egg yolk—dan huang
Omelet—jian dan
Preserved duck egg—xien dan
Thousand-year-old egg—pi dan

DESSERTS—Tian Dian Xin

Almond bean curd—xin ren dou fu
Eight-Treasure rice pudding—ba bao
   fan
Ice cream—bing qi lin

Pronunciation Guide

a	vowel as in *far*	**s**	consonant as in *sister*
b	consonant as in *be*	**sh**	consonant as in *shore*
c	consonant as in *chip;* strongly aspirated	**t**	consonant as in *top;* strongly aspirated
d	consonant as in *do*	**u**	vowel as in *too;* also as in French *tu* or the German München
e	vowel as in *her*		
f	consonant as in *foot*		
g	consonant as in *go*	**v**	consonant used only to produce foreign words, national minority words, and local dialects
h	consonant as in *her;* strongly aspirated		
i	vowel as in *eat* or as in *sir* (when in syllables beginning with c, ch, r, s, sh, z and zh.)		
		w	semi-vowel in syllables beginning with u when not preceded by consonants, as in *want*
j	consonant as in *jeep*		
k	consonant as in *kind,* strongly aspirated		
l	consonant as in *land*	**x**	consonant as in *she*
m	consonant as in *me*	**y**	semi-vowel in syllables beginning with i or u when not preceded by consonants, as in *yet*
n	consonant as in *now*		
o	vowel as in *law*		
p	consonant as in *par;* strongly aspirated		
q	consonant as in *cheek*	**z**	consonant as in *adze*
r	consonant as in *right* (not rolled) or pronounced as *z* in *azure*	**zh**	consonant as in *jump*

Selected Bibliography

Aero, Rita. *Things Chinese*. Garden City, N.Y.: Dolphin Books, 1980.

Anderson, E. N. *The Food of China*. New Haven: Yale University Press, 1988.

Ball, J. Dyer. *Things Chinese*. Hong Kong: Oxford University Press, 1982.

Blofeld, John. *The Chinese Art of Tea*. Boston: Shambhala Publications, 1985

Bredon, Juliet, and Igor Mitrophanow. *The Moon Year*. Hong Kong: Oxford University Press, 1982.

Chang, Chi-yun. *A Life of Confucius*. Taipei: Hwakang Press, China Academy, 1971.

Chang, K. C., ed. *Food in Chinese Culture: Anthropological and Historical Perspectives*. New Haven: Yale University Press, 1977.

Chen, Pearl Kong, Tien Chi Chen, and Rose Tseng. *Everything You Want to Know about Chinese Cooking*. Woodbury, N.Y.: Barron's, 1983.

Courtauld, Caroline. *Collins Illustrated Guide to Fujian*. London: William Collins Sons & Co. Ltd., 1988.

———. *A Guide to Nanjing, Suzhou and Wuxi*. Hong Kong: China Guide Series Limited, 1981.

Destenay, Anne L., ed. *Nagel's Encyclopedia Guide to China*. Geneva: Nagel Publishers, 1978.

Gong, Dan. *Food and Drink in China: A Visitor's Guide*. Beijing: New World Press, 1986.

Hsiung, Deh-ta. *Chinese Regional Cooking*. New York: Mayflower Books, 1979.

Kaplan, Fredric, Julian Sobin, and Arne de Keijzer. *The China Guidebook*. Boston: Houghton Mifflin/Eurasia Press, 1989.

Kong Demao, and Ke Lan. *In the Mansion of Confucius' Descendants*. Beijing: New World Press, 1984.

Lai, T. C. *At the Chinese Table*. Hong Kong: Oxford University Press, 1984.

————. *Chinese Food for Thought.* Hong Kong: Hong Kong Book Centre, 1978.

Lai, T. C., Husein Rofe, and Phillip Mao. *Things Chinese.* Hong Kong: Swindon Book Company, 1971.

Lee, Gary. *Chinese Tasty Tales Cookbook.* San Francisco: Chinese Treasure Productions, 1974.

Leeming, Margaret, and May Man-hui Huang. *Chinese Regional Cookery.* London: Rider and Company, Ltd., 1983.

Lin, Hsiang Ju Lin, and Tsuifeng Lin. *Chinese Gastronomy.* London: Thomas Nelson and Sons, Ltd., 1969.

Lo, Kenneth. *Peking Cooking.* New York: Pantheon Books, 1971.

Lu Niangao, Li Tiefei, ed. *China Tianjin.* Beijing: China Travel and Tourism Press, 1983.

————. *China Guilin.* Beijing: China Travel and Tourism Press, 1983.

————. *China Jinan, Mount Taishan.* Beijing: China Travel and Tourism Press, 1983.

————. *China Nanjing.* Beijing: China Travel and Tourism Press, 1983.

————. *China Hangzhou.* Beijing: China Travel and Tourism Press, 1983.

Malloy, Ruth Lor, and Priscilla Liang Hsu. *Fielding's Republic of China.* New York: Fielding Travel/William Morrow & Company, 1987.

Matsumoto, Kakuko, ed. *Authentic Chinese Cuisine: Beijing I.* Tokyo: Shufunotomo Co., Ltd., 1984.

————. *Authentic Chinese Cuisine: Beijing II.* Tokyo: Shufunotomo Co., Ltd., 1984.

————. *Authentic Chinese Cuisine: Beijing III.* Tokyo: Shufunotomo Co., Ltd., 1984.

————. *Authentic Chinese Cuisine: Guangdong I.* Tokyo: Shufunotomo Co., Ltd., 1984.

————. *Authentic Chinese Cuisine: Guangdong II.* Tokyo: Shufunotomo Co., Ltd., 1984.

————. *Authentic Chinese Cuisine: Shanghai I.* Tokyo: Shufunotomo Co., Ltd., 1984.

————. *Authentic Chinese Cuisine: Shanghai II.* Tokyo: Shufunotomo Co., Ltd., 1984.

————. *Authentic Chinese Cuisine: Sichuan I.* Tokyo: Shufunotomo Co., Ltd., 1984.

————. *Authentic Chinese Cuisine: Sichuan II.* Tokyo: Shufunotomo Co., Ltd., 1984.

Passmore, Jackie, and Daniel Reid. *The Complete Chinese Cookbook.* New York: Exeter Books, 1982.

Perkins, David W., ed. *Hong Kong and China Gas Cookbook.* Hong Kong: The Hong Kong & China Gas Co. Ltd., 1978.

Rolnick, Harry. *Eating Out in China.* Hong Kong: South China Morning Post, 1979.

Sakamoto, Nobuko. *The People's Republic of China Cookbook.* New York: Random House, 1977.

Simonds, Nina. *Chinese Seasons.* Boston: Houghton Mifflin, 1986.

———. *Classic Chinese Cuisine.* Boston: Houghton Mifflin, 1982.

Summerfield, John. *Fodor's Beijing, Guangzhou, Shanghai.* New York: Fodor's Travel Publications, 1989.

Williams, C. A. S. *Outlines of Symbolism and Art Motives.* New York: Dover Publications, 1976.

Wu, Guang. *Shandong Local Dishes.* China: Shandong Provincial Tourism Bureau, 1986.

Zhang, Wei'e, and Wu Li. *A Guide to Shanghai.* Hong Kong: Joint Publishing Co., 1984.

Index